THE DRUZE

REALITIES
& PERCEPTIONS

Druze Heritage Foundation

The Druze
Realities & Perceptions

Edited by Kamal Salibi

Druze Heritage Foundation

Published in 2005
by the Druze Heritage Foundation
48 Park Street, London W1K 2JH, UK
Tel: 020 7629 7761
Fax: 020 7499 3386
Email: info@druzeheritage.org

ISBN 1-904850-06-5

Cover Design by Mohamad Hamady
Printed by Calligraph, Beirut, Lebanon

Table of Contents

Preface vii

Foreword ix

Sami Makarem
The Druze Faith 1

Tony P. Naufal
Sylvestre de Sacy on the Druze 9

David R. W. Bryer
Druze Religious Texts 29

Naila Kaidbey
Al-Sayyid Jamal al-Din al-Tanukhi as a Druze Reformer 43

Fuad I. Khuri
Aspects of Druze Social Structure: 'There Are No Free-Floating Druze' 61

Bernadette Schenk
Druze Identity in the Middle East: Tendencies and Developments
in Modern Druze Communities since the 1960s 79

Intisar Azzam
Druze Women: Ideal and Reality 95

Leila Fawaz
The Druze-British Connection in 1840-1860 105

Abdul-Rahim Abu-Husayn and Engin D. Akarli
The Subordination of the Hawran Druze in 1910:
The Ottoman Perspective 115

Kamal Salibi
Jebel Druze as Seen by Rustum Haydar 129

Michael Provence
Druze *Shaykhs*, Arab Nationalists and Grain Merchants 139

Leslie McLoughlin
Fuad Hamza as an Observer of the Kingdom of Saudi Arabia 155

Eyad Abu Chakra
The Druze and Arabism 171

Amir Taheri
Remarks on Some Communities with Druze-Like Affinities 183

Judith Palmer Harik
Coping with Crisis: Druze Civic Organization during the Lebanese Civil War 197

Index 217

Preface

IT WAS MY GREAT PLEASURE to welcome the scholars whose work appears in this volume to the Druze Heritage Foundation's conference on "The Druze: Realities and Perceptions," which took place in Oxford in 2001. The research, presentations and discussions of the participants were impressive and these articles will undoubtedly be helpful to those who seek to know more about the Druze—their faith, identity and society, and the role that they have played in the history of the Middle East.

It seems there is something special and appealing about the Druze, who have been discussed quite extensively in scholarly and popular works. We aim to give the right and true picture of the Druze and to preserve their valued traditions.

With materialism dominating modern life, it is so rewarding to look into the spiritual side of life and to join in the quest for knowledge. The Druze Heritage Foundation (DHF) strongly supports these virtues and was established to sustain them in a practical way: to advance learning and to promote the study of Druze history and culture; to collect Druze literature wherever such literature exists; to accommodate an information centre and a library; and to sponsor academic activities including conferences and publications.

The conference in 2001 represented one step toward these aims. Moreover, within the short period since its inception, the DHF has also commissioned and published two books. Three others are in press, and a further seven due shortly for publication. It is my hope that such works, will and others to come, help to create a more profound understanding of the Druze as well as genuine dialogue between cultures.

For their guidance, encouragement and collaboration in making the 2001 conference possible, I would like to extend my personal gratitude to Dr. Eugene Rogan and to the Middle East Centre at St. Antony's College, the University of Oxford. I would also like to give special thanks to Professor Kamal Salibi and his team at the Royal Institute for Inter-Faith Studies, Amman, Jordan, for all of their excellent work in organizing and supervising this conference. I further appreciate the considerable efforts of Mr. Nadim Shehadi and his assistants to make our meetings and stay memorable, and the board of trustees of the DHF for their great support. Finally, warm thanks are also due to Professor Sami Makarem for the wonderful calligraphy that he designed for each conference participant.

At a time when studies of global scope are in fashion, we feel that there are many interesting areas of research to pursue concerning a transnational people like the Druze. We welcome all suggestions and contributions.

Salim Kheireddine
Oxford, 12 July 2002

Foreword

IN THE PLANNING of the first international academic conference of the Druze Heritage Foundation (DHF), held in collaboration with the Middle East Centre at St. Antony's College, Oxford, in July 2002, it was thought best not to concentrate on any single aspect of the Druze legacy, but to attempt to cover the widest possible range of themes, the better to bring out the Druze ethos as understood by the Druze themselves and as perceived by others. Thus, of the fifteen papers presented in this volume, which were the ones ultimately received in publishable form, the first four relate to religious issues. An explanation of the Druze faith by Sami Makarem (American University of Beirut) is followed by a critical assessment of the pioneering work of the French Orientalist, Sylvestre de Sacy, on the subject, contributed by Tony P. Nawfal (independent scholar). Next, David R. W. Bryer (former head of OXFAM) presents a survey of Druze religious texts, while Naila Kaidbey (American University of Beirut) describes the career of the fifteenth-century Druze reformer, al-Sayyid Jamal al-Din al-Tanukhi, commonly regarded as the founder of what one may call normative Druzism.

The next three papers treat social themes: a paper on the structure of Druze society by the late socio-cultural anthropologist, Fuad I. Khuri (author of the DHF publication, Being a Druze); another on tendencies and developments in modern Druze communities since the 1960s, with emphasis on the question of Druze identity, by Bernadette Schenk (Free University of Berlin); and a third on the status of Druze women between the ideal and the reality, by Intisar Azzam (American University of Beirut).

These are followed by four papers on historical themes: the Druze-British connection in the middle decades of the nineteenth century is assessed by Leila Fawaz (Tufts University); the Ottoman perspective on the subordination of the Hawran Druze in 1910 is presented jointly by

Abdul-Rahim Abu-Husayn (American University of Beirut) and Engin D. Akarli (Brown University); a picture of Jebel Druze and its people as depicted in the 1918 diary of the Arab nationalist, Rustum Haydar, is sketched by Kamal Salibi (American University of Beirut); and an in-depth study of the relationships between the Jebel Druze chiefs and the grain merchants and Arab nationalists of Damascus at the onset of the mandatory period is ably provided by Michael Provence (University of California, San Diego).

Of the remaining four papers in this volume, the first, by Leslie McLoughlin (independent scholar), is biographical, dealing with Fuad Hamza: a Druze who rose high in the service of King Abdul-Aziz ibn Saud and left descriptions of Saudi Arabia in his time that remain invaluable for scholars today. The second, by Eyad Abu Chakra (Al-Sharq al-Awsat Magazine), surveys the Druze role in the emergence and development of Arab nationalism. The third, by Amir Taheri (Middle East specialist based in London), surveys the diverse but little known communities with Druze-like affinities in different parts of the Muslim world. And the fourth and last, by Judith Palmer Harik (American University of Beirut), is a study of Druze civic organization during the Lebanese civil war.

In preparing this volume for press, it was decided to unify the transliteration of Arabic technical terms as they appear in different papers but, normally to leave personal and place names in the spellings given by the different authors. As a help to the reader, the index lists the variant spellings of these names.

The Editor

Sami Makarem

The Druze Faith

THE DRUZE MOVEMENT sprang from Isma'ili Shi'i Islam in the year AH 408/AD 1017, during the time of the sixth Fatimid caliph-*imām*, al-Hakim bi-Amr Allah. Headquartered in Cairo, the movement soon took hold in Mount Lebanon and the Anti-Lebanon range, in northern and southern Syria, in and around Damascus and in northern Palestine. Most of the adherents to this faith were members of those Arabian tribes, such as the Tanukh, Kalḅ, Kilab and Tayyi', who had already come under the political and creedal impact of Isma'ili Fatimid hegemony. Druze epistles were also sent to the Hijaz, to the eastern part of Arabia and to Yemen. They reached as far as India. This suggests that adherents to the Druze movement may have existed in those countries.

The name by which the Druze like to be known is *Muwaḥḥidūn* (sing. *Muwaḥḥid*), which reflects their central belief in a mystical oneness (*tawḥīd*) with the One. Ironically, however, the followers of this movement acquired their popular name, the Druze, from a certain Muhammad ibn Isma'il al-Darzi (also known as Nashtakin or Anushtagin al-Darazi). He was a high state functionary enrolled in the movement in its early stages, but who came, before long, to have major differences[1] with other of its leaders: this prompted Hamza ibn 'Ali, the movement's head, together with Caliph al-Hakim, to expel him from it, causing him to rise up against Hamza ibn 'Ali and to ally himself with the non-adherents to the faith among the Cairenes. He led an insurrection that ended with his defeat on 29 Dhu l-Hijja AH 409/9 May AD 1019 and his execution on the following day.[2]

In order to understand the Druze faith, we must step back to consider the evolution of Islamic approaches to the Qur'an. As Muslims came into greater contact with Greek philosophy, Persian thought, Indian mysticism, and Jewish and Christian theology, they began to interpret the literal message of the Qur'an in order to gain insight into its deeper ramifications.

This new approach to Islam became more distinctive as Muslims increased their acquaintance with Sufism. An interaction between Greek rationalism and Oriental mysticism, which was intensified by the emergence of Sufi sages, especially in the ninth and tenth centuries AD, prepared the way for the emergence, at the beginning of the eleventh century (fifth century AH), of the Druze movement as an offshoot of the esoteric Ismaʿili approach to Islam. Adherents to the movement believed that a third and last stage of Islam had begun: namely, *al-ḥaqīqa*, 'self-realization,'namely, as true a feeling of unity with the One as is humanly possible. The first stage, *al-sharīʿa* (literal or exoteric Islam), had paved the way for the second one, *al-ṭarīqa* (inner or esoteric Islam), but now it was the time of *al-ḥaqīqa*. These three Sufi terms—*al-sharīʿa, al-ṭarīqa,* and *al-ḥaqīqa*—were used by the Druze synonymously with *islām, īmān* and *iḥsān* (or *tawḥīd),* the latter three being common among other Muslims as well, Sunni and Shi'i alike. *(Islām* here refers to the first stage, not to the religion as such.)

For the Druze, this third and last stage, variously known as *al-ḥaqīqa, islām,* or *tawḥīd* (oneness with the One), is reached by passing through the states of gnostic preparedness instilled during the preceding two stages. It is the nature of *tawḥīd* to lead the adherent to behold his or her divine reality where no relative is mystically apart from the absolute and no outward existence is independent of divine reality. The *Muwaḥḥid* is thus led to identifying him or herself and, consequently, every existing being, with the One. At this stage, the *Muwaḥḥid* is mystically subsumed into the all-inclusiveness of the One, whose existence is the only real existence.

The role of al-Hakim

The Druze doctrine maintains that, four hundred years after the advent of Islam (one thousand years after Christ), esoteric interpretation of the Qur'an achieved its task and the stage of *īmān* or *al-ṭarīqa* terminated with the arrival of the caliph-*īmān*, al-Hakim bi-Amr Allah. Just as the Prophet Muhammad had delivered the divine message (literally, *islām* or *sharīʿa*) and was the last conveyor (*nāṭiq*) of it, so was al-Hakim the last of the esoteric *īmān*s who, starting with ʿAli ibn Abi Talib down through the Fatimid caliphs, took upon themselves the task of interpreting God's message and implementing the second stage (*īmān* or *ṭarīqa*) by establishing the Fatimid state, thus transmitting the esoteric meaning of the divine Word to mankind. (Hence, the Fatimid *īmān* was known as the *maqām* or 'station' of the esoteric divine Word.) With al-Hakim, the third stage started.

Consequently, on 1 Muharram AH 408/30 May AD 1017, al-Hakim, according to the Druze, relinquished the esoteric Imamate and appointed

Hamza ibn ʿAli as the *īmān* of the third stage (*tawḥīd*). He also appointed a distant cousin, ʿAbd al-Rahim ibn Ilias, as heir presumptive of the Muslims (*walī ʿahd al-Muslimīn*) and another Fatimid personality, Abu Hisham ʿAbbas ibn Shuʿayb, as heir presumptive of the Muʾmins (*walī ʿahd al-Muʾminīn*). The Fatimid *imām* was thus replaced by the holders of three different positions, the first dealing with the Muslims (in other words, the followers of exoteric Islam), the second dealing with the Muʾmins (the followers of *īmān*) and the third dealing with the *Muwaḥḥidūn* (the followers of *tawḥīd*.)[3] Al-Hakim was now solely the *maqām*.

The Druze concept of God

The doctrine of *tawḥīd* maintains that God is not an entity in Himself (*dhātiyya*); nor is He merely above this existence. For the Druze, God is absolute existence. Consequently, He is not a creator in that He created the universe *ex nihilo*. Rather, physical existence is God's expression, His manifestation (*badū*). Since God is absolute, He has not created the world outside of Him for, as absolute, He has no limit: similarly, the world did not emanate from Him in time. He is the One: there is none other than God; He is the only Existent. The world is a constant projection from Him, by Him, within Him and to Him. This is what the Druze doctrine means by *ibdāʿ*, not an act that occurred outside of God.

The world is, therefore, in existence due to God's divine nature (*amr*). The Qurʾanic verse, "His *amr*, when he wills a *shayʾ*, is to say to it, 'Be,' and it is,"[4] lies at the basis of the Druze doctrine of existence according to Hamza ibn ʿAli. The word *amr* in this verse means *shaʾn* ('affair', 'activity') and is equivalent to the Latin word *res*.[5] According to the Druze interpretation of this Qurʾanic verse, the *amr* of God, that is, His will, activity, is transformed into the divine imperative: "Be!" For the Druze, God is to His *amr* as a word's meaning is to the word. As meaning both transcends the word that it expresses and is immanent in it, the absolute Existent transcends the world while being immanent in it. Hence, God is referred to by the Druze as both transcendent (*munazzah*) and immanent (*mawjūd*). *Tawḥīd* is defined as *tanzīh wa wajūd*, that is, transcendence and immanence.

Hamza ibn ʿAli refers to God's *amr* as *ʿaql*, an Arabic verbal noun that originally meant 'to bind': equivalent to the Greek *nous*, it should not be misunderstood as 'mind' or 'reason'. As an intelligent and purposive principle, however, the *ʿaql* is inclusive of all existing beings. The *ʿaql* or *amr* of God binds and encompasses (*ʿaqala*) the whole world. It is the finite projection, so to speak, of the absolute One (*al-mubdaʿ al-mahdūd min al-mubdiʿ al-aḥad*).

Just as a word is in constant union with the meaning which it expresses, so God's *amr* or *ʿaql* is, by its very nature, in constant union with God. However, as a finite projection of the absolute, the *ʿaql* is also, by its very nature, aware of being projected (*mubdaʿ*) by the One. This awareness made it feel that it was an entity in its own right, although one within the absolute oneness of God: the *ʿaql* had become aware of its self.

By being aware of its self, the *ʿaql* was deflected, so to speak, from its original course, for self-awareness impeded it from full awareness of the One. This deflection from feeling in union with God to 'focusing upon' and 'enjoying' its self made the *ʿaql* feel that it was separate from God. This deflection, however, was nothing more than relative absence from the One, the absolute Existent, an absence of light (*nūr maḥḍ*) that is the same as utter darkness (*ẓulma maḥḍ*). This is a delusion (*ʿadam*). The absence of divine light is what the Druze call adversity (*ḍidd*). It is a selfish attitude, the origin of discord, contrariety and division.

However, the *ʿaql* realized that it had been deflected from the One and developed an imploring passion to return to Him. I say 'imploring' because the *ʿaql* realized that it is, by its very nature, completely dependent upon the One. It has no power of its own. Hamza called this passion *nafs* ('wish', 'desire', 'endeavour', 'eagerness' or *himma*).[6] and it is the *shayʾ* mentioned in the Quʾranic verse quoted above. Here, *shayʾ* is the verbal noun of the Arabic verb *shāʾa* ('to desire'). For the Druze, it is the second cosmic principle. The first is the *ʿaql*; the third, according to the Druze interpretation of the verse, is the 'saying' (*al-qawl, al-kalima*) implied in the phrase, *an yaqūla*; the fourth is the imperative "Be!" ("*Kun!*"). This imperative precedes its implementation, *yakūn*, which is the fifth cosmic principle. Hence, the *amr* or *irāda* corresponds to the *ʿaql*; the *shayʾ* corresponds to the *nafs*; the *qawl* (in the phrase *an yaqūla*) corresponds to the *kalima*; the imperative *kun* to the *sābiq*; and the implementation of *kun*, namely, *yakūn*, corresponds to the *tālī*, in other words, that which follows. These are the five cosmic principles (*al-ḥudūd al-khamsa*) that are always associated with the Druze. They are derived from the Druze's esoteric interpretation of the Qurʾanic verse (36:82) "*Innamā amruhu idhā arāda shayʾan an yaqūla lahu kun fa yakūn.*" (His *amr* ('nature', 'activity'), when he wills a *shayʾ* ('desired thing'), is to say to it, 'Be', and it is.)

The world

From the fifth cosmic principle, therefore, came forth the world. The world is the expression of the fifth cosmic principle, which is, in turn, the expression of the fourth cosmic principle, and so on, all of the way back to the first cosmic principle, the *res divina*, the divine will, the *ʿaql*, the finite projection of the absolute.

Now, since man is the quintessence of this world, which originated as a spark from the *ʿaql* and, since the *ʿaql,* as the finite projection of the absolute, is eternal, then so is man's reality—his soul. The human soul is to the human body as its meaning is to a word. Just as a meaning makes sense only when expressed through its word, so must the human soul be expressed in a human body. The human soul realizes itself in the human body. The human body, therefore, serves as the sole medium for the human soul to achieve actualization and to participate in the progress of man toward knowledge and self-realization. The true knowledge of the oneness of God, through which man realizes his purpose of feeling as much in union with the One as is humanly possible, can only be achieved through man's gradual yet continuous spiritual experience and through his constant preparedness for the gnostic discovery of human union with the One. For the Druze, the span of a single life is not enough for an individual to realize this ultimate purpose.

God and man

Since man is the only being who possesses the faculty to comprehend this gnostic reality, he alone can strive to discover it. He is the only being who can check the egotistic drive that throws him into the delusion of plurality and, consequently, deflects him from his true nature. Here lies the seed of vice in man: taking joy in his own ego and living in the delusion of plurality. Virtue, on the other hand, lies in living in this plural world, but without taking it as an aim, that is, in moving away from one's own ego toward unity with the rest of humanity and, therefore, in union with the One, inasmuch as it is humanly attainable. Those who succeed in reaching this goal do so through divine love. Hence, love is seen by the Druze as a mystical feeling of endless striving for such a union with the One, whereas hatred is understood as a product of metaphysical egotism in which one separates one's own being and interests from the being and interests of the whole.

Union can be reached if man believes in and spiritually realizes the following: the non-dualism and absoluteness of the One; that God's *amr,* the *ʿaql,* is the finite manifestation of the absolute; and that the cosmic principles are the source of all being, with the *ʿaql* as both their origin and their goal.

In addition, man should practice, truly and through the exercise of his free nature, the following virtues:

1 Veracity in the broadest sense of the word, that is, to profess the truth, to act according to the truth and to live for the truth.

2 Safeguarding, helping and guiding his fellow men or seeking their guidance along the path of truth and real knowledge.
3 Renouncing all beliefs leading to repudiation of the oneness of God and, consequently, to falsehood.
4 Dissociation from those who transgress against righteousness and justice, that is, those who hinder man from knowing the truth and treading upon the path of real knowledge.
5 Striving endlessly to achieve the real purpose of man, namely, to be in union with the One as much as is humanly possible.
6 Contentment (*riḍā*) with the divine law.
7 Submission (*taslīm*) to God's will and deeds.

In order, these seven tenets are the true meanings of the seven Shi'i pillars of Islam, namely, the two testimonies, prayer, almsgiving, fasting, pilgrimage, strife in God's way (*jihād*) and allegiance (*walāya*).

It is by means of these pillars that man moves away from egotism and plurality toward union with the One. In the Druze faith, the aim of ethics is not merely to acquiesce to a superior will, but to lead man, rationally and spiritually, to the natural fulfilment of his being through virtuous behaviour.

This approach is what led the Druze to call for complete equality among human beings, including equality of opportunity: it is only thus that man may realize himself, to the highest possible degree, in the One. This is why the Druze doctrine strictly condemns polygamy. The Druze law of domestic relations stipulates that, when a man marries a woman, he must put her on the same footing as himself, materially as well as spiritually. Husband and wife must treat one another with complete equality and justice. In case of divorce, the spouse proven to have been unjust must pay the other half of what he or she owns.

This approach stems from the central position that the Druze doctrine gives to the human being.

In order to try to live up to such a standard, men and women must strive to attain the purpose of their being, which is self-realization in the One and living accordingly, in real love.

The individual's capacity to reach such oneness with the One depends upon his or her intellectual and spiritual preparedness.

True discovery of the self will enable the individual to behold the One, as if he or she looked into a mirror and saw his or her own image.

It was through such manifestations that the presence of God was revealed to man, just as a word reveals its meaning to the reader inasmuch as the reader is prepared to receive it.

God is infinite and transcendent in His boundless immanence and omnipresence. The onus is on man, through intellectual and spiritual preparedness, to behold such immanence and omnipresence.

As is stated in my book, *The Druze Faith*[7]:

> [T]he impetus for man's evolution comes from two sources. One source is imposed by the cosmic order and prods man on his way; the other is within man and comes from man's being endowed with reason, which makes him endeavour to know and to be at one with the universe. These inner and outer forces work in conjunction, so that man may fulfil his own nature. Unless man has the will to strive to implement this inner force he is left with an imbalance. If the inner force, which should buoy him up, is not acting properly then man will be at the mercy of the cosmic forces. In other words, he will lose his freedom of will. . . . On the other hand, with the two forces acting simultaneously man freely works towards self-realization.

Man can achieve the harmony of these two forces only if he opens his heart to divine love.

No one, however, can walk the path of self-realization without a guide to show him that God, in His oneness, is both inside and outside of him, both transcendent and immanent, both divine and human.

Notes

1 Marshall G. S. Hodgson, "Al-Darazi and Hamza in the Origin of the Druze Religion," *Journal of the American Oriental Society* 82 (1962): 5-20. See, also, Kamal Salibi, "Introduction," to *The Druze Heritage: An Annotated Bibliography*, compiled and edited by Talal Fandi and Ziyad Abi-Shakra (Amman: Royal Institute for Inter-Faith Studies, 2001), 1ff.

2 Sami Makarem, *The Druze Faith* (Delmar, NY: Caravan Books, 1974), 19-22.

3 Cf. Sami Makarem, "Al-Hakim bi-Amrillah's Appointment of His Successors," *Al-Abhath* 23 (December 1970), nos. 1-4.

4 Qur'an 36:82; Makarem, *The Druze Faith*, 43.

5 Cf. Sami Makarem, *"Al-Amr al-Ilāhī wa mafhūmhu fi al-ʿaqīda al-Ismāʿilīyya," Al-Abhath* 20, no. 1 (March 1967): 3-16.

6 E. W. Lane, "Nafs," in *An Arabic English Lexicon* (London: William and Norgate, 1893).

7 Makarem, *The Druze Faith*, 115.

TONY P. NAUFAL

Silvestre de Sacy* on the Druze

In memory of Shaykh Sulayman Salim Alamuddin

ON 15 JULY 1700, a physician from Aleppo by the name of Nasrallah ibn Gilda[1] presented King Louis XIV of France with a very unusual gift: three manuscript volumes of letters and documents concerning the beliefs of the *Muwaḥḥidūn* ('Unitarians' or Druze). The manuscripts, which came from Baʿqlin,[2] were kept with all of the other collections that formed the Bibliothèque royale. In 1701, the secretary of state issued an order to have them translated and the task went to François Pétis de la Croix,[3] holder of the royal chair in Arabic. It did not prove to be an easy one. Ultimately, Pétis de la Croix failed to understand the order of the documents, bridged the gaps in erroneous ways and even tried to rework the title of a major section of the text, completely confusing the issue. Many years later, when attempting to give a systematic description of the translation to the Académie des inscriptions et belles-lettres, Antoine Silvestre de Sacy was confronted with its shortcomings. It was clear to him that, in his desperate struggle to disentangle the web, Pétis de la Croix had falsified the text[4] and wreaked havoc: "Il est plus que vraisemblable que ce désordre ne régnait point encore dans ce manuscript, quand Pétis de la Croix en a rétabli les lacunes."[5] It became incumbent upon Silvestre de Sacy, the leading Arabist of his day, to try his hand at the challenging task of making sense of the manuscripts.

Silvestre de Sacy worked on the Druze manuscripts for over forty years, with interruptions, until he decided to release them for publication in 1838. He was eighty then and died before the year was out. His study on the Druze, to which he gave the title *Exposé de la religion des Druzes* (2 volumes), crowned a long and brilliant career. To the body of the texts, he added a life of the Fatimid caliph, al-Hakim bi-Amr Allah, an excursus on the origin of the Fatimid dynasty (which included two excerpts from the work of the historian al-Nuwayri) and capped the whole with a long, considered introduction on the philosophical developments that had paved the way for Unitarian thought. This totalled one thousand four hundred and fifty-six pages in all, to which he had planned to add a third volume[6] that was being prepared when he died.

Silvestre de Sacy's *Exposé* set a precedent and became a work of the utmost importance. It unveiled secret beliefs related to an esoteric system of ideas and laid the cornerstone for further studies. Sami Makarem, commissioned to write on the Druze by their highest religious authority, referred sixteen times to Sacy's work in his monograph, *The Druze Faith*, more than he did to the texts that he has on hand from his father's collection. Even granting that the *Exposé* contains a number of mistakes, eventually pointed out by Sacy's numerous colleagues and students,[7] its importance remains undiminished. In a work published in 1928, Philip Hitti states that this "monumental work . . . has not been superseded though it appeared some ninety years ago and before many original sources were brought to light, [and it] gives us an excellent internal interpretation of the Druze religion." However, forgetting that Sacy's aim was to elucidate the royal manuscripts, Hitti reproaches him for not going far enough "in disentangling the various strands of the intricate and complex web of the Druze system and in tracing them back to their remote origins in various religions or philosophical and metaphysical schools of thought."[8] Hitti's own approach, which was not quite convincing, relying too much upon the Persian connection of the Unitarian creed, now appears dated. Yet, Sacy sensed the tensions in the Unitarian movement at a much earlier date and, by returning to his work, one may find the seeds of a fresh interpretation. The purpose of this paper is to examine Sacy's method and his findings in the *Exposé* and to show, in particular, how the latter were inextricably linked to this exceptional man's personality and background.

The achievements of Silvestre de Sacy

Antoine Isaac Silvestre de Sacy (1758-1838) may be justifiably considered the father of French 'Orientalism.' Before his entry into the field, it was restricted to dragomans who dabbled in Oriental languages to serve the embassies of France in the Levant and to travellers who were animated by a sense of curiosity and a taste for the exotic. During his long and brilliant career, Silvestre de Sacy changed all of that by bringing the Near East within the scope of Western scholarship. Without leaving Paris, the sedentary scholar established rigorous standards of research with a marked emphasis on original manuscripts, prepared the tools of his discipline and pointed the way for further research to instruct "Europe savante." Sacy was undoubtedly the single most influential figure in the formation of the field of 'Oriental' studies in Europe and arguably the father of European 'Orientalism' as well, since he monitored its course in the Netherlands, Germany, Austria, Sweden, Denmark, Spain and Russia either directly, by training scholars from these countries, or indirectly, through his impact on them.

There are three spheres in which Sacy distinguished himself and played a significant role in 'Oriental' studies: first, as a prolific scholar who published a great number of works; second, in various institutional settings, not only as a teacher of Arabic and Persian, but also as a mentor to many of his peers; and, third, as a focus of the bustling activity in his contemporary milieu and through his regular contributions to leading European journals. By the end of his career, Sacy's influence was felt as far as the Near East itself, which prompted some of its local writers to present him with their recent works. Without manuscript sources, however, the achievements of Sacy would have been impossible. The manuscripts at the Arsenal and the depository of St. Germain des prés provided Sacy with the raw material that informed his vast knowledge and grounded his authority, while simultaneously governing his choice of texts. Sacy was, then, fundamentally a product of the library and essentially an editor. His works, which total more than four hundred and fifty in number, deal with both primary (original Arabic, Persian, Hebrew, or Turkish manuscripts) and secondary (Orientalists' publications) sources. Sacy dominated the field of Near Eastern studies by publishing on religion, literature, languages, etymology, epigraphy, prosody, geography, jurisprudence, numismatics, onomastics and other subjects. Nor did he limit himself to considerations of period or genre. His scope encompassed classical and contemporary topics alike and the several forms that he used illustrate his broad interests and versatile approaches: "*exposé,*" "*mémoire,*" "*recherche,*" "*dissertation,*" "*considération,*" "*observation,*" "*aperçu,*" "*compte-rendu,*" "*lettre*" and "*notice.*" Each form corresponded to a level of authority and erudition and was intended for a certain audience.

In addition to the collections of excerpts that he put together for use in teaching, like the "*anthologie*" or "*chrestomathie,*" Sacy also published full original texts by Near Eastern authors, which were enriched by his annotations, variant readings, collations and rectifications.[9] Equally important were the bilingual editions of basic texts, in which the translations were either in French or Latin, and occasional volumes featuring the translations alone. By no means absent from his publications, Sacy made personal contributions that were efforts at synthesis and expressed in the form of "*mémoire,*" essay, or even letter. Sacy also left numerous reviews ("*comptes-*

rendus") of works by 'Orientalists,' spanning an impressive gamut of topics, from a Syriac version of the New Testament found in China to commerce in the Levant. In the rising science of epigraphy, Sacy played a noteworthy role in the race to unveil the mystery of the Rosetta stone, providing some of the keys needed to decipher hieroglyphics, decisively refuting von Hammer's erroneous lead and following up on Champollion's progress with guidance and encouragement.

Sacy went beyond his immediate area of expertise to address administrative and governmental problems and to discuss larger issues informed by his wide-ranging studies, such as linguistics, the art of translation and general questions of method (relating to sinology, for instance). During Sacy's early career, it was still common practice to approach Arabic studies as *ancilla theologiae*. After proving himself in biblical scholarship with contributions to Eichhorn's prestigious *Repertorium für biblische und morgenländische Literatur*, Sacy was instrumental in making Arabic studies into a separate field. However, Sacy never abandoned his biblical research, which he published in several journals, including the other famed Eichhorn publication, the *Allgemeine Bibliothek der biblischen Literatur*.

In addition to his writings, Sacy attained unprecedented stature in the great establishments of learning in Paris, instituting his own teaching method. Appointed the expert in Arabic at the Ecole des langues orientales vivantes, created in 1795 by the revolutionary Convention nationale, he became the school's administrator from 1824 until his death. In 1806, he was appointed expert in Persian at the Collège de France, where he eventually became its administrator (in 1823). An associate of the Académie des inscriptions et belles-lettres beginning in 1785, he became a full academician in 1792 and served five terms as president. Although Sacy had never followed any existing school or method in his early years, he gradually devised one of his own, which was adopted in Europe and Russia. It was empirical in nature, relying heavily upon detail and the use of illustrative texts. In the development of semantics, Sacy would occupy an interesting position between the logic of Port-Royal and the 'universal grammar.' Familiar with more than a dozen languages,[10] Sacy composed the *Grammaire arabe* (1831) for his students, which set out the theoretical framework of the language, as well as the earlier (1829) *Anthologie grammaticale arabe*, which presented a selection of texts, translated and annotated, written by classical Arab grammarians of the calibre of Ibn Hisham, al-Zamakhshari and Sibawayh. His many students (and auditors) and the important posts that they held in their own countries increased Sacy's influence. Among them were the Germans, Bopp, Steudel, Mohl, Vullers,

Freytag, Flügel, Habicht, Kosegarten, Stickel, Dorn, Olshausen, Mitscherlich, Middeldorpf, Allioli, Fleischer (his follower) and others; the Spaniard, Dom Pascual de Gayangos; the Swiss, Jean Humbert; Denmark's Rasmussen; Norway's Holmboe; the Swede, Tornberg; and the English Sanskritist, Chamney Haughton. The most illustrious of his numerous French students (some were followers) included Quatremère, de Slane, de Chézy and Garcin de Tassy. The famous biblical scholar of Strasbourg, Reuss, was also his student, as were two lesser scholars who participated in Napoleon's expedition to Egypt, J. J. Marcel, the director of the printing press in Cairo, and Amedée Jaubert, who occupied the post of interpreter upon the death of Venture de Paradis at the siege of Acre. At the request of the Russian minister, Uvarov, Sacy sent two of his followers, Charmoy and Demange, to Russia to build up 'Oriental' studies there. Sacy also exercised his influence on Austrian 'Orientalism' by contributing to (and monitoring) the *Fundgruben des Orients*. In France, he founded the Société asiatique (1822), publisher of the *Journal asiatique*, which is still in circulation.

Finally, to Sacy's roles as a scholar and educator must be added his leading position at the centre of contemporary European intellectual activity and in French political and governmental circles. Through regular contributions to the leading journals of Europe, Sacy secured his position as an intellectual, particularly as a revered and inexhaustible critic; at times, he even dominated such publications as the *Journal des savants, Magasin encyclopédique, Moniteur universel* and *Bibliothèque française*. In the realm of the exotic, for which the age showed no less fervour than its predecessors, Sacy's hand was equally felt, endowing voyages and discoveries with realism through his annotations and frequent articles in the *Annales des voyages*. The circle around Sacy was not only composed of 'Orientalists,' but also included scientists, such as Fulgence Fresnel of the scientific mission in Mesopotamia and the biologist, Cuvier, whose Paris salon Sacy occasionally attended. The Hellenists, Thurot and Larcher, were among his friends. He kept a correspondence with a variety of people in the diplomatic corps, especially those posted to Constantinople, Cairo, Aleppo and Basra. Although he never became an impressive political figure, his presence was felt at the state level beginning in 1808, when he joined the Corps législatif and, more significantly, during the Restoration and under Louis-Philippe. Napoleon elevated him to the rank of baron in 1814 and he was awarded a number of other titles, the most noteworthy being Peer of France, when Louis-Philippe named him, along with Cuvier, to the French 'House of Lords' in 1832. He remained, however, primarily a scholar whose international renown prompted academies to solicit his membership and, thus, belonged to the academies of Göttingen, Berlin, Frankfurt, Munich, Würzburg, London, Copenhagen, Amsterdam, Leyden, Utrecht, Uppsala, St. Petersburg, Kasan, Cambrai and Abbeville (in France), Naples, Pisa, Torino, Worcester (Massachusetts), Calcutta and Corfu. Sacy was equally important as a witness to his times and a biographer of his contemporaries, colleagues and followers, many of whom he outlived. He contributed sketches to the *Biographie universelle* of Michaud and became the historian of the Académie, reading the funerary orations of Champollion, Rémusat, Chézy, Anquetil-Duperron and others.

Establishing the Druze text

It is surprising to find in Europe so many manuscripts or portions of the writings of a Near Eastern religious group which did its utmost to remain secret. In order to establish the texts that would allow him best to understand the Unitarian creed, Sacy had to survey all of the manuscripts available at the time, describe them, organize them and make a final choice. His "Notice des Manuscrits" is an invaluable classification of the Druze collections held by different libraries at the time: there were two volumes at the University of Leiden, four at the Bodleian (at Oxford, brought by Shaw), one in the Vatican and one in the Imperial Library of Vienna. Other manuscripts were in private hands, such as the one of Berggren (of the Swedish legation in Constantinople), which Sacy consulted when they met in Paris. Caussin de Perceval, another 'Orientalist,' also owned a manuscript, but it was imperfect, whereas that of Dr. Picques of Paris (d. 1699) was extremely valuable. Sacy himself possessed a few pieces and he was in contact with the French consular agent in Beirut, Dupont, who kept a good collection that he intended to donate to the Bibliothèque du roi. Dupont died prematurely, however, and his collection was lost, but he had fortunately given a list of his manuscripts to Sacy, who had taken note of those that were unknown to him, as "ces indications pourront servir à diriger les recherches futures des voyageurs."[11] The ones that he ultimately chose to work on were the three volumes brought over by Nasrallah ibn Gilda, a fourth volume containing Dr. Piques' collection and excerpts from the Bodleian volumes. As Sacy notes, the curator of the Bodleian, Mr. Cureton, "had the kindness to copy most of this manuscript for me."[12] That was how it worked: copies were made for scholars, as had been the practice for centuries. At one point, Sacy states with jubilation: "Je m'en suis procuré un fac simile!"[13] The Benedictine congregation of St. Maur housed the collection of Dom Berthereau on the historians of the Crusades and related matters, among which were Unitarian documents, but these were no longer available by the time that Sacy turned his attention to the Druze: they had been looted during the turmoil of the Revolution. No matter what form this scramble for manuscripts took, one thing remained clear to Sacy, "que nous ne possédions qu'une partie de leurs livres sacrés."[14] This explains why he deferred publication and also governed his careful, almost apologetic, approach.

Sacy's major concern, in fact, was to establish a kind of 'definitive' text of the Unitarian creed that would show the 'real' beliefs of the Druze and not the later corruptions and additions invented by their religious opponents. This is the reason why Sacy discarded controversial material composed in defence of Christianity against Druze beliefs. More importantly, he was very careful not to include later Druze manuals that he grouped together as catechism (questions and answers or "*formulaire*"). He focused, then, only upon "le doctrine primitive des Druzes, qui est l'unique objet de mon travail."[15] Again, when assembling the texts that would form his first chapter, in which he explained the Druze understanding of the unity of God, Sacy adds "pour que l'on puisse se faire une idée de l'enseignement des premiers fondateurs de cette religion."[16] The only *formulaire*[17] that Sacy allowed was the one of Venture de Paradis (1739-1799), for he needed it as a sounding board, but he never quoted from it as an authoritative source. Among its other uses, Venture's *formulaire* served to highlight a number of obscure points, to confirm some views and to verify the soundness of Sacy's conjectures. Sacy was vigilant, however, to ensure that no general points of dogma slipped through from the *formulaire* to taint the original set of Druze beliefs, for he held that "la preuve que ce formulaire contient des choses contraires à l'enseignement primitif de la religion des Druzes" meant that "il est permis de soupçonner que son auteur se sera écarté en cela de la doctrine de Hamza."[18] During the forty or so years that Sacy awaited new material from the Near East to broaden the basis of his study, many pieces related to the Druze reached him, but were discarded for the same reason: they were quite unlike the teachings of the sect's founders. In a *mémoire* that he read to the Académie in 1818, he says: "J'ai eu plus d'une fois occasion de me convaincre que les Druzes d'aujourd'hui sont bien éloignés du véritable esprit de leurs institutions primitives, et que même, sur certains points de leur croyance, ils professent une doctrine diamétralement opposée à celle de leurs livres sacrés."[19]

In the body of the *Exposé*, which is quite distinct in tone and purpose from its introduction, Sacy set himself as the preserver of the authenticity of the Druze creed, accepting only the teachings that came from Hamza and his circle, admitting solely the early texts. He became, then, a kind of 'fundamentalist,' a purist looking back at the earliest days of the creed in an effort to capture their spirit and the first unmediated message. How was one to preserve the spirit of the original teachings? By dint of critical perseverance and exegetical acumen. As for the title of these collected texts, Sacy believed, after some argument and hesitation, that the whole ought to carry the title written on some of its parts: *Kitāb al-mashāhid wa'l-asrār al-tawḥīdiyya*. Although the term *ḥikma* (wisdom) abounds in the letters,[20] it is not part of this title.

Sacy's insistence on the importance of the text and the purity of the original creed were characteristic of his Jansenist upbringing. Although it had become a curious relic by the time of the Regency, Sacy had remained a reserved but firm adherent to this Catholic tendency. The Jansenists lay great store by the text, putting the scriptures before tradition and the Bible before the pope.[21] They insisted that the Bible should be accessible to everyone and emphasized, therefore, individual study and interpretation. As their position obviously came close to Calvinism, the Jesuits attacked them for heresy. But the Jansenists wanted to stay within the Church and merely strove to bring it back to the purity of its origins. Sacy undertook the same search for origins regarding the Druze and even in relation to other religious groups, particularly the Samaritans. Because his contemporaries believed that the Samaritan scrolls were capable of shedding light on Hebraic religious texts and early Christianity, Sacy started a correspondence with the Samaritans of Nablus in 1808. This culminated in the uncovering of the Samaritan Pentateuch, which allowed scholars to compare it with the Torah and, thus, open up a new approach to Old Testament studies. The same interest in early sources had led Sacy to focus upon the Book of Enoch[22] as early as 1799.

There is, however, another possible motive for Sacy's drive toward a reliable and recognized text delimiting the Druze creed; namely, 'enlightened' Europe's desire to measure its own progress by assembling all of the world's religious texts, a huge corpus that it was proud to own, exhibit and contemplate in order to obtain knowledge of the world. Both notions, that of Jansenist purity and that of 'enlightenment' and progress, were relevant to Sacy's quest.

Periodization and authorship

Sacy was very familiar with the work of Joseph Scaliger and had even translated some of the Samaritans' letters to him for the *Morgenländische Repertorium* (published by Eichhorn). He held Scaliger's method of historical criticism in high regard and used it skilfully to date the Druze manuscripts. Each text was studied in terms of its place relative to the others and the historical record, as well as the tone of its author.[23] Sacy further applied Scaliger's critical method to cleanse the 'original' text of the writings of Druze renegades like al-Darazi, al-Bardhaʿi, Sikkin, al-Muhalla, Ibn al-Kurdi, Ibn ʿAmmar, Ibn al-Barbariyya and Lahiq (also called al-Mukhtar). To do this, he needed to determine the date and author of each piece. Fortunately, some of them already had dates, for instance, the document entitled *Al-Kitāb al-maʿrūf bin-naqd al-khafī,* which is dated AH 408 or the first year of Hamza's reign. Every new religion brings its own calendar with it and Sacy noticed that the dates mentioned in the texts referred either to Hamza's rule or his 'absence' (Sacy uses the term 'occultation'). The question of authorship was just as important if Sacy was to discard the 'frauds.' Some of the pieces were signed (usually at the end) but, when the signature did not appear, he attempted to establish authorship from internal evidence, such as the style of composition or the ideas expressed in the piece. For instance, *Manshūr al-sharṭ wa'l-baṭṭ* is attributed to Muqtana, who must have practiced medicine,[24] and the same author, in Sacy's opinion, undoubtedly penned *Manshūr ilā'l-maḥall al-azhar al-sharīf* as well.[25] Sacy was unable to identify the authors of some texts with any degree of certainty, leaving the door open for future scholarship.

By separating 'text' from 'counter-text,' Sacy acknowledged two important points: that religions develop from one creed to another and that later developments or positions can betray the spirit of the founding fathers and their writings. Hence, he believed that the secrecy and need for dissimulation (*taqiyya*) imposed upon the Unitarians were a false innovation, an iniquity and "une impiété. Un pareil ordre est absolument contraire aux écrits de Hamza et de Moktana, et je n'en fais mention ici que pour le faire remarquer."[26] In another instance, commenting upon Hamza's writings concerning "resurrection," Sacy observes "il y a quelque différence dans ces écrits, suivant l'époque à laquelle ils ont été composés."[27]

The *Exposé*: Some preliminary problems

Sacy approached the collection as "Recueil des Druzes" and his procedure in the *Exposé* was to translate the components of the "Recueil" and then string them together in a narrative divided into chapters according to seven main themes. The first involves the Unitarian approach to the divinity and the way Hamza explains God's unity. The second treats the metaphysical setting and its hierarchies, the five principles of the Unitarian dogma which Sacy calls the five "ministers." Since the metaphysics delineate the theological space, so to speak, he habitually referred to this as the theogony of the Druze (theogony being a term borrowed from classical Antiquity, specifically, from Hesiod). In the third chapter, he discusses the notion of the transmigration of souls. The fourth chapter revolves around central theological concepts, like *tanzīl* and *taʾwīl*, and the seminal position of the Unitarians on free will, "libre arbiter." The Last Judgement and the Druze view of resurrection are the subject matter of the fifth chapter, while the sixth looks at the seven pillars of the Unitarian creed and the ethical conduct required of adherents. Sacy ends with a short seventh chapter on legal matters, such as marriage and divorce, and here includes the oath taken by confirmed Unitarians.

Sacy's enterprise was fraught with difficulties since he had to translate or paraphrase the texts into French, the language most familiar to "Europe savante" at the time, before he could begin dividing the material into chapters. And no translation comes without its pitfalls. To be able to translate one must first understand the text and then find the right word or corresponding term. When the text exhibits a wealth of esoteric terms and unfamiliar ideas, like the ones that Sacy faced, the challenge of translation is compounded. Sacy arrived at his solutions by trial and error, by staying alert and flexible, and by being willing to go back on earlier decisions. The word *ḥudūd*, for example, is rendered as 'ministers' because of two passages in a fragment outside of the collection mentioning *wuzarāʾ Hamza* and *asmāʾ al-wuzarāʾ al-khamsa*.[28] Knowing that the term pertained to the law in the Qurʾan, he first translated it as 'to exercise penal law,' but the other two passages led him to revise his translation to read 'principal ministers of religion.'[29] When uncertainty did exist, Sacy sometimes included an entire passage in Arabic in his work, just to be on the safe side: for instance, he does this to clarify, in a footnote, the meaning of the term *ḥijjat al-qāʾim*.[30]

Sacy's problems in transforming his Arabic text into French are reversed for those critically assessing the *Exposé*. Given Sacy's inaccurate system of transliteration, scholars are forced to guess what the original Arabic term was and if Sacy correctly grasped it. It takes some stretch of the imagination to read "réka" as *rakʿa,* while some names written in Latin script are nearly impossible to identify. For a sounder critique of the *Exposé,* one would need to compare the French rendering with the Arabic original, which unfortunately lies dormant at the Bibliothèque nationale in Paris (MSS number 1580, 81, 82, 83).

Sources and tools

Perhaps Silvestre de Sacy's most stupendous achievement regarding the *Exposé* concerns the fact that he worked almost exclusively with unpublished manuscripts—both the Druze texts and secondary sources. Although there are today evident shortcomings in his work connected to his inability to consult additional sources, he did succeed in examining the largest number available at the time. Other than the obvious Arab historians, like Maqrizi and Nuwayri, he looked at works by Ibn al-Athir, Severus of Ushmuneyn, Jaʿfari, Ibn Taghri-Birdi, Tilmisani, Ibn Hibatallah, Ibn Khallikan, Ibn Wasifshah, Mirkhond (*Rawḍat al-safā*), Khondamir, Abu'l-Fida, Abu'l-Faraj, Ibn al-ʿIbri and many more.

His vast knowledge of Arabic was the prerequisite for such an undertaking: we need only recall that W. Wright's *A Grammar of the Arabic Language* (Cambridge, 1896), which is still used in leading Western universities, is a translation of Caspari's work based, in turn, upon Sacy's *Grammaire arabe*. Sacy used to teach his students Arabic from the "Banat Suʿad," Kaʿb ibn Zuhayr's poem eulogizing the Prophet, and Labid's "Muʿallaqah," both of which are difficult pieces of literature. Sacy was, moreover, amazingly proficient in Qurʾanic studies. John Penrice's glossary to the Qurʾan, called *Silk al-bayān fi manāqib al-Qurʾān,* relies heavily upon Sacy's linguistic work, indicating its importance to this field. The Druze manuscripts are laden with details (allusions and ideas) that refer back to the Qurʾan, as well as citing whole passages from it. Sacy traced each of these thoroughly, stating their provenance, determining both the *sūra* and *ayā* (part) and discovering, sometimes, that the original reference was actually to a combination of *āyas* from different *sūras*. He also indicated when these references conformed to classical interpretations and when they had apparently been taken out of context. For example, when Tamimi (Ismaʿil ibn Muhammad, the second minister) explains the incarnation, comparing it to a mirage, he refers his reader to a Qurʾanic passage, but Sacy recognized the verse and was able to show how its meaning had been skewed.[31] In another of his argumentative footnotes, this time concerning *nihāyat al-ḥudūd,* which he understood as "the highest degree of excellence," Sacy observed that the word *nihāya* does not appear in the Qurʾan.[32] This bold assertion is all the more amazing when one realizes that general reference works or indices to the Qurʾan were not available in his day.

Affinities

Silvestre de Sacy possessed an uncanny ability to identify with his subject matter, so much so that Napoleon called him "l'Arabe" whenever they met. What distinguished his approach to Arabic grammar and made it drastically different from the ones of his predecessors (such as Erpenius) is that it relied completely upon Arab grammarians, garbed in a Latin cloak. Sacy's esteem for Arab learning, especially the Arabs' literary output, and for its position in the world corpus was so high that it led him to assert that the Arabs had been great in spite of Islam![33]

A similar identification is observable in Sacy's dealings with the Druze manuscripts. Often there is only a barely perceptible break between the Unitarian text (Hamza's or Muqtana's) and his own explanation, as if he were continuing the thought. His tone is deferential, barring indignant outbursts at the notion of al-Hakim's self-declaration as the Godhead. Yet, even these assertions could be attributed to misconstrued elements in the Arabic text. (The classic Unitarian view is to see al-Hakim as the manifestation of the divinity—a chosen figure or medium.) But despite the fact that Sacy obviously disliked this side of Unitarianism, he remained objective, staying close to the text and interacting with it in an equitable fashion.

Sacy never let his Christian convictions hamper his work as a scholar, for he saw religion as a personal matter. Although he revealed his faith at times, it was never to pose it as the strongest model against which to judge other religions. He was nevertheless very pious. There is no other way to explain his translation of the testament of the guillotined king, Louis XVI, into Arabic (*Al-durr al-manzūm fi waṣāya al-sultān al-marḥūm*). He apparently wished to show how devout, simple and charitable his beloved monarch had been. But despite his piety, his voluminous work on the Druze was a balanced treatment that mentioned Christianity only twice. The first of these references occurs when his argument compels him to draw a parallel between the Unitarian and Christian dogmas of incarnation and he apologizes in the footnote for offending the reader.[34] On the second occasion, he reveals his Christian affiliation through a slip of the tongue, when he notes that Muqtana knows "our" books.[35] It is his attitude toward the same Muqtana that furnishes the best proof of Sacy's religious detachment. Sacy was intrigued by Muqtana's knowledge of the Christian scriptures and the subtlety of the arguments that he used to win Christians over to the Druze faith. These points led Sacy to conclude that Muqtana was a Christian apostate. Nevertheless, he had positive feelings toward him and was not offended by his frank zeal: "Tout me porte à croire que Moktana était un enthousiaste de bonne foi."[36]

Jansenists and Druze

Strange as it may seem, there were still other elements that linked Sacy to the Unitarians, affinities beyond the ones that may form between a scholar and his subject, namely, the common features between Sacy's religious background and that of the Druze. This is not to say that the Jansenism of

Sacy was similar to the Druze faith, but that there was a general ambience that attracted Silvestre de Sacy and explains his perseverance in studying the Druze. The first of these affinities involved minority feeling: religious and social isolation—the necessity of keeping a low profile in a sea of incomprehension and adversity—were features common to both sects. Among the Druze, this imperative was clearly indicated by their continued secrecy. Sacy also had convictions that went against the grain, causing him to constantly feel alone and at odds with events. He was a royalist in an era of revolution and empire; a devout man who held mass in his home when revolutionary anti-clericalism banned it; and a Jansenist—a member of a group on the brink of extinction. Despite all of the honours that he received, he remained withdrawn. The observation that "le Jansenisme est un calvinisme honteux, qui se cache et se dissimule"[37] accurately describes Sacy and his circle.

The most striking common feature, however, of both Jansenists and Druze is the flood of 'apocalyptic literature' that members of both groups released against their incredulous detractors. In the *Exposé,* Sacy kept returning to the apocalyptic Unitarian vision of Judgement Day,[38] which echoes the Jansenist sense of the coming end and retribution. Much as Druze teachings described their enemies as cursed and facing transformation into bulls or other animals, Jansenist doctrine assimilated the sect's foes, the Jesuits, to the "ten-cornered beast" or the "locust." Also common to both are the moral features that they highlighted: austerity and truthfulness.

Deciphering

Sacy lived during one of Europe's most exciting eras of archaeological and linguistic discovery, one that left the traditional approach to historical chronology in a shambles and had a staggering cultural impact on the continent. During this time, Egyptian antiquities finally revealed their secrets, unlocking the world of the pharaohs, while the ground was prepared for the study of Assyriology. Sacy had a foothold in both fields and contributed to the latter by deciphering the inscriptions on the rock of Behistun (in Kirmanshah) before turning his attention to hieroglyphics and the feverish race to discover the language of ancient Egyptian civilization. With his first success—deciphering the names 'Ptolemy' and 'Arsinoe'—Sacy seemed unstoppable, but he soon ran out of clues. The victory ultimately went to J. F. Champollion (1790-1832), who was a student of Sacy's, but one with whom he had had a stormy relationship.[39] Sacy had many reasons to dislike and distrust a young (Jacobin) revolutionary like Champollion. Not only were their political views opposed, but their characters clashed as well. The staid, withdrawn professor was alarmed by the extremes of temperament exhibited by his wild student; however, he could not ignore his genius and hard work. He soon took the noble decision to put aside their differences and to assist Champollion by means of his own learning and patronage, enthusiastically acknowledging the former student's advances.

What Champollion did with the Rosetta stone, Sacy repeated with the Druze manuscripts. Champollion's breakthrough had relied upon two fundamental processes: dismantling the cartouches in the writings (understanding how the hieroglyphic elements were used) in order to make substitutions; and determining the language in which the text was written (which turned out to be Coptic). Sacy followed the same procedure. In part, he broke the Druze 'code' when he fortuitously came upon a gloss by Tamimi entitled *Shiʿr al-nafs*, which provided the necessary keys for replacing coded words with their explanations. Much like Champollion, who was able to make his substitutions work once he hypothesized that the Rosetta stone was inscribed with a written form of Coptic, Sacy sensed that the Druze texts depended upon Ismaʿili concepts and terminology. (One takes this for granted today, but it was not obvious then.) As he discovered more glosses and compared several texts, Sacy succeeded in 'deciphering' most of the coded terms and in understanding the meaning of words and phrases like *tanzīh, tasbīḥ, nāṭiq, asās,* the four books, the four women and so on. Thus, readers of the *Exposé* were able to draw up a full list of the keys as Sacy guided them through the Druze epistles using his system of quick substitution; once the code was broken, the equivalent terms could be applied 'mechanically'; for greater clarity, Sacy sometimes provided the original Arabic text alongside the decoded French.[40] Recognizing the role and rank of the ministers in the Druze hierarchy and how they corresponded to the ones in the Ismaʿili order took considerable exertion, the fruits of which occupy a good part of the second volume of the *Exposé*.

Among the terms that Sacy had to explain were *tanzīl* ('revelation') and *taʾwīl* ('analogy'), two complex notions that work on different levels. Sacy had started focusing his attention upon these concepts in 1805, in a Latin treatise published in Göttingen.[41] At its most basic level, *tanzīl* in the Druze epistles refers to the text of the Qurʾan as well as to all of those who accept the literal meaning of holy texts. It describes a first stage of belief that is common to Sunnis and to Jews. Analogy brings believers to a higher level since reason is involved in interpretation. This second level is the one of the Shiʿa and the Christians. According to Hamza, however, true religion lay at a third level, that of *tawḥīd*—the unification of the emanations of the Godhead, which is the Druze way. In the Unitarian system, the principle of Intelligence reigns supreme. The use of reason is, therefore, the characteristic that determines the level of any given religion and establishes the hierarchy of faiths. In Hamza's view, the partisans of *tanzīl,* who take revelation literally and are directed by external law (*ẓāhir*), are forced into anthropomorphism since God speaks, sits on a throne, has hands and so on; hence, they stand open to accusations of unbelief (*kufr*). Those who merely allegorize (*ta'wīl*) and interpret and who have internalized the law (*bāṭin*) are driven to polytheism (*shirk*). These two camps are referred to in the Druze texts as the *Muslimūn* (Muslims) and the *mu'minūn* (believers). The Druze creed considers the first form of revelation to have been abrogated and the second to have been overtaken and transformed by the final manifestation of Divinity.

Sacy contended that, despite their subtlety, Hamza's arguments were not always logical since they tended either to force the point or to employ *non sequitur* fallacies. He felt, moreover, that allegorical interpretation as a method of seeking meaning was open to abuse. Sacy believed in reason; his entire system of learning languages centred upon it. When it came to religious texts, he insisted that conjecture should be bound by strict rules: "Ce n'est pas que j'entends proscrire toute allégorie dans l'exégèse sacrée; mais je pense que, pour être juste, elle doit être extrêmement réservée et toujours fondée sur un sens littéral bien développé; jamais elle ne doit le suppléer."[42] These issues were important to Sacy because of their bearing on biblical interpretation and were part of the greater controversy concerning biblical exegesis that was raging at the time. It might, in fact, be argued that Sacy had turned to the study of 'remote' religious groups, like the Druze, which had no link to Christianity, in order to avoid the kind of textual scrutiny of the scriptures (biblical 'higher criticism') being pursued by his German colleagues, Eichhorn, Ewald and Gesenius. Whether or not this was the case, it is clear that Sacy was aware of the limits to interpretation and of the ideological stands that it could serve, asking "de nos jours, l'allégorie n'a-t-elle pas été la resource des théologiens allemands, qui ont voulu trouver partout, depuis les livres de Moïse jusqu'a l'Apocalypse, les idées de Kant?"[43]

Despite his reservations concerning Hamza's arguments, Sacy expressed great admiration for the spirituality of his teachings and his insistence on ethical conduct. For this reason, Sacy dismissed accusations that the Druze worshipped the figure of a calf or that they were lewd: he believed that their spiritual and highly moral 'legislator' would not have permitted such practices. In addition, Sacy was unable to hide his enthusiasm for the imaginative way in which Hamza illustrated the doctrine, which was often strange or subtle to the point of extravagance. Several of these curious notions are highlighted in the section devoted to the soul in the *Exposé*. Concerning the transmigration of souls, for instance, the soul's elevation is compared to the act of pronunciation, to the proximity of the word to the uvula (*lahāt*, plural *lahawāt*): the soul describes the movement between the tongue and the uvula. Sacy explains the term *fī al-lahawāt* ("dans les glottes") as the soul's peregrination between elevation and debasement so long as it clings to the uvula (that is, remains attached to a body).[44] From the *lahawāt,* however, come the velars *kāf* and *qāf* and Sacy was unaware that his observation was still the more interesting because it touches upon a fanciful explanation for the Unitarians' distinctive pronunciation of the *qāf*: reaching for 'q,' the soul is elevated.

Sacy made other observations—drawn from dogma, to be sure—that might also shed light on some distinctive features of Druze society. The most interesting of these is Muqtana's injunction to adherents to carry their weapons at all times.[45] This was probably a precaution that developed owing to persecution in the early days of the sect, but it has textual authority. Combined with the hierarchical organization of Druze society, possibly reflecting the rigid ranking of the 'ministers' at the sect's inception, this might explain the traditional view of Druze society as paramilitary in nature. Moreover, Sacy was aware that the Druze traditionally admired moral courage or manliness (still expressed today by the term *rujjāl*), although without linking it to military prowess or physical strength: rather, it is seen as the virtue of upholding one's principles since "les hommes ne sont véritablement hommes que par la justesse de leurs sentiment, et non par le mensonge et par des actions honteuses."[46] Another Unitarian virtue close to Sacy's heart was their fortitude: no matter what befell them, they accepted it with resignation and a peaceful soul. Finally, among the many clues to be found in Sacy's work and that might lead to a new interpretation of the Druze creed, is its link to the ancient Egyptian mysteries and, especially, to the cult of Hermes.[47]

Silvestre de Sacy's ultimate stance

It is the introduction to the *Exposé* that best indicates Sacy's own opinion of the Druze 'system.' Sacy wrote the introduction much later than the body of the text because he was still expecting additional Druze manuscripts to arrive from the Levant. For this reason, the introduction possesses a different spirit and focuses upon another problem. How had a messianic faith like the one professed by the Druze grown in the staunchly monotheistic environment of traditional Islam, which did not allow any mediation between God and man. What kind of change had Islam undergone to allow "des sectateurs [Druze] parmi les disciples de Mahomet, ennemis declarés de toute sorte d'idolâtrie."[48] Sacy found the answer in his traditional nemesis—philosophy. He was convinced that the subtlety (and extravagance) of philosophical arguments had prepared the way for the Druze system by virtue of their destructive and levelling action. With the translation and wide circulation of Greek philosophical works during the Fatimid period, this 'calamity' had entered the intellectual fabric of society and introduced "parmi les Musulmans l'esprit de dispute et un scepticisme dangereux."[49] The dissemination of philosophical ideas and trends was accompanied by an ever-growing number of sects, thoroughly enumerated and reviewed by Sacy in his introduction. Moreover, the sharpest weapon deployed by philosophy to corrupt the faithful was allegory, a blade that struck "également à la loi de Moïse, à l'Evangile et à l'Alcoran."[50] In the final analysis, philosophy surreptitiously led to disorder and to a general lack of respect. Philosophy's treacherous aim, for Sacy, was "apprendre à mépriser jusq'aux premiers principes éternels de l'ordre et de la justice, gravés dans le cœur de l'homme par l'auteur de son être, et, à plus forte raison, toute idée de révélation et d'autorité divine."[51] Here, Sacy comes to the defence of revelation against the attacks of philosophy and its consort, reason. By the same token, he defends traditional Islam against all movements that meant to corrupt its adherents. Thus, although Sacy approaches the study of the Druze in a detached fashion—and often with an undercurrent of warmth—in the body of the *Exposé,* his stance is reversed in the introduction. For Sacy, revelation cannot be opposed to reason since they belong to two different realms. Just as God had given man mental acuity, he had also endowed him with an internal moral imperative strengthened by revelation. As far as religious belief was concerned, Sacy could not separate reason from revelation and took a middle position, one that tried to instil harmony between the two; when forced to choose, he made reason subservient to revelation.

Sacy's introduction may be seen, then, as a clear warning against the misuse of reason and was probably aimed not only at the Druze, who posited Intelligence as their primary principle, but even more so at rational and sceptical inquiries into the scriptures, which had started with the Wolfenbüttel fragments of Reimarus, published by Lessing in 1774, and was still a daring intellectual activity during Sacy's final years. In the "Avertissement" of the *Exposé,* dated 1837 (less than three months before his death on 19 February 1838), Silvestre de Sacy expressed the wish that his work on the Druze might serve as a lesson to all those who glorified intelligence.

Left on its own, reason, for Silvestre de Sacy, was capable of the worst aberrations.[52] It always needs the support and guidance of revelation.

NOTES

* His name is sometimes spelt with a 'y'" (Sylvestre), but he personally wrote it with an 'i' (Silvestre) as is shown on the title page of the *Exposé*. Silvestre was his family name and Sacy an additional place name. Although it is, therefore, incorrect to refer to him as Sacy, the present paper uses this short form for the sake of convenience.

[1] The gift was possibly in appreciation of the French king's decree, dated 1700, providing stipends for twelve young Christians from the Near East to study at the Collège Louis-le-Grand in Paris. Nasrallah ibn Gilda made a special trip to Lebanon and used the favour accruing from his healing skills to obtain the manuscripts. Cf. H. Guys, *Théogonie des Druses* (Paris, 1863), 14.

[2] Silvestre de Sacy, *Exposé de la religion des Druzes* (Paris, 1838), 1:456.

[3] It should be noted that there were two François Pétis de la Croix, father (1622-1695) and son (1653-1713), who successively held the same position as the King's Arabists. It was the son who worked on the Druze; he also left a translation of *1001 Days*.

[4] *Exposé*, 1:463.

[5] Ibid., 1:493.

[6] Ibid., 1:6; 2:704 (note).

[7] See, for example, H. Guys, "Observations critiques sur quelques passages de l'ouvrage intitulé *Exposé de la religion des Druzes*," in *Théogonie des Druses*, 131-41.

[8] Philip Hitti, *The Origins of the Druze People and Religion* (New York: Columbia University Press, 1928), 25-26.

[9] For instance, the literary classic, *Calila et Dimna, ou Fables de Bidpai, en arabe, précédée d'un mémoire sur l'origine de ce livre. . .* (Paris, 1816).

[10] Sacy received a solid grounding in Greek and Latin through private tutoring. He then acquired Syriac and Hebrew before moving on to Arabic and Persian. He later added Amharic, Coptic and Turkish as well. His critiques show that he also knew German, Italian, Spanish and Russian.

[11] "Notice des Manuscrits," in *Exposé*, 1:516.

[12] Ibid., 1:515; the translation is mine.

[13] Ibid., 1:496.

[14] Ibid., 1:360.

[15] Ibid., 1:516.

[16] Ibid., 1:66.

[17] It exists in English translation in *Appendix to the Memoirs of the Baron de Tott* (London, 1786).

[18] *Exposé*, 1:24-25.

[19] "Mémoire sur l'origine du culte que les Druzes rendent à la figure d'un veau" in *Histoire et mémoire de l'Institut royal de France* (Paris, 1818), 74.

[20] *Exposé*, 1:30, 57, 168 ff.; 2:83, 185, 373.

[21] J. Carreyre, *Le jansénisme durant la Régence*, 3 vols. (Louvain, 1929-33), 1:391.

[22] Sacy, "Notice du Livre d'Enoch" in *Magasin encyclopédique* (1799), 1:369-98.

[23] For an example of the problem of dating that Sacy faced and his conjectures, see *Exposé*, 2:358-59.

[24] Ibid., 1:510.

[25] Ibid., 1:512.

[26] Ibid., 2:399.

[27] Ibid., 2:596.

[28] "Notice des Manuscrits," in *Exposé*, 1:516.

[29] *Exposé*, 1:205 (note).

[30] Ibid., 1:78 (note).

[31] Ibid., 1:45 (note).

[32] Ibid., 1:76 (note).

[33] Académie des inscriptions et belles-lettres, séance du 5 mars 1810, 7.

[34] *Exposé*, 1:76 (note).

[35] Ibid., 2:200.

[36] Ibid., 1:508.

[37] Carreyre, *Le jansénisme durant la Régence*, 1:391.

[38] *Exposé*, 2:524 ff.

[39] For the relationship between Silvestre de Sacy and Champollion, cf. Hermine Hartleben, *Champollion, sein Leben und sein Werk* (1906); French translation by D. Meunier (Paris, 1983).

[40] For a clear example of substitution in which Sacy cites the Arabic coded text and its decipherment, see *Exposé*, 2:635.

[41] "Commentatio de notione vocuum 'tenzil' et 'tawil' in libris, qui ad Druzorum religionem pertinent," in *Commentationes Societatis regiae scientarum göttingensis* 16 (1805).

[42] *Exposé*, 1:33 (note).

[43] Ibid.

[44] Ibid., 2:428-29.

[45] Ibid., 2:663.

[46] Ibid., 2:660.

[47] Ibid., 2:423 (note); 2:705 (note).

[48] Ibid., 1:4.

[49] Ibid., 1:32.

[50] Ibid., 1:35.

[51] Ibid., 1:34.

[52] "Avertissement," in *Exposé*, 1:8.

David R. W. Bryer

Druze Religious Texts

Before beginning, I should like to offer two caveats. The first is that most of my research on the Druze religion was done some thirty years ago and that it largely focused upon origins, that is, the Ismaʿili roots of the Druze faith. Second, and more important, it is virtually impossible for someone who is not an adherent to present a complete picture of a religion, particularly when its inner truths are known only to a minority of community members—the initiates. When one has not been part of a religious oral tradition that interprets and reinterprets the original body of doctrine, one can only comment on the traces that are visible and cannot pretend to do more.

The writings peculiar to the Druze community may be conveniently classified according to seven headings. The first two types, which are the ones that I will look at here, are the collection of canonical scriptures which, taken together, form the Druze 'Bible'[1] and the glosses explaining and expanding certain points in those scriptures and written at a later date in the manuscripts of the canon.

Beyond these are, third, the commentaries[2] on the scriptures penned by later scholars, of whom the most famous is ʿAbd Allah al-Tanukhi, and, fourth, a group of non-canonical writings[3] dating from the first centuries of the Druze era that are mainly concerned with expanding the philosophical ideas outlined by Hamza, al-Tamimi and Bahaʾ al-Din. The fifth type is composed of certain apocryphal writings, such as the *Kitāb al-Yūnān,* attributed to one or another of the ministers, but dating, in fact, from a later period[4] and containing, in at least two instances (to be found in de Sacy[5]), information that is actually opposed to the teaching of Hamza. What is common to all of these writings today, however, is the fact that most, to the best of my knowledge, are available solely to the *ʿuqqāl*. The rest of the Druze writings are, with certain restrictions, open to the *juhhāl* as well. They include the sixth type, namely, catechisms, prayers and sermons, and the seventh, various secular writings, including many poems.

The canon

Of all of these, the canon of scriptures is, of course, the most important group of writings. It consists of one hundred and eleven pieces, normally divided into five or six volumes, the last two volumes sometimes being combined into a single one. With only a few exceptions, the division of the epistles into volumes and their order in those volumes is constant in all manuscripts.

As for the authorship of the epistles, there are few difficulties concerning the later works. Epistles XXXVI to XL are, without any doubt, by the second minister, al-Tamimi, while XLI to CXI are all by Baha' al-Din, with the possible exception of XLIV, which de Sacy assigns to Baha' al-Din in one place, but to Hamza in another. His reasons for attributing it to Hamza—the style and the lack of honorifics following Hamza's name—do not, however, seem sufficient justification for thinking that the compiler of the canon may have made a mistake.

The authorship of the first thirty-five pieces presents more difficult problems. The first four pieces are not specifically Druze, but their connection with al-Hakim has led to their being included. Piece I is a *sijill* written in Dhū'l-Qa'da 411, immediately after the disappearance of al-Hakim. Its writer calls himself the "Lord of the Daʿwa of the Commander of the Faithful" and al-Hakim's name is followed by the epithet normally used by the Ismaʿilis for the *imām*, something specifically forbidden by Hamza in a later epistle. Indeed, the terminology of the whole piece is non-Druze and it has obviously been written for all Muslims and not just the *Muwaḥḥidūn*. These points have led Muhammad Kamil Husayn to suggest that the writer was a Fatimid scribe or perhaps even the great Ismaʿili scholar, Hamid al-Din al-Kirmani.[6] But such a conclusion does not necessarily follow. Hamza was quite capable of adapting his teaching to the group that he was addressing. If he is indeed the author of the refutation of the Nusayris, for example, he displays in it an attitude toward the *ẓāhir* and *bāṭin* that differs greatly from what he preaches elsewhere in his epistles. The title of 'Lord of the Daʿwa of al-Hakim' would, from Hamza's point of view, fit himself as well as al-Kirmani and it seems, therefore, not at all improbable that Hamza himself wrote this document and in such a way as to appeal to the largest possible audience and to cause the least offence to the feelings of the Cairene public. Certainly, the ability to write on quite different levels and in a way that appears contradictory to the outsider is typical of most Isma'ili writers, not least Qadi al-Nu'man who, according to Isma'ili tradition, wrote not only the *Da'ā'im al-Islām,* but the very different *al-Risāla al-mudhhiba*! As for Hitti's suggestion that the writer's injunction against any investigation of al-Hakim's disappearance may indicate that Hamza "had a hand in the conspiracy that resulted in the murder of al-Hakim,"[7] it can be completely discounted. Amid all of the uncertainties that surround the early days of the Druze, Hamza's loyalty and faith in al-Hakim stand out clear and sure. If he indeed plotted the murder of al-Hakim, then everything that he preached was a gigantic hoax intended solely to buttress his own power and prestige—a possibility which no one who has read his writings can possibly entertain.

Piece II is a *sijill* of al-Hakim dated Dhū'l-Qa'da 400 and it was no doubt included because it was the only document written by al-Hakim that was available to the compiler of the canon. Similar motives also led to the inclusion of the next two pieces. The account of the discussions between al-Hakim and the Jews and Christians probably dates from the period of their most serious persecutions, AH 403 or 404, and is presumably included to demonstrate al-Hakim's wisdom, while Piece IV, a supposed exchange of letters between the Qarmatian leader and al-Hakim at the time of a threatened Qarmatian invasion of Egypt, is apparently meant to show his power. The latter, however, can hardly be what it purports to be, for no record of such an invasion in the reign of al-Hakim exists. Perhaps it dates from the Qarmatian expedition in AH 363, during the reign of al-Mu'izz.

Pieces V to XXXV have traditionally been accepted as the work of Hamza and, certainly, the compiler of the canon must have considered them as such since he placed them all together between the works of al-Hakim and al-Tamimi. The certainty with which one can assign them to Hamza, however, varies considerably from one piece to another. Thirteen of them name Hamza as author. The title of XXV also shows the work to be his. Another nine are probably his owing to the doctrines that he introduces, his use of the first person, the definition given of his own position, or his reference to another of his writings. XXXV is presumably Hamza's last epistle, being placed by the founder of the canon at the end of his writings and bearing the same title as Baha' al-Din's own final work. Piece V, the *Mīthāq,* was probably authored by him as leader of the community. There is little about the prayers (epistles XXIX-XXXI) to suggest their authorship except the title of the first, which seems to indicate that it was written by Hamza. In most manuscripts, only the style suggests that Epistle XI is by Hamza, but the Bodleian one, Arab e213 (which I discuss below), actually has a colophon naming Hamza as the author, which would carry much weight if the manuscript is not a forgery. Epistle XV, the refutation of the Nusayris, has little to suggest that it is by Hamza except its position in the canon. If he is indeed the author, then its list of the *ḥudūd*, its attitude toward the *bāṭin* and the *ẓāhir* and its favourable references to the *Ta'wil* and *Majālis al-Ḥikma* suggest an early date, probably AH 408, and perhaps an audience that, while accepting the special nature of al-Hakim, still considered itself to be Isma'ili.[8] Finally, XXXII is almost certainly not by Hamza, for the writer speaks of Hamza as "My Lord."

As with their authorship, so with their dating, for only some of the early epistles present special problems. With the exception of pieces II, III and IV, which date from AH 400, perhaps 403 and perhaps 363 respectively, the rest of the canonical writings were composed during the period AH 408 to 434. Dates, when given, are usually given according to the Druze era, in which AH 408 corresponds to the Year 1, but in which AH 409 is excluded so that AH 410 is Year 2. Although only a fraction of the epistles are so dated, they permit us to hazard a reasonable guess concerning the ones that are not. The writings of Baha' al-Din stretch over the longest period—from AH 418-434; al-Tamimi wrote only in the year AH 411 and, perhaps, 412; and Hamza's epistles are from the years AH 408, 410 and, possibly, 413.

Of Hamza's writings, twelve or, if one accepts the colophon of MS Arab e213, thirteen are dated: Epistles VI and VII are from AH 408; IX to XIII, XVI, XVII, XIX and XXVIII from AH 410; and XXII and XXIV from AH 411. Of the rest, VIII and XV are probably from AH 408, XXXV may be from AH 412 and the remainder are from AH 410 or 411. Against this comparatively simple scheme, however, certain objections have been raised. In an attempt to show that Imam al-Hakim was in no way involved with Hamza, an Isma'ili, Mr. Assaad, has suggested[9] that all of the Druze writings except XXVIII, Hamza's letter to the chief *qāḍī*, date from after the time of al-Hakim and that the dates found in the colophons were added later. To support this theory, he put forward three pieces of evidence: first, the *sijill* written after the disappearance of al-Hakim makes no mention of any other Druze writings; second, Epistle VI contains two lines of a poem that also appear in the *Majālis al-Mu'ayyadiyya*, written half a century later; and, finally, Epistle IX contains a passage which suggests that al-Hakim's son has already succeeded his father.

Such evidence, however, seems rather slender against the testimony both of the writings themselves and of the historians, for if Hamza and his followers were as active in the last years of al-Hakim's reign as the historians make out, it seems inconceivable that Hamza began to write his epistles only after the *ghayba* of al-Hakim. The absence of any mention of other Druze writings in the *sijill* is quite understandable if one accepts that Hamza was writing here for the whole Cairene population and not merely his own followers. As for the two lines of poetry in Epistle VI, they might have come from an earlier source, as Hamza himself claims, and been quoted both by Hamza and al-Muʾayyad or, less probably, they might have been added to the rest of the epistle at a later date, a suggestion made by Muhammad Kamil Husayn.[10] If they were indeed copied from al-Muʾayyad, then it would almost certainly mean that the writer was not Hamza and that this epistle and, presumably, all of the others claiming Hamza as their author were actually written half a century later, at a time when all connections between the Druze and Egypt had been cut—a complete impossibility if one consider the obvious Egyptian and Ismaʿili ambience of all of these early epistles. Regarding the passage in Epistle IX, it may well be an insertion made after the disappearance of al-Hakim against those who believed that the divine manifestation had passed to *al-Ẓāhir*. It is also likely that such an insertion would have been made by Hamza himself, for there is no reason to doubt the genuineness of his belief that al-Hakim would soon return to initiate the triumph of his followers. If the epistles were read and re-read to the faithful much as the *majālis* were to the Ismaʿilis, the possibility that Hamza might later have inserted short passages like this seems quite plausible.

Although the six volumes of the scriptures contain all of the extant writings of the first, second and fifth ministers—Hamza, al-Tamimi and Bahaʾ al-Din—together with the handful of works by or about al-Hakim, it is clear that Hamza, at least, wrote other works that were not included in the canon and are no longer extant. In Epistle XV, he mentions a book that he had written on marriage; in Epistle XVII, he speaks of the *Kitāb al-munfarid bi-dhātihi*, apparently a polemic against those who do not accept that the divine was fully manifested in al-Hakim; in Epistle XXI, he mentions a code of rules that he has drawn up and also a previous letter appointing al-Qurashi as *dāʿi* before he was promoted to the rank of *kalima*. Finally, Epistle XXII, the letter of appointment of the fifth minister, refers to another letter that names the fourth one.

Just as the order of the epistles is constant in most manuscripts of the scriptures, so, too, is their text. Although the Druze have traditionally not printed their sacred books (indeed, printed versions of the canon are still rare), relying instead upon handwritten copies continually being made by otherwise inactive *ʿuqqāl*, there is quite remarkable agreement among the manuscripts thus produced: almost all of the variants are of an orthographical or grammatical nature and of little importance. It would thus seem that both the form of the canon and the details of the text were established very early. In the years immediately following the disappearance of Hamza, several versions of each epistle were probably in circulation but, before long, presumably once the contents of the canon had been fixed, one version of the text was accepted as correct. This must then have become the archetype for all succeeding manuscripts. The Bodleian manuscript Arab e213, to be discussed below, is possibly, if genuine, one of the pre-archetypal manuscripts.

This leads us to the question of who gathered the one hundred and eleven epistles, fixed their texts, put them in order and divided them into volumes. It is likely that one man did all of this (although the division into volumes may have come a little later), with the work being done early enough to prevent too many discrepancies from appearing in the text, yet long enough after the break-up of the community in Cairo for some of Hamza's writings to have disappeared. The Druze scholar, al-Tanukhi, suggested by Mr. Assaad as the founder of the canon, is certainly too late a figure to be considered. At least three of the Paris manuscripts contemporary with al-Tanukhi show evidence of being nothing more than links in an already long tradition which, if we can rely on the ancient Bodleian manuscript, goes right back to the fifth/eleventh century. Much more probable is the figure generally accepted by the Druze as the founder of the canon, Baha' al-Din. The later Druze work, *Mukhtasar al-bayān fi majra al-zamān,*[11] explicitly states that, before his *ghayba,* Baha' al-Din put together his own works with those of Hamza and al-Tamimi. Certainly, Baha' al-Din, as de facto leader of the community for more than twenty years, was in by far the best position to settle both the contents and the order of the canon. Indeed, the only real argument against accepting Baha' al-Din as the canon's compiler is the position of piece XXXII.

The first two volumes begin with works connected with al-Hakim and end with the epistles of al-Tamimi; as suggested above, the central group of writings (V-XXXV) are probably by Hamza. The order of all of these pieces is more or less chronological, although sometimes those with similar content have been placed together even if this conflicts with the chronological principle. The position of XXXII, which contains an interesting list of the names, ranks and titles of the five higher ministers, within the group of works by Hamza, although certainly not by Hamza, thus militates, at first sight, against the proposition that Baha' al-Din was the compiler of the canon, for surely the *tālī* must have had a detailed knowledge of everything that Hamza had written and would not have wrongly inserted a piece by another author among Hamza's writings. One possible explanation is that Bahaʾ al-Din inserted it as a necessary guide to the surrounding works, much like a map or plan drawn by someone other than the author might be inserted into a book. Certainly, all of the other evidence favours accepting the fifth minister as the compiler of the scriptures.

The division of the *rasāʾil* into volumes was no doubt largely a matter of convenience and may have occurred at any time during the first century or two of the Druze era (the ancient Bodleian manuscript here being of little help in fixing the date). The only internal evidence for thinking that this division may date back to the earliest times are the words found at the end of Epistle XIV, the last epistle of the first volume: "Here endeth the first section and the second will follow it if Our Lord wills." If these words are an addition and not by Hamza, they must clearly have been inserted before the archetype of the extant manuscripts became fixed, for they appear in all of the manuscripts that I have seen.

The glosses

I would also like to discuss briefly the glosses be found in certain manuscripts of the canon. They are written above or beside the line and explain difficult words, give *taʾwīls* of certain words to show that they actually refer to the *ḥudūd*, provide figures, such as the number of *daʿis*, or show how certain words used to refer to Muhammad or ʿAli really have a much stronger meaning than might be assumed. Although they are only found in a minority of the manuscripts, there is such similarity between the various glosses that they, too, must date from the first centuries of the Druze era. On the other hand, they were certainly written by Druze scholars who knew nothing of Ismaʿilism and who were far more hostile to the Prophet and Islam than Hamza ever had been.

The fact that the writers of the glosses were unfamiliar with Ismaʿili theology may be seen, for example, in a reference to Maryam in Epistle VI, where she is called the "Hujja Sahib Zamanihi." According to the Ismaʿili writers, the Sahib Zamanihi was Zakariyya.[12] The writer of this gloss, however, gives the perhaps more expected—but non-Ismaʿili—interpretation that the Sahib Zamanihi was ʿIsa. The writers of the glosses show their ignorance of Ismaʿilism more clearly in Epistle XVII, when the gloss explains references to *Kitāb al-daʿāʾim, Mukhtasar al-athār* and *Al-Iqtisār,* three of the most well-known books on *fiqh* by Qadi al-Nuʿman, as denoting the Qurʾan. The hostility to Islam is shown in glosses like those in Epistle XV: the *nāṭiq* is Iblis; the *asās* is al-Shaytan.

Clearly the glosses date from those early centuries when the Druze had become a closed community in the foothills of Mount Hermon and in Mount Lebanon, often struggling to exist alongside their frequently hostile Muslim neighbours. Their main interest lies in their being one of the few ways in which one may see how the religion of Hamza developed in those centuries.

The manuscripts

I would now like to move on to the physical form of the Druze scriptures, the manuscripts themselves and, especially, the ones that are publicly available. More than two hundred fifty manuscripts of Druze writings are mentioned in the catalogues of European and North American libraries. Most of these were acquired in the mid-nineteenth century, following the conflict between Druze and Christians in Lebanon; at that time, many Druze *khalawāt* were ransacked and their manuscripts stolen and sold to Europeans in Damascus. Some, however, were acquired earlier either by European travellers in the Levant or, occasionally, by Syrians who brought them as gifts to Europe. The earliest known of all such acquisitions came about through the presentation of a set of the scriptures to Louis XIV in 1700 by a Syrian doctor, Nasrallah Ben-Gilda, who had stolen them from the home of Shaykh Nasreddin in Bʿaqlin, the chief town of the Druze in Mount Lebanon.

The manuscripts whose existences are confirmed by catalogues are to be found in twenty-five libraries in Europe and several in the United States. However, these certainly represent only a fraction of the ones not in Druze hands. Even in libraries, there are often many manuscripts that have not yet been catalogued. The Bodleian, for example, had only four of its fifteen Druze manuscripts listed in its catalogues in 1970 while, in Berlin, it is still not clear what happened to all of the manuscripts that were in the State Library before World War II. Apart from these, there are many Druze manuscripts in Lebanon, particularly in some Lebanese monasteries; doubtless there are others to be found in Syria, Palestine and Egypt. At the moment, however, the major collections available for study remain those of Paris and Berlin, followed by Munich, the Vatican, the British Library and Oxford and Cambridge.

Almost all of these manuscripts are ornamented to a greater or lesser degree. At the very least, the titles and the first words of sentences are coloured red. More often, the decoration is still more ornate, with many colours—gold, blue, green, red, yellow and purple—and even glitter used to decorate the titles and distinguish new topics. This has led Martin Sprengling to suggest that "the neat, clear but not ornate handwriting and illumination in gold, blue, green, red and yellow is another case of Manichaean influence."[13] However, the complete absence of any overt connection with Mani or Manichaeism, as pointed out by Hodgson,[14] suggests that this superficial similarity is a coincidence, rather than an effect. Much more probably it is in imitation of the Qur'an.

A system of coloured dots is also used as a type of punctuation, red ones usually signifying new sentences, green ones quotations from the Qur'an. In a number of manuscripts, the system is taken much further, with different coloured dots and dashes used as glosses. The complete system is not entirely clear, but the meaning of certain signs can be guessed at with reasonable certainty. Five red dots above a word, for example, mean that it refers to the five true *ḥudūd*, while five green ones signify the five false ones. The 'code' system is normally much more complicated than this, however, with dots of different colours interspersed along a line or grouped in circles in ways that make it nearly impossible for anyone outside of the *ajāwīd* (the initiates) to guess their meaning. There is considerable, but by no means total, agreement among manuscripts as to which words are further explained by such markings.

Another feature of the manuscripts—which, while not, of course, confined to Druze manuscripts, is invariable among them—is that there is an odd number of lines to each page.

The orthography, morphology and syntax of the manuscripts is basically that of 'classical' Arabic, but modified by the influence of the spoken language.

As I have said, despite occasional differences, the manuscripts are clearly from one tradition and, notwithstanding variations in age and provenance, there is remarkable uniformity among them. The one exception to this is the Bodleian Library manuscript, Arab e213, described by Professor A. F. L. Beeston in the *Bodleian Library Record* in 1956[15] and also referred to by Marshall Hodgson in 1962.[16] The Beeston article suggests that the manuscript is, in fact, an autograph of Hamza and it is sad that a closer analysis of the text does not appear to confirm this.

The manuscript contains seven epistles (VI-XII), with IX-XII being followed by VI-VIII. There are considerable portions of the text missing—more than a third of Epistle XII, for example—but, in most cases, the missing portions are from either the beginning or the end of the epistles. The curious order might be quite early as the owners' marks are on the first folio.

Until the Bodleian bought the manuscript in 1956, the earliest known Druze manuscripts were the fifteenth-century ones in the Bibliothèque Nationale in Paris. Certain aspects of Arab e213, however, point to its being some four centuries older than these. Indeed, if we leave aside, for the moment, the suggestion that it is an autograph of Hamza, there are only two possibilities concerning its date: either it is a very old copy dating from the early eleventh century AD or a forgery of the mid-twentieth century. If the former is true, Arab e213 has great importance for indicating the early date at which the epistles began to be collected together and the canon formed; for demonstrating the comparative stability of the text over nearly a thousand years; and for adding a few details of information, such as the authorship and date of Epistle XI, and altering some accepted views, for example, about the claims of al-Darazi. On the other hand, if it is a forgery, it is an interesting addition to a group of manuscripts of doubtful authenticity that appeared on the market in the 1950's, but is of far less interest for a study of the Druze.

The main reason for thinking that the manuscript is an autograph is a colophon on folio 33 saying that the epistle was completed in the hand of Hamza ibn ʿAli, Guide of the Obedient, in the second year of his era. This replaces the usual ending and the usual disclaimer: "This was copied from the writing of the *qaʾim al-zamān* without any distortion or changes," a phrase that clearly would not have appeared in Hamza's original letter. One possible explanation for this difference is that the text was copied by a scribe before agreement had been reached on an authoritative version. Beeston also calls attention to the grammatical variants in the text, of which there are some four hundred. He suggests these may be due to Hamza's Persian origin but, while this might excuse the writer's ignorance of correct case endings, it cannot explain the fifty or so instances in which the variants are obvious copying errors and make no sense or where vital words have been omitted.

But even if Arab e213 is not an autograph, there is still considerable evidence to suggest that it dates from the eleventh century AD. First, the script, the so-called Rhomboid or East Persian Kufic, is found only in manuscripts of the tenth and eleventh centuries. Moreover, it has various owners' marks, including one of ʿAbdullah ibn Shihab, dated AH 785/AD 1383. More interesting still is the signature, Muhammad ibn al-Alqami, the *wazīr* to the last ʿAbbasid caliph, who died in AH 655/AD 1257. There are also fragments of Arabic poetry in an early script and a twelve-line Persian poem in a script Professor Beeston places in the seventh/thirteenth century or earlier.

All of this would suggest that the manuscript is an early copy of some of Hamza's writings, written by a scribe with little understanding or learning some time before the archetype was finally established. Somehow the manuscript soon left Druze hands and, within two centuries, had reached the Iraq library of Muʿayyad al-din Muhammad ibn al-ʿAlqami, noted for his interest in and favour to the Shiʿa. From there, it presumably travelled to Persia and, finally, to Dublin, where a dealer called Khonsari sold it to the Bodleian in February 1956. Such a history is unique for a Druze manuscript for, without exception, all of the other manuscripts in European libraries have been acquired in the last three centuries from the present Druze homeland in Lebanon, Syria and Palestine.

And there the story would end were it not for the fact that, in the early 1950s, a number of rare manuscripts in this same Rhomboid or East Persian Kufic script[17] appeared on the market. In 1952, what was purported to be an autograph of otherwise unknown writings by the tenth-century Iraqi mystic, Muhammad ibn ʿAbd al-Jabbar al-Niffari,[18] was bought in Dublin. Two years later, the British Museum acquired from the same Dublin dealer a collection of philosophical treatises dated AD 330, which became the earliest secular manuscripts that it holds.[19] Not only was this collection in the same Rhomboid script as the Druze manuscript, but it also appears to be in very similar handwriting and on identical paper. Most interesting is a copy of the *Madīna al-fādila* by al-Farabi that apparently dates from the author's own lifetime, which was offered for sale for $10,000 by a Persian dealer in New York called Rabenou in about 1955. It is in a script that is extraordinarily similar to the one used in the Niffari manuscript and, as was definitively shown in 1969 by Stern and Walzer, is quite certainly a forgery of the mid-twentieth century.

But does the falsity of the al-Farabi manuscript in any way help us to decide the truth about the manuscripts that appeared in Dublin in the early 1950s, notably, the Niffari, the British Museum miscellany and the Bodleian Druze manuscript? In the final analysis, after stating their peculiarities, one can only rely upon intuition: sadly, there has been no scientific analysis to back my own hunch that they are all products of the mid-twentieth century. But certain points can be stressed. First, all of the manuscripts, quite apart from their script, are of remarkable importance to their own fields. All claim to be written within the lifetimes of their authors and some, for instance, the Niffari and, perhaps, the Druze one, claim to be actual autographs. Next, three of them antedate the earliest known manuscript in the Rhomboid script that is undoubtedly genuine: an Istanbul Qurʾan of AH 361/AD 971. Both the Niffari and Druze manuscripts are arranged in ways that differ from all other manuscripts of the text and both have surprising lacunae. More important is the similarity of the handwriting in the Niffari and the Farabi, although this, of course, might simply reflect the fact that the Niffari was used as a model for the Farabi. More surprising still is the even greater similarity in handwriting and paper between the British Museum miscellany and the Druze manuscript—writings which, if genuine, were separated in time by eighty years and in space by many hundreds of miles. It would be interesting to know the price asked for such manuscripts but, apart from the *Madīna al-fādila* at $10,000, it has been impossible to find out how much they cost: the Chester Beatty Collection and the British Museum apparently having no record of the expenditure, while the Bodleian "was not willing to divulge the price." At present, it is difficult to go much further than this in deciding the date of Arab e213. It remains the most fascinating of Druze manuscripts and, even if a forgery, one that may be based upon an as yet untraced early manuscript as was the copy of the *Madīna al-fādila*.

NOTES

[1] For the best account of the formation of the canon, its dating and the authorship of the epistles see H. Wehr, "Zu den Schriften Hamza's im Drusenkanon," *Zeitschrift der Deutschen Morgenländischen Gesellschaft* 96 (1942): 187-207.

[2] For example, Bodleian (Oxford) Marsh 563; British Museum (London) Add. 22485 and Or. 6852; Bibliothèque Nationale (Paris) 1436-1440; Munich State Library 228 and 232; and Austrian State Library (Vienna) MS 1578.

[3] H. Guys, *Theogonie des Druzes* (Paris, 1863); Seybold, *Die Drusenschrift: Kitāb al-Nuqat wal Dawā'ir* (Leipzig, 1902); M. Sprengling, "The Berlin Druze Lexicon," *American Journal of Semitic Languages* 56 (1939): 402-07.

[4] For example, Austrian State Library (Vienna) MS 1577; *Kitab al-Yunan*, cf. Petermann, *Reisen im Orient* (Leipzig, 1860), 1:377; Wehr, "Zu den Schriften Hamza's," 201-06; cf. Cambridge University Library Add. 1902, 1-5.

[5] De Sacy, *Exposé de le Religion des Druzes* (Paris, 1838; republished Amsterdam, 1964), 495-96.

[6] Muhammad Kamil Husayn, *Tā'ifat al-Durūz* (Cairo, 1962-68), 90.

[7] P. Hitti, *The Origins of the Druze People and Religion,* Columbia University Oriental Studies, vol. 27 (New York, 1928), 62.

[8] For the importance of this epistle in connection with Nusayri history, see C. Cahen, "Note sur les origines de la communauté syrienne des Nusayris," *Revue des Etudes Islamiques* 38, fas. 2 (1970): 249.

[9] School of Oriental and African Studies, London, 1970.

[10] Muhammad Kamil Husayn, *Ta'ifat al-Durūz* (1968), 91.

[11] See Guys, *Theogonie des Druzes*, 67-68; and Wehr, "Zu den Schriften Hamza's," 190-91.

[12] For example, al-Qadi al-Nu'man, *Kitāb asās al-ta'wīl*, edited by Arif Tamir (Beirut, 1960), 291-97.

[13] M. Sprengling, "The Berlin Druze Lexicon," *American Journal of Semitic Languages* 61 (1939): 410.

[14] M. Hodgson, "Al-Darazi and Hamza in the Origin of the Druze Religion," *Journal of the American Oriental Society* 82 (1962): 15.

[15] A. F. L. Beeston, "An Ancient Druze Manuscript," *Bodleian Library Record* 5 (1956): 286-90.

[16] Hodgson, "Al-Darazi and Hamza," 10.

[17] E. Schroeder, "What Was the Badi' Script?" *Ars Islamica* (1937): 232-48; M. Minovi, "The So-Called Badi' Script: A Mistaken Identification," *Bulletin of the American Institute for Iranian Art and Archaeology* 5 (1937): 142-47; Nabia Abbott, "The Contribution of Ibn Muqla to the North-Arabic Script," *American Journal of Semitic Languages* 56 (1939): 70-83; S. M. Stern, "Review of Istanbul Universitesi Kutuphanesi Arapca Yazmalar Katalogu, Vol.1, Fas.1, Istanbul, 1951," *Bulletin of the School of Oriental and African Studies* 6 (1954): 398-99; S. M. Stern, "A Manuscript from the Library of the Ghaznavid Amir Abd al-Rashid," in *Paintings from Islamic Lands*, edited by R. Pinder-Wilson, Oriental Studies, vol. 4 (Oxford, 1969), 18.

[18] A. J. Arberry, "More Niffari," *Bulletin of the School of Oriental and African Studies* 15 (1953): 29-42; Professor Ettinghausen of the Metropolitan Museum, New York, at a seminar in June 1971, stated that, in his view, the manuscript was of twentieth-century origin.

[19] G. Meredith-Owens, "A Tenth-Century Arabic Miscellany," *British Museum Quarterly* 20 (1955-56): 33-34.

NAILA KAIDBEY

Al-Sayyid Jamal al-Din al-Tanukhi as a Druze Reformer

ASIDE FROM THE *ḤUDŪD* and the scholars who founded and propagated the Druze religion, Emir Jamal al-Din ʿAbdullah al-Tanukhi (AD 1417-79), better known as al-Sayyid, is the person most venerated in Druze history.[1] Taken together, his documented interpretations of some of the Druze epistles, his theological writings and ethical treatise, and the example of his own life serve as an enduring model of Druze faith.

In this paper, I will focus upon Emir ʿAbdullah al-Tanukhi, first, as a spiritual leader of the Druze community and, then, as a jurist and social reformer. Next, I will proceed to discuss the contributions of his disciples and the power struggle that followed his reforms. The question being considered here is as follows: what was the role of al-Sayyid in preserving the religious and social identity of the Druze and was it as vital as commonly believed?

Background

In the years following the disappearance of the *ḥudūd,* many of the Druze epistles were scattered, destroyed, or kept hidden.[2] The centre of authority had gone and many of the remaining fragments of the *ḥikma* (Druze scriptures) were too mystical to be understood by any but the most dedicated. As a consequence, few were able to attain spiritual fulfilment.

The earliest Druze concentrations in Lebanon were in the regions of Wadi al-Taym, al-Gharb and the mountains of al-Shuf. Clans of the Tanukh tribal confederation were among these early settlers. Since the eighth century, some 300 years before the commencement of the *daʿwa* or 'call', the nascent Druze community had been entrusted with the protection of coastal and mountain roads by ruling dynasties in Damascus.[3] Their task was to ward off invaders and keep watch over important harbours. In the centuries that followed, the experienced Tanukh warriors, in particular, led by their traditional chieftains, proved invaluable to the defence of the Lebanese coast.

These and other circumstances forced the Druze to practice an intense degree of in-group solidarity and secretiveness and to emphasize military skills and values, leaving very little room for intellectual pursuits. Matters connected to their faith were safeguarded and overseen by pious elders in each region of Druze habitation, with almost no effort at harmonization or coordination. The epistles were kept in their original forms without any scrutiny or research into their esoteric connotations. The community as a whole would have to wait for almost four centuries before its code of ethics and much of its doctrine was structured and organized under the aegis of Emir ʿAbdullah al-Sayyid.[4]

While the Tanukhi emirs played an important role in keeping the Druze community within its religious boundaries and while many of them were members of the *ʿuqqāl* (the 'class' of sages or initiates), none of them ever reached the status of Emir ʿAbdullah al-Sayyid, who possessed, in the words of his biographer, both *jamāl al-dīn wal-dunya* (physical and spiritual radiance).[5]

Spiritual leader

Al-Sayyid was born in ʿAbey to a Tanukhi family on 22 Rabiʿ I AH 820/ 29 April AD 1417.[6] He grew up in dire poverty, having lost his father while still young. From an early age, he showed not only promise, but signs of greatness. His first concern was to memorize the entire Qurʾan, a task which he accomplished early in his youth. He was able to recite it from start to finish and even in reverse. As his biographer, Ibn Sibat, comments, with evident awe and admiration: "To memorize the Opening alone in reverse is miraculous, let alone the whole Qurʾan!"[7]

Al-Sayyid's approach to his studies was very disciplined. He would set himself a goal and neglect even the most basic of his needs until he had achieved it. Nothing, not even sorrow or elation, was capable of swaying him from his purpose. Denouncing worldly temptations, he occupied himself with worship and almost ceaseless contemplation. By the time that he reached early manhood, his pre-eminence among his fellows had become well-established. Ibn Sibat describes him as "decent, deliberate, steadfast in his opinions, precise and laconic except where matters of the *ḥikma* were concerned; a wise man who rarely blundered."[8]

Al-Sayyid sought to follow the path of the ascetics in his life and his counsel. He asked of people only what he himself was capable of and forbade only what he himself avoided. He encouraged his followers to wear simple and coarse clothing, emphasized that money was always best spent in charitable endeavours and urged moderation in all aspects of human life.[9]

In this way, he set the standard for his contemporaries and all who came after him. For example, the initiates of the Druze community, the *ʿuqqal*, still wear the simplest attire in accordance with the tradition set by al-Sayyid. His ascetic teachings are even more impressive when we consider that he was an emir and might easily have acquired wealth and lived in relative luxury by capitalizing upon his rank and prestige.

Al-Sayyid advocated a strict moral code, even for the prominent members of the community who followed in his path. He enjoined them to avoid the pleasures of this world and to focus their attention upon the hereafter. His biographer reports:

> Al-Sayyid taught them to act virtuously and to distinguish between the good hearts and the bad, to prohibit lustful and malicious behaviour. His commendable actions were many and his virtues beyond count.[10]

The arbitrator

The ascetic and austere life of al-Sayyid gained him the respect of all. Because he did not possess an *iqṭāʿ*[11] and the power and wealth that it would have entailed,[12] he was independent of the ruling emirs and of the Mamluks. His prominence stemmed solely from his position as the foremost Druze religious scholar and theologian of his time. His habit of practicing what he preached soon came to personify the Druze code.

The power of scholarship and edification proved to be more important than the clout of emirs or dignitaries. Al-Sayyid was recognized as the community's sole and unequalled arbitrator, a privilege previously exercised by the appointed judicial authorities alone.[13] This recognition would later create a rift between al-Sayyid and the rest of the Tanukhis—one with significant ramifications.

Biographers cite many examples that attest to the respect accorded to al-Sayyid by members of other religious communities in addition to the Druze. Not only did members of his own faith seek his arbitration, but Christians and Jews also came to the village to obtain his advice on non-religious disputes.[14]

An incident mentioned by Ibn Sibat is indicative of al-Sayyid's reluctance to bring local conflicts between Druze before the Mamluk judiciary. Ibn Sibat reports that a notable *shaykh*[15] of the region who was a disciple of al-Sayyid brought a dispute with one of his neighbours to the attention of the local authorities. The matter was settled when his opponent was coerced into agreeing to unjust terms: after being arrested and flogged, he had to pay a large sum as a penalty.

When the man was advised to bring his case to the attention of al-Sayyid, he recoiled: "Who am I to be listened to when my opponent is one of the emir's closest and most prominent disciples?" He was told: "Oh! But you are so ignorant! Emir Jamal al-Din puts no one above justice, not even his own son."

After hearing both parties, al-Sayyid expressed astonishment and concern that his follower had behaved in such a reprehensible manner. He reprimanded the *shaykh* by saying:

> You brought your case before officials who know no justice. They insulted the man and took the money he needed to support his family; then you forcibly chased him out of his home. This is an act of tyrants. Had this man any nails to scratch [you] with, you would not have dared [to act thus]. Have you forgotten the teachings of your faith?
>
> Know this, if you still trust in us, want to remain amongst us, then obey and abide by our verdict. Give the man back his money and let him return to his village.[16]

The *shaykh* complied.

Al-Sayyid became known for such impartiality and wisdom in arbitration, which was the source of the respect and reverence accorded him by members of his community. His counsel was sought by rich and poor alike, as well as notables and dignitaries of all faiths, and his equitable verdicts were always accepted.

Majālis (councils)

Al-Sayyid established a weekly council or *majlis* for spiritual matters and worship. Any member of the assembly who committed a transgression was barred from attending the *majlis*. People came to dread this banishment more than any penalty enforced by government officials. Ibn Sibat comments on this by saying: "The reprimands of al-Sayyid were more powerful than the fury of sovereigns."[17]

Self-discipline was mandatory as members of the *majlis* were expected to confine themselves to their homes if they committed any transgression. This self-confinement would continue until a word from al-Sayyid brought it to an end. Some of his followers went even further by banishing themselves from their villages and seeking refuge in remote regions as penance for their misdeeds.

One such ill-fated man said:

> Never have I faced such anguish. Death would have been easier. I have confronted merciless governors; I have been imprisoned and lost two sons; but never have I been in a more daunting situation.[18]

Among the devout, such self-discipline and self-deprivation continue to this day—testimony to the lasting nature of al-Sayyid's teachings.

Al-Sayyid encouraged the establishment of *majlis* in all of the areas inhabited by Druze. He appointed to the *majlis* of every village a dedicated administrator or *sāyis*, a pious man who followed the example set forth by al-Sayyid. This *sāyis* had the authority to receive new members into the *majlis* and to banish transgressors from it.

The result was a significant improvement in the quality of the moral and overall social fabric. Theft and other forms of wrongdoing soon became rarities as old and young alike sought the blessing and approval of their local *majlis.*[19]

It is worth noting that the weekly meetings of the *majlis* became venues for diverse deliberations, both religious and social. The confidential nature of their proceedings allowed for the frank discussion of all matters related to the general welfare of the community. The incessant interchange of advice, suggestions, opinions and even thoughts among the *ʿuqqāl* was a source of both unity and strength. In times of adversity, this practice proved to be very valuable in maintaining Druze cohesion.

Disciples

Prior to the fifteenth century, the Druze did not have any religious institutions. The *ʿuqqāl* were a spiritual élite distinguished only by their piety and strict morality. In principle, they had no regulatory role in the community or authority over its members. Al-Sayyid, however, endeavoured to change all of that. He enjoined his many disciples to carry his mission into their *majālis* and to advocate virtue, renounce evil and transmit his instructions regarding observance of the *sharīʿa.*

It was this effort which assured the continuation of the message of Hamza ibn ʿAli, the founder of the Druze faith. The *dāʿīs* (missionaries) of yesteryear almost seemed to have been reincarnated as al-Sayyid's disciples preached the *ḥikma* and taught tenets of the faith that had been forgotten or controversially transmitted. Al-Sayyid's followers were instructed to be fair, to help the oppressed and to clarify ambiguities in Druze teachings. Gradually, they attained new heights of prominence and importance and, as people sought their mediation in local disputes, took over the role of the appointed *qādis* (judges). The latter were adherents to the strict code of the Sunni *sharīʿa* whereas al-Sayyid, through his disciples, advocated Druze ethics and jurisprudence.

Al-Sayyid gave his followers, who were to emulate him in all of their actions, considerable authority.[20] In this way, he ensured that he had a representative in each village who would answer to no temporal power.[21] This semblance of a clerical establishment continued for some time after his death. Later years saw the stronger ruling emirs erode and eradicate what they considered to be a parallel authority and the *ʿuqqāl* resume a more pastoral role within the community.

The social and religious reformer

We find many references in the biographies of Emir ʿAbdullah al-Sayyid describing the era into which he was born as a time of abuse of power and moral laxity. Because of these circumstances, al-Sayyid played an indispensable role as a social and religious reformer. He considered every aspect of Druze life and directed the Druze to increase communal cohesion through austerity, piety and honest work. In this section, I will limit myself to those social reforms which had the most profound and lasting effects on the Druze.

Al-Sayyid's principal concern, besides the moral standard of the community, was to raise the level of education among his coreligionists. He constantly spoke of the necessity of learning and even paid the expenses to school orphans in all Druze regions. Although he lived in a community in which books were rare and at a time when they were very expensive to obtain, al-Sayyid collected over 300 volumes concerned with all fields of study then known.[22] He also composed many works dealing with religious and social issues, including *Subul al-akhyār* (The path of the righteous), a valuable treatise that gives details about the path that initiates should follow in their lives and worship, and an essential lexicon of the Arabic language entitled *Safinat al-lughā* (The vessel of language).[23]

Al-Sayyid's most important contributions, however, are his commentaries on three of the Druze epistles: *Al-Mīthāq* (The covenant); *Kashf al-ḥaqāʾiq* (The revelation of the truth); and *Sharṭ al-imām* (The *imām*'s proviso).[24]

Al-Mīthāq is the pledge by which every Druze binds him or herself to the faith. Perhaps because the covenant's meaning was not fully appreciated during his time, al-Sayyid found it necessary to explain and comment on its every word. The result was a comprehensive treatise on what it meant to be a Druze. Al-Sayyid reiterated that man's real purpose is union with the One and that deflection from the route leading to this goal results in separation from God, remoteness from His light, deprivation of His goodness and absence from genuine Existence. As avowed by *al-Tawḥīd* (Unitarianism),[25] man is the only being who can repress the egotism that leads him away from his real purpose and alienates him from his true nature. Accordingly, al-Sayyid enjoined the faithful to use each human limb (*al-jawāriḥ*) in accordance with its purpose and nature and, thus, to attain virtue.[26]

Kashf al-ḥaqīqa is one of the principal epistles for it contains the basic principles of the Druze faith. In it, Hamza ibn ʿAli expounds upon the Druze perception of God, the universe and the *ḥudūd*. The esoteric connotations of this epistle were beyond the comprehension of those whom de Sacy calls "*les simples unitaires,*"[27] however, because of the presence of philosophical terminology needing clarification.[28] Al-Sayyid explained and simplified many of these terms in an effort to make the epistle accessible to anyone dedicated enough to seek *al-ḥaqīqa* (the truth).

The commentaries of al-Sayyid on *Sharṭ al-imām,* a short treatise that focuses upon the institution of matrimony in the context of the Druze faith, were still more comprehensive. Al-Sayyid dealt with every aspect of this relationship and clarified any ambiguity that might have resulted from the epistle's misinterpretation. He also included an extensive exposition on the need for moderation in individual conduct within the community.

Al-Sayyid encouraged erudition in all Islamic disciplines. He believed that without a deep understanding of Islam one could not comprehend the true meaning of *al-tawḥīd* and *al-ḥaqīqa.* For this reason, he was unwavering when it came to the proper recitation of the Qurʾan. In addition, he ordered the construction of new mosques and the renovation of old ones. Upon his recommendation, funds were set up for charitable and religious endeavours.

As a social reformer, al-Sayyid was a pioneer and pathfinder on the subjects of marriage, divorce and the rights of women. Even though the Druze community already possessed codes and laws on these questions, they seem to have been neglected or misunderstood by al-Sayyid's time. Many people followed Sunni laws or modified versions of them that had been adapted at the discretion of regional Druze leaders. Al-Sayyid found it necessary to clarify, refine and update Druze regulations in order to try to simplify them as much as possible. The result was a coherent amalgam of Islamic law, acceptable Druze social norms and al-Sayyid's own interpretations based upon religious scriptures.

According to *al-Tawhīd,* matrimony is sacred.[29] Al-Sayyid was keen to the point of excess about a woman's right to refuse or consent to marriage (*al-riḍā wal-taslīm*).[30] He was known for strictly upholding this principle: anyone found to have forced a woman into marriage bore the brunt of his wrath. He went so far as to declare that any union based upon coercion was adulterous and that children born of such a union were illegitimate.[31]

A related point that indicates his concern for the community's welfare is his insistence that a man should not take a wife unless he possessed the means to meet his future obligations. Al-Sayyid was aware of the financial burdens of marriage and sought to secure a healthy environment for the family.[32] At the time, the Druze community was not affluent and additional expenses only increased the misery of the people. To assure compliance, al-Sayyid permitted certain important exceptions, such as the marriage of poor orphans, male or female.

Al-Sayyid also emphasized compatibility in character and social standing if both parties to the marriage were to fulfil their responsibilities toward one another. The education of the woman was paramount, particularly if her prospective husband was a scholar. For al-Sayyid, it was unacceptable for a man to seek knowledge in matters of religion while leaving his wife in ignorance: both had to have an equal opportunity to learn about *al-ḥaqīqa*. Hence, at a time when women were deemed to be inferior to men, al-Sayyid advocated greater equality between the sexes.

In all aspects of their relationship, al-Sayyid argued, a man should treat his wife with kindness and respect so that she would learn to love and honour him. Without love, he said, obedience can never be assured. In addition, a man had to provide for his wife and never deny her anything within his means. She was seen as an equal partner who shared in the most smallest details of her husband's life. These teachings gave Druze women a sense of self-esteem in the context of their marital relationships—something that endures to this day.

Al-Sayyid was also an advocate of family planning, favouring small families, especially for those who could not afford to raise many children. The family's breadwinner was not only expected to educate his offspring, but also to set aside something for charitable giving—a challenge for those with large families. Moreover, too many children might distract parents from their religious obligations. To quote al-Sayyid:

> If man comprehends the true meaning of *al-tawḥīd* and perceives the glory of the creator, his interest in offspring and other material pleasures will be greatly reduced.[33]

Al-Sayyid advocated one child for the poor and two or three for the more affluent with a four-year interval between children.[34] This enabled the parents, especially the mother, to give undivided attention to each child. In a detailed treatise, al-Sayyid enjoined parents to bring up their children to be pious, truthful and faithful to the principles of mutual assistance and solidarity (*ḥifiẓ al-ikhwān*) between members of the community.[35]

For al-Sayyid, as for all Muslim scholars, divorce was a last resort. However, consistent with his efforts to organize and reform socio-religious practices, he was obliged to address this problem and set out some basic precepts to regulate it. In a move indicative of his progressive thinking, he first reaffirmed that Druze women, as well as men, had a legitimate right to initiate divorce proceedings. His second point of emphasis was the necessity of avoiding hasty emotional decisions. In al-Sayyid's view, divorce should never result from one word or sentence spoken in anger. He reaffirmed the necessity of exhausting all possible venues for reconciliation before any thought of separation was seriously entertained and he instructed the *sāyis* of each *majlis* to play a conciliatory role on such occasions.[36]

In the unhappy event that divorce is seen to be the only solution, there are important prerequisites that must be met. Primary among these are indications that one of the two parties has engaged in blasphemy or the denial of *al-mīthāq*, in adultery or dishonesty, is mentally unbalanced, or has neglected his or her marital or social duties. If none of these has occurred, then the party initiating the divorce must forfeit half of his or her assets as a penalty. While all of this is mentioned in the epistle entitled *Sharṭ al-imām,* al-Sayyid paid particular attention to explaining the full meaning and significance of divorce.

Once divorced, husband and wife can never—under any circumstances or for any reason—remarry one another. Polygamy is also out of the question. Oral history has it that al-Sayyid refused the invitation of a prominent Druze in Safad because the man had more than one wife: this indicates that polygamy was still practiced in some Druze communities until the fifteenth century.

During the time of al-Sayyid, the Druze encouraged endogamy—marriage within one's own group. This was fundamental for the Druze since conversion to the faith had been suspended with the closing of the *daʿwa.* Marriage outside of the faith meant a loss of membership in the community.[37] The Druze have repeatedly found themselves in serious conflict with a variety of outside groups and have had to cope with many threats to their existence. One such threat involved their assimilation into the larger Sunni Muslim society. To avoid such a possibility, al-Sayyid re-emphasized the practice of endogamy in his commentaries.

Further supporting the equality of female members of the *ʿuqqāl*, al-Sayyid affirmed that women wishing to devote themselves to religion could be exempted from bearing and rearing children. Ultimately, such a decision was their own, in concert with their guardian (if single) or husband, with all parties to it being rewarded in the next world.[38] Al-Sayyid was actually reiterating the position of the *ḥudūd* concerning the education of woman[39]; however, his deep concern about this issue leads us to conclude that few Druze women were encouraged to pursue their own spiritual development at the time.

Al-Sayyid's position toward inheritance also shows his concern for equality among the *ṣālihīn* (righteous) of the community, irrespective of gender. For the Druze, a last will and testament is mandatory[40] and each person has the right to dispense of his or her wealth as he or she sees fit. What draws our attention here is the fact that al-Sayyid gave *al-imraʾa al-ṣāliḥa* (the virtuous wife) the same right to a share of her husband's wealth as their children; in other words, he recognized her intrinsic right to own property.

He also did not differentiate between male and female children in matters of inheritance, although he did encourage parents to be more generous toward the most virtuous of their children.[41] He further specified that wills should allocate a sum as a donation to the *ʿuqqāl*, with the size of the gift being directly proportional to the wealth of the deceased. If the *ʿuqqāl* are not mentioned in the will, a stipulated amount is allocated to them by the family of the deceased. Such directives attest to al-Sayyid's concern about social disparities in the community. The *ʿuqqāl*, most of whom lived the lives of ascetics, were always in need of financial assistance. Al-Sayyid stressed, however, that no one should accept charity unless he or she needed it,[42] a teaching that survives until the present.

Like all Muslims, the Druze strongly censure the drinking of wine and other alcoholic beverages. Al-Sayyid pronounced drinking alcohol to be a heretical practice and ostracized anyone who drank or produced wine. Upon his instructions, vines were uprooted. He even opposed the sale of raisins to Egyptian merchants for fear they might be used to make wine. He said: "It is more appropriate to sell raisins locally and offer [the juice] to guests as cold drinks."[43]

Power struggle within the community

Al-Sayyid's religious rigor and moral inflexibility ultimately led to a noticeable polarization between the religious and political authorities. By promoting the *ʿuqqāl,* he undermined the authority of the emirs, who were apprehensive at the former's newfound influence.

Several references indicate that al-Sayyid avoided those who socialized with government dignitaries and the officials responsible for tax collection.[44] He saw the Tanukhi emirs as sharing responsibility for social injustice with their associates, the Mamluks. Hence, al-Sayyid was reluctant to accept contributions from the emirs and encouraged his disciples to refuse them as well. This became a tradition among the Druze faithful. To this day, the *ʿuqqāl* exchange currency that they receive from government officials for money from someone that they know and trust. By advocating such behaviour, al-Sayyid was in effect rejecting the norms that had been set by the ruling *muqātiʿjīs*. It was not within his power to challenge the Tanukhis as tax collectors, but he refused to vindicate their actions.

Damascus interlude

Inevitably, strife and division have always accompanied reform movements. Al-Sayyid was opposed by those who stood to lose because of the changes that he had initiated. To avoid dissent among the Druze, al-Sayyid decided to leave his home in ʿAbey and settle in the Shaghur district of Damascus.

Historians have offered numerous explanations and justifications for al-Sayyid's extended absence.[45] The one most repeated—and which he himself might have encouraged—was that he was there to ensure the proper education of his son, ʿAbd al-Khaliq. However, the length of his stay in Damascus and the fact that his adherents sent petitions appealing to him to return suggest otherwise.

The ruling emir in al-Gharb at the time was Badr al-Din al-Husain (d. 1456), a close ally and personal friend of the Mamluk governor of Damascus, Jilban al-Mu'ayydi (1439-1454).[46] Ibn Sibat tells us that Badr al-Din imitated the Mamluks in dress and behaviour to such an extent that he was considered one of them. When Jilban paid a visit to ʿAbey, Badr al-Din was keen to demonstrate to his guest that the Druze community adhered to Islamic rituals.[47]

As noted above, al-Sayyid encouraged the outward observance of Sunni tenets; however, at the same time, he was working to revitalize *al-Tawḥīd,* a heterodox teaching by Sunni standards.[48] Hence, if the Tanukhis condoned his actions openly, they risked jeopardizing their position vis-à-vis the Mamluks, who had demonstrated their intolerance of heterodoxy on more than one occasion. The only way that they could survive in a hostile environment was by practicing *al-taqiyya* (dissimulation).[49]

I believe that al-Sayyid was coerced into leaving ʿAbey because of this dynamic. Otherwise, why would Ibn Sibat have overlooked this period of al-Sayyid's life? As the author of al-Sayyid's most detailed biography, he must have been aware of the circumstances behind the Damascus interlude. However, Ibn Sibat was writing at a time when Emir ʿAbdullah's pre-eminence among the Druze was well-established. Any allusion to al-Sayyid's exile, voluntary or otherwise, would have exposed Emir Badr al-Din to criticism—something that a scribe in the service of the Tanukhis could not risk.[50]

Another curious fact is that Ibn Sibat never refers to Emir ʿAbdullah as 'al-Sayyid,' a title bestowed upon him in Damascus owing to his considerable scholarship and piety.[51] Recognition of that title would have served as acknowledgement of the time that he had spent in exile.

Historical sources are vague about the social and religious fabric of al-Shaghur. It is possible that al-Sayyid was there in order to extend his reform program to the Druze of that region. The conflict between al-Sayyid and a certain Ahmad bin Abi al-Furn supports this possibility. Ahmad and his cohorts contested al-Sayyid's position on excluding transgressors from religious circles, favouring more tolerant prescripts instead.[52]

After years of separation from family and friends, al-Sayyid sent a letter to the *ʿuqqāl* of his homeland that is referred to in the sources as *Kitāb ilā jamāʿat al-buldān*.[53] While the text of this letter is full of reprimands and reproachful toward any who may have deviated from his teachings, the undertone is conciliatory. The *ʿuqqāl* were elated by this communication and stood in reverence each time it was read in the *majālis*.[54] The letter is now a sermon and an integral part of Druze doctrine. To this day, the *ʿuqqāl* stand when it is read—testimony to al-Sayyid's lasting influence.

Al-Sayyid returned to ʿAbey and gradually passed his duties on to his son, ʿAbd al-Khaliq, withdrawing into the background.[55] However ʿAbd al-Khaliq was soon killed in a tragic accident. Al-Sayyid's famous sermon to his fellow believers during his son's funeral became an enduring symbol of pious conviction and self-restraint.[56] It went as follows:

> Hear ye. All life is fleeting and there is no escaping death. When you stand before God, your deeds, good and bad, are your only testimony. We are all in the realm of the Lord and His mercy is our sole salvation. Self-indulgence is our darkest abyss, denying the One Truth our downfall. For God's will is the ultimate wisdom and seeking His forgiveness the ultimate quest. To obey God and to seek His grace and forgiveness in patience is our blessing.

> Blessed is he who submits to God's will and devotes his life to God's worship. [Blessed is] he who accepts, he who makes wisdom his beacon and he who comes to realize that life is but a gift from God and His to take away. Blind is he who forsakes the word of God, for he shall answer for his negligence on the day when all accounts are due and blessing as well as condemnation are perpetual and absolute.
>
> Hear ye all who see me before you. Let none of you think that my submission to and acceptance of the loss of my son are signs of desperation and lack of resolve; that I have forgotten my son's goodness, his candour and his keenness. He was God's gift to me, my solace and my companion.
>
> Submission to the will of God is my resolve as it was my son's. For how can I also forget my son's piety, sincerity of belief and devotion? Accepting what God dictates whenever He dictates it is our conscious decision and our emphatic belief. My son and I have always sought God's mercy and deliverance, the apex of our humble existence and the very essence of our souls. For God has created you and blessed you with his infinite mercy; God has been bountiful to you and asked that you seek only the true and the good. You have been warned against disobedience and woe to him who disobeys! For you can only will what God has willed for you.
>
> You are like a fish created by God and given seven seas to wander. He gave you life and the gift of pursuing what you may, day and night. Are you not satisfied or do you actually think rebellion or disobedience to be your salvation? You whom He has made and He can at any time will not to be. For you are also like a bird in the cage of His will, His discretion and His mercy.
>
> Hear me all, for the day will come when the centuries will fade. Soon all will stand before the Maker, the Judge of the Infinite on the day when no good deed will go unrewarded. On that day, when time is stilled, you shall know what you have done.
>
> Triumph be to the [God-fearing] and joy to the [virtuous].[57]

Resigned to the will of God, al-Sayyid spent the last years of his life in meditation and spiritual exercise. He died on Saturday, 17 Jamada II AH 884 (4 September AD 1479).[58]

Conclusion

Had the Druze faith depended solely upon the epistles, it could not have survived eight hundred years of trial and danger, hated by Muslims and Christians alike, assailed on political and doctrinal grounds, and seeking no converts—yet, at the close of that long period, a subject of firm belief and a bond of union.[59] Al-Sayyid and the scholars who emulated him introduced into the faith elements that strengthened it and increased its attractiveness to the community.[60]

Suffice it to reiterate what one of al-Sayyid's biographers wrote:

> His heart was true without falseness, his utterance friendly and kind, and his striving ever to observe the *ḥikma.*
>
> Undeniable, too, was his deep piety, his pursuit of *tawḥīd* virtues and devotion to knowledge, his rectitude, his self-scrutiny, his probity and readiness to conciliate and mediate disputes, his hatred of trimming, his singleness of purpose and his rare intellectual acumen.[61]

NOTES

1 The word *ḥudūd* (guardians of the faith) has been translated as 'cosmic principles,' 'limitaries,' 'luminaries,' 'superiors' and 'dignitaries'. While all are correct, I prefer to use the original Arabic term as it is the one used by the Druze. On the *ḥudūd,* see Malik al-Ashrafani, *ʿUmdat al-ʿārifin,* MS in 3 vols. (private collection of Sami Makarem), 3:80-115; Zayn al-Din 'Abd al-Ghaffar Taqiuddin, *Kitāb al-nuqat wal-dawāʾir,* edited by Anwar Abu Khizam, introduction by Sulayman Taqiuddin (n.p.: Dar isharat, 1999); Silvestre de Sacy, *Exposé de la religion des Druzes,* 2 vols. (Paris: Imprimerie Royale, 1838), 2:101-297; and Nejla Abu-Izzuddin, *The Druzes* (Leiden: Brill, 1984), 101-122.

2 The principal *ḥudūd* went into concealment in AH 411/AD 1020. Bahaʾ al-Din al-Muqtana was entrusted with all matters pertaining to the faith. In AH 435/AD 1043, Bahaʾ al-Din wrote *Risālat al-ghayba* (epistle no. 111), which is considered to be the last of the epistles, before bidding the faithful farewell and going into retirement. See al-Ashrafani, *ʿumdat al-ʿārifin,* 3:106; ʿAbbas Abu-Salih and Sami Makarem, *Tārīkh al-Muwaḥḥidīn al-Durūz al-siyāsī fil-Mashriq al-ʿArabī,* (Beirut: By the authors, 1984), 66, 92; and Robert B. Betts, *The Druze* (New Haven: Yale University Press, 1988), 16.

3 On the history of the Tanukhis, see: Kamal Salibi, "The Buhturids of the Garb: Mediaeval Lords of Beirut and of Southern Lebanon," *Arabica* 8 (1961); Nadim Hamzeh, *Al-Tanūkhiyūn* (Beirut: Dar al-nahar lil-nashr, 1984); and Sami Makarem, *Lubnān fi ʿahd al-umarāʾ al-Tanūkhiyīn* (Beirut: Dar Sadir, 2000).

4 Al-Sayyid collected 111 epistles; Sulayman Alamuddin, *Al-Mādaris al-fikriyya* (Beirut: Nawfal, 1998), 566.

5 Ibn Sibat, *Tārīkh al-Durūz fi akhir ʿahd al-Mamālīk,* edited by Naila T. Kaidbey (Beirut: Dar al-'awda, 1989), 84.

[6] In Vatican MS no. 270, the date of al-Sayyid's birth is given as 12 Rabi' I AH 820. This MS is the earliest extant copy of *Ṣidq al-akhbār, also compiled by Ibn Sibat, author of the most extensive biography of al-Sayyid. See Ibn Sibat, Tārīkh,* Introduction, 17.

[7] Ibid., 70.

[8] Ibid., 69.

[9] 'Abdullah al-Tanukhi, *Sharḥ mīthāq walī al-zamān,* MS (my private collection), 324.

[10] Ibn Sibat, *Tārikh,* 81.

[11] The English equivalent for *iqṭaʿ* is fief and a *muqāṭiʿjī* is a feudal lord. I prefer to use the Arabic words because they express the specificities of the feudal system as it applied in Mount Lebanon during that era.

[12] Sulayman bin Nasr, *Durrat al-tāj w-sullam al-miʿrāj fī tārīkh al-amīr Jamal al-Dīn ʿAbdullah al-Tanūkhī,* American University of Beirut MS no. 922.97, 15.

[13] Ibn Sibat refers to al-Sayyid as *amīr al-umarāʾ* to indicate the reverence which he inspired in the community; Ibn Sibat chose to ignore the fact that this title was officially used to designate Emir Sharf al-Din Musa (d. AH 892/AD 1486). See Ibn Sibat, *Tārīkh,* 24-25, 43; Makarem, *Lubnān,* 244.

[14] Ibn Sibat, *Tārīkh,* 77.

[15] Although the word sheikh appears in English-language dictionaries, I prefer to use the Arabic *shaykh* to differentiate between the feudal lords of Mount Lebanon and present-day Arab sheikhs.

[16] Ibid., 76-77.

[17] Ibid., 73.

[18] Ibid., 78.

[19] Ibid., 73.

[20] ʿAbdullah al-Tanukhi, *Sharṭ al-īmām,* MS (my private collection), 154-156.

[21] For a list of the names and biographies of the most prominent disciples see ʿAjaj Nuwayhid, *Al-Tanūkhī al-Amīr Jamal al-Dīn ʿAbdullah wal-Shaykh Muhammad Abu Hilāl* (Beirut: Dar al-sahafa, 1963), 183-254.

[22] Ibn Sibat, *Tārīkh,* 70.

[23] Many of al-Sayyid's works are not available. Some are lost, while others are kept hidden by the *ʿuqqāl* in an effort to maintain the secrecy of the faith. For the most extensive list of his works, see Fuʾad Abu-Zaki, *Al-Amīr al-Sayyid Jamāl al-Dīn ʿAbdullah al-Tanūkhī* (Lebanon: By the author, 1997), chapter 3.

[24] These are epistles 5, 13 and 25 respectively. Al-Ashrafani reports that al-Sayyid wrote 13 volumes of commentaries on these epistles; only a fraction of these are available, the remainder being either hidden or lost. See al-Ashrafani, *ʿumdat al-ʿārifīn,* 143; and Nuwayhid, *Al-Tanūkhī,* 130-34.

[25] The Druze prefer to be known as *Muwaḥḥidūn* (Unitarians: those who have

knowledge of the unity of God or *al-Tawḥīd*). They believe that the name Druze comes from the discredited Anajtekin (commonly pronounced Nashtakin) al-Darazi and probably became attached to the movement owing to the stir that he created. See Sami Makarem, *The Druze Faith* (Delmar, NY: Caravan Books, 1974), 12; Kamal Salibi, *Syria under Islam: Empire on Trial, 637-1097* (New York: Caravan Books, 1977), 102; and Abu-Izzuddin, *The Druzes*, 104.

[26] On the Druze position with regard to questions of good and evil, see al-Tanukhi, *Sharh al-mithaq*, 126-265; and Makarem, *Druze Faith*, 50-52.

[27] De Sacy, *Exposé*, 2:407.

[28] On these basic principles, see Makarem, *Druze Faith*, 41-113.

[29] Al-Tanukhi, *Sharṭ*, 148-49.

[30] Ibid., 149, 157.

[31] Ibid., 160-61.

[32] Abu-Zaki, *Al-Amīr al-Sayyid*, 343-50.

[33] *Tawḥīd* is translated as 'the true knowledge of God's unity'. See al-Tanukhi, *Sharḥ al-mīthāq*, 329-33; Makarem, *Druze Faith*, 91.

[34] Al-Tanukhi, *Sharḥ al-mīthāq*, 329.

[35] Ibid., 330-34.

[36] Al-Tanukhi, *Sharṭ*, 178.

[37] Al-Tanukhi, *Sharṭ*, 189; and Nora Alamuddin and Paul Starr, *Crucial Bonds: Marriage among the Lebanese Druze* (Delmar, NY: Caravan, 1980), 39.

[38] Al-Tanukhi, *Sharḥ al-mīthāq*, 331.

[39] In epistle 47, entitled *Taqlīd al-shaykh abī al-katā'ib*, there are clear instructions from Baha' al-Din to one of the *da'is* that young girls should be taught to read from the *ḥikma*; see al-Tanukhi, *Sharḥ al-mīthāq*, 328.

[40] Ibid., 308.

[41] Ibid., 305.

[42] Ibid., 309.

[43] Ibn Sibat, *Tārīkh*, 72.

[44] Al-Tanukhi, *Sharḥ al-mīthāq*, 170-76; and Ibn Sibat, *Tārīkh*, 70, 80.

[45] Al-Sayyid spent twelve years in Damascus. The dates of his departure and return are not known. See Nuwayhid, *Al-Tanūkhī*, 117-23; Makarem, *Lubnān*, 233-234; and Abu-Zaki, *Al-Amir al-Sayyid*, 205.

[46] Al-Sakhawi, *Al-ḍaw' al-lāmi'*, 12 vols. (Cairo: n.p., 1934), 3:78; and Ibn Tulun, *I'lām al-warā*, edited by 'Abd al-'Azim Khattab (Cairo: 'Ain Shams, 1973), 52.

[47] Ibn Sibat, *Tārīkh*, 23.

[48] Al-Tanukhi, *Sharh al-mīthāq*, 464.

[49] *Al-taqiyya* (dissimulation) is the principle by which individuals are permitted to deny their faith in order to avoid persecution or to safeguard their beliefs from the 'undeserving.' See 'Ali Shimlawi, *Al-Taqiyya fi iṭāriha al-fiqhī* (Beirut: By

the author, 1992); Fathiya ʿAtwi, *Al-Taqiyya fil-fikr al-Islāmī al-Shīʿī* (Beirut: Dar al-Islamiyya, 1993).

[50] Hamza ibn Ahmad ibn Sibat was a scribe in the service of the Tanukhi emirs. His father, Ahmad ibn Sibat, was one of the disciples of al-Sayyid and the *imām* of his mosque in ʿAbey. See Ibn Sibat, *Tārīkh*, 11.

[51] Makarem, *Lubnān*, 235.

[52] Al-Sayyid regarded drinking wine and adultery as being among the great sins (*al-kabāʾir*) and as sufficient grounds for expulsion from the *majlis*. Anonymous, *Mukhtārāt min al-hikam wal-mawaʾiẓ*, MS (my private collection), 193-207; al-Ashrafani, *ʿUmdat al-ʿārifīn*, 3:144; Nuwayhid, *Al-Tanūkhī*, 121; and Abu-Zaki, *Al-Amir al-Sayyid*, 574-78.

[53] Badr al-Din died in AH 863/AD 1458 and his successor, Sayf al-Din Yahya, died in AH 864/AD 1459; both were considered 'enemies' of al-Sayyid. See Anonymous, *Mukhtārāt*, 106; Nuwayhid, *Al-Tanūkhī*, 124; and Makarem, *Lubnān*, 236.

[54] Abu-Zaki, *Al-Amir al-Sayyid*, 220.

[55] About the life of ʿAbd al-Khaliq, see Ibn Sibat, *Tārikh*, 64-67; Ibn Nasr, *Durrat al-tāj*, 30-36; and Nuwayhid, *Al-Tanūkhī*, 94-95.

[56] ʿAbd al-Khaliq died on the day of his wedding, but his father concealed the news from the guests until all of the festivities were over. Biographers give different dates for the death of ʿAbd al-Khaliq. An earlier biographer, Abu ʿAli Mirʿi, says that it took place in AH 876/AD 1471; Ibn Sibat says it was in AH 874/AD 1469. The funeral address is frequently read within religious circles as an example of al-Sayyid's sanctity. See Ibn Sibat, *Tārīkh*, 64-67; Ibn Nasr, *Durrat al-tāj*, 30-36; and Nuwayhid, *Al-Tanūkhī*, 118-21.

[57] Two words in the Arabic text, *muttaqīn* and *muḥsinīn*, are both from the Qurʾan. For the translation of these words, see Arthur J. Arberry, *The Koran Interpreted* (London: Oxford University Press, 1975).

[58] Abu ʿAli Mirʿi and Ibn Sibat describe his funeral and the eulogies delivered on that day in detail. See Nuwayhid, *Al-Tanūkhī*, 127-28; and Ibn Sibat, *Tārīkh*, 82-84.

[59] Henry H. Carnarvon, *Recollection of the Druses of Lebanon and Notes on Their Religion* (London: J. Murray, 1860), 59.

[60] Emir Sayf al-Din Abu Bakr bin Zanki was chosen by the *ʿuqqāl* as al-Sayyid's successor; see Ibn Sibat, *Tārīkh*, 82.

[61] This is quoted from Abu ʿAli Mirʿi who wrote the earliest biography of al-Sayyid. See Nuwayhid, *Al-Tanūkhī*, 93, 102-04; and Bin Nasr, *Durrat al-tāj*.

FUAD I. KHURI

Aspects of Druze Social Structure: 'There Are No Free-Floating Druze'

EXCEPT FOR SOME BRIEF INTERRUPTIONS, the Druze have displayed throughout their history a clear internal cohesion and a strong attachment to ethnic identity. Practically everyone who has written on the Druze, past and present, has stressed their internal cohesiveness and solidarity. Louis Périllier, in his book, *Les Druzes*,[1] Philip Hitti, who lived among the Druze as a child,[2] Gabriel Ben-Dor, who worked among the Druze in Palestine,[3] Colonel Charles Churchill, who was an eyewitness to the sectarian clashes in Mount Lebanon between 1842 and 1860,[4] the late Hanna Batatu in his last book on Syria[5]—all have made the same observation.

During Lebanon's prolonged civil war (1975-90), every religious sect, every political party, every paramilitary organization split into warring factions at some point or another except the Druze, who took a united stand throughout the conflict. This united stand was not confined to the Druze of Lebanon alone, but extended across the country's frontiers to include the Druze of Syria and, particularly, the Druze of Palestine. In his book, Z. Atashe, one of two Druze representatives in the Israeli Knesset (the other being Salah Tarif), reviewed in detail how the Druze of Palestine were mobilized to defend their brethren in Lebanon when their safety was at jeopardy immediately following the Israeli occupation of central Lebanon in 1982.[6] The open letter that the Druze author, Salman Natur, sent to the Israeli prime minister summed up their attitude:

> I discovered my *ḥamula* in Lebanon, some ten thousand people, Druze and the descendants of Druze spread out over several villages, from Beirut in the north to Hasbayya in the south. They told us about the bloody civil war, the suffering, the hunger and fear. They appealed to us to rescue them from death and from the shame of war. Is this possible, they asked? I wrote the Prime Minister and requested him to allow us to help our

brethren. He wrote to me saying that he read my letter with great attention. I, too, read his reply with great attention.[7]

The Druze image of themselves as a cohesive force is well reflected in the metaphor that likens them to 'a plate of copper that resonates as one if a single edge is touched.'[8] In my forthcoming book, *Being a Druze,*[9] I attribute this internal cohesiveness to a number of interconnected factors. The first of these is the belief in reincarnation, which continuously creates positive and amicable relationships between families. The impact of reincarnation is exemplified by the statement: 'We are born in each other's house.'[10]

The second factor is the influence of self-appointed, freelance *shaykh*s of religion who serve as role models; as they advance in religious worship, these upholders of ethics withdraw from factional politics and present themselves as the voice of consensus. They are innumerable, comprising, on the average, between 10 to 20 percent of the population of individual Druze communities. They lead in prayer; deliberate on who is eligible to join the congregation; officiate on questions of family law; reconcile conflicts and quarrels within the community (and sometimes beyond); disseminate aspects of *tawḥīd* among the Druze; and evaluate the worth of a person upon his death by uttering blessings during his funeral. The greater the number of *shaykh*s attending the funeral and the larger the number of blessings uttered, the higher the dead man's religious and/or social standing—and vice versa.

Third, counting altogether about one million souls, the majority of Druze live in relatively close proximity. About half of all Druze live in Jabal al-ʿArab (Syria),[11] 250,000 in Mount Lebanon,[12] 100,000 in Upper Galilee (Palestine),[13] 25,000 in al-Ghuta (on the outskirts of Damascus), 15,000 in Jabal al-Summaq (also called Jabal al-Aʿla, in the vicinity of Aleppo), 8,000 in the Golan highlands, 5,000 in al-Azraq in the kingdom of Jordan, and some 50,000 immigrants overseas, 30,000 of them in the United States. It is said that, barring those who live in Jabal al-Summaq, all of the Druze in Syria, Lebanon and Palestine were capable of communicating by means of a beacon lit atop one of the hills of Mount Hermon. They generally live in compact adjacent villages composed either almost exclusively of Druze (58% of all settlements) or of a Druze majority with a Christian or Sunni Muslim minority (in 33% of cases). Only 8% of the Druze live as minorities in villages dominated by others. The late Kamal Junblat's contention that "the Druze are a minority without minority feelings" carries much truth.[14]

Fourth is their emphasis on brotherhood. One of the main pillars of religion as taught by Imām Hamza ibn ʿAli is *hifẓ al-ikhwān,* that is, rendering support and protection to brethren. When two Druze meet, they cross their fingers and raise their hands upward to kiss each other's thumbs; they often kiss each other on the shoulder to underscore their mutual support: 'shoulder to shoulder' is an expression that indicates the height of collaboration. The Druze see themselves as a community made up of brothers and sisters, which induces in them a strong sense of equality. Indeed, 'equality' is as central a theme to the Druze as 'love' is to Christians or 'justice' to Muslims. It is no wonder that a good number of the Druze of Lebanon readily accepted the principles of the Progressive Socialist Party founded by the late Kamal Junblat. Among those who objected to the party was none other than Sitt Nazira Junblat, Kamal's mother. In this connection, Igor Timoviev relates the following anecdote in his book, *Kamal Junblat: Al-Rajul wal-ustūra:*

> When Nazira Junblat, Kamal's mother, heard of the foundation of the Progressive Socialist Party, she went to Beirut to meet with Shaykh ʿAbdullah al-ʿAlayili whom she blamed for having cooperated with her son in this matter. She protested: "Whoever has a strong party, like the Junblats, does not need to establish a socialist party." Two weeks later, she was visited by a party member inquiring about 'comrade' Kamal. She snapped: "When Kamal became a 'comrade,' I stopped knowing his whereabouts."[15]

The emphasis given by religion to mutual support and protection is consistently reinforced by a series of rituals during which food is communally consumed—an activity which further strengthens the bonds among participants. For lack of a better term, I shall refer to these rituals as examples of 'consumality'—that is, the collective and ritualistic consumption of food. Consumality is a widespread practice, especially during holidays, such as the Eid at the conclusion of Ramadan, or at weddings or funerals; it may also involve the sharing of salt or of coffee. In the first meeting to launch their mutual aid society, the founders of al-Bakura al-Durziyya in Seattle brought a bowl of salt and requested each member, in turn, to dip his finger into the bowl and eat the salt, a ritual signifying an unshakable bond between participants. For the same purpose, coffee is served to guests from a single cup. When I quietly suggested to my host in Suwayda that it would be more hygienic to serve coffee in separate cups, he asked sharply: "Do you want to destroy our bond?"[16]

The Druze grant individuals freedom of choice in the practice of religion since they consider religion to be a private experience rather than a public right—a sort of 'secret' between man and God that should not be divulged publicly to others. However, not all aspects of Druze religious tradition are optional: in particular, being or not being a Druze is not a matter of choice. Born Druze, a person remains Druze: it is a public right. In this sense, religion is at the heart of ethnic identity. Being a Druze is a foregone conclusion that cannot be altered by death, conversion to other religions, or marrying exogamously (outside of the religious community). The soul of a Druze who converts to another religion or who alienates him/herself from the community by exogamous marriage reverts back to its natal patrikin upon death and is instantaneously reborn as a Druze.

The Druze have no kings, popes, or patriarchs and no seminaries or colleges, but still display an impressive degree of social solidarity and a strong sense of ethnic identity. Just as internal cohesiveness is maintained in the absence of a graded authority structure, a strong sense of ethnic identity is achieved in the absence of institutions that openly and publicly teach dogma and ways of worship. *Tawḥīd* beliefs and practices are the privileges of those who seek to acquire them. This suggests that, in order to explain their sustained social cohesion and persistent attachment to ethnic identity, it is necessary to look into the socializing process, namely, how a Druze 'learns' his or her culture. 'There are no free-floating Druze!' What does this statement mean?

Every Druze, young or old, adult or adolescent, is slotted into some sort of religio-cultural category. When he is a *raḍīʿ* ('suckling'), living on his mother's milk, his parents and close relatives begin to observe his gestures and body movements to see if these remind them of the body language of a person known to them, but recently deceased. When he enters the *nuṭq* (remembering past experiences) stage, between the ages of two and 12, they pay particular attention to his speech in the belief that the soul that he acquired at birth will identify itself through language. From adolescence through adulthood, he joins the 'uninitiated' or 'ignorant' (*juhhāl*), who take no part in the practice of religion, as opposed to the *ʿuqqāl* or 'initiated' who do.

The difference between *ʿuqqāl* and *juhhāl* is very arbitrary. It does not necessarily reflect the extent of religious knowledge since many persons classified as 'ignorant' may know more about religious tenets than the majority of the 'initiated.' It is entirely a question of whether or not a person participates regularly in religious rituals. In other words, the *ʿuqqāl* practise religion regularly: the *juhhāl* do not. In this paper, rather than calling them *ʿuqqāl* and *juhhāl,* which are emotionally-loaded terms, I shall refer to them as 'initiated' and 'uninitiated,' respectively.

To practice religion, a person has to be admitted to a *majlis* that is subject to the strict authority of the religious *shaykhs* and headed locally by a *sāyis*. The procedure is not simple. In the process of seeking admission, the supplicant has to humble himself before the *sāyis* and the congregation, not only by repenting past misconduct, but also by appearing before them more than once to ask to be admitted to the ranks of worshippers, saying, 'I am here to beg your kindness.'

The various stages through which the uninitiated pass while being exposed to the scriptures are not clear-cut. They overlap and intersect and tend to vary from one *majlis* to another, depending upon the person concerned and the *shaykh* (*sāyis*) in charge. Customarily, when the *sāyis* officially opens the assembly with a brief invocation and instructs each member of the congregation 'to search for his or her self,' the uninitiated candidate wishing to join the congregation as a permanent member is supposed to leave the *majlis*, a gesture that signals his or her interest. This is referred to as *taswīf,* meaning 'postponement', and is intended to humble the soul. If the candidate possesses the right qualifications for admission, he or she will be permitted to join the *waʿz* stage of worship, which does not qualitatively differ from the first stage. At the *waʿz* stage, the candidate is presented with a wide variety of traditions, sayings and words of wisdom associated with the Prophet Muhammad, his companions, the orthodox caliphs, some Sufi writers and poets, and those Greek philosophers (for example, Pythagoras, Socrates, Plato and Aristotle) discussed by Arab writers, notably, Ibn Rushd. Included in the *waʿz* are stories told of the admired four—namely, Salman al-Farisi, al-Miqdad ibn Aswad al-Kindi, Abu Dharr al-Ghifari and Ammar ibn Yasir, who are known among the Druze as the 'ministers of truth' (*ḥudūd ahl al-ḥaqq*).[17] The Druze believe that love of the admired four was ordained by God through the Prophet Muhammad as indicated in the Qurʾanic verse: "Send not away those who call on their God morning and evening, seeking His face."[18]

Sometimes the telling of these stories is interspersed with recitations of Sufi poetry praising the prophets, the saints and the Druze ministers. The bulk of this introductory material focuses upon fear and hope—fear of God and of the forbidden, and hope for the mercy of divine manifestation. Two themes dominate: the virtue of austerity and the value of self-control. Many of the stories told at this stage are tragic in character and concern the rich king or prince who, after meeting the pious poor, gives up perishable worldly pleasures for eternal life. "To acquire everything (eternal life) we have to abandon everything (worldly pleasures)," says Shaykh Ghalib Qays of Hasbayya.[19]

Women are repeatedly told the stories of the famous Sufi mystic, Rabiʿa al-ʿAdawiyya, and Sitt Shaʿwani. Rabiʿa is seen as exemplifying the woman who, as princess or concubine, enjoys all sorts of earthly delights, but accidentally meets a devout, godly person dedicated to worship and abandons the profane for the sacred. She is described as dreaming of the Prophet Muhammad, who asked her, "Oh, Rabiʿa! Do you love me?" She replied, "I do, but my heart is full with the love of God." Just as Rabiʿa is an exemplar of the sensualist who has become righteous, Sitt Shaʿwani epitomizes the righteous woman who devotes herself to worship and supports those in need, yet is unjustly accused of wickedness. Perceived in this way until her death, she was posthumously rewarded by angels preparing her coffin, divine music playing during her funeral and a heavenly voice crying at her burial: "She is innocent, she is innocent."[20]

Men are urged to emulate the admired four mentioned above. These companions were known for their love of the Prophet, their early and total devotion to Islam, their active participation in the early military expeditions to spread the word of God and their austere, almost Sufi lifestyles. As a measure of austerity, none of them married and none had children.

Of Persian origin, Salman al-Farisi is noted for his love for and devotion to the holy House of ʿAli and is admired for having left his home at an early age in search of religious truth. Following in his footsteps today, many of the *shaykh*s of religion refrain from eating meat, fast for long periods and shave their heads. Abu Dharr al-Ghifari is well-known for his animosity toward the Umayyads, whom he accused of having treacherously accumulated enormous riches during the early Islamic conquest. Whatever money came into his hands was quickly dispensed to the poor.

It is said of Ammar ibn Yasir, whose mother, Sumayya, was the first female martyr in Islam, that he suffered severely and consistently at the hands of anti-Islamic circles in Mecca, but his convictions did not waver. The Prophet Muhammad is quoted as saying: "Ammar is full of faith from head to toe: faith runs in his blood."[21] Al-Miqdad ibn Aswad al-Kindi is also renowned for his unwavering commitment to Islam, in addition to his exploits in the early battles waged against 'infidels.' He consequently became known as 'the knight of the Prophet' and several of his heroic deeds are often narrated during Druze assemblies. While preparing for the battle of Badr, which marked the commencement of the conquest, al-Miqdad lent support to Muhammad by uttering these words:

> I swear by He who sent you [to us] as the prophet of truth, if you order us to advance with you to pools of blood [meaning death] we will not hesitate to do so until you realize your aim.[22]

At the popular level, these four are joined by two others: the second Druze minister, Abu Ibrahim Ismaʿil al-Tamimi and the venerable Sitt Sarah. Al-Tamimi, nicknamed Abu Ibrahim, was appointed by Imām Hamza as his successor. He was a high-ranking officer in the Fatimid army and well-known for his writings and courage on the battlefield. He is still thought of as a guardian and protector by the Druze, who call out *Ya Abū Ibrāhīm* (Oh, father of Abraham) whenever they face personal crises or danger. Sitt Sarah, Bahaʾuddin's niece, exemplifies the righteous disciplinarian; acting upon her uncle's instructions, she headed a delegation to quell the disruptions that erupted in Wadi al-Taym in her day and to teach Druze women the essentials of the doctrine.[23] Even today, when disciplining a disobedient child, Druze parents threaten to refer him or her to Sitt Sarah.

When the ritual at the *majlis* moves to the *sharḥ* stage, which involves the interpretation of the scriptures, the *sāyis* instructs those candidates who have not yet been admitted to leave the assembly and clear (*saffū*) the house. Admission to the congregation, which is rarely granted automatically, normally occurs in middle age and attendance continues until death. During this period, the 'initiated' devote themselves to worship and the study of *tawḥīd* doctrine, seeking 'the knowledge of unity in God, the only existent.'

There are exceptions to the age rule: aside from the children of religious *shaykh*s, who are initiated at a very early age, people blessed with extraordinary powers or stricken by uncommon misfortunes, like an accident or sickness, might also join in early. The word *shaykh*, which means 'elderly', is used by the Druze to refer to all regular practitioners of religion, irrespective of age. Women, who are called *shaykha*s, are generally admitted to the *majlis* at an early age—at any rate, when younger than men. They attend the Thursday congregation, listen to religious treatises and join in the chanting if the *majlis* is composed solely of women. Under no condition may the chanting of women be heard by men.

Once initiated, a person is expected to observe a rather strict ethical behavioural code much like the one expected of religious *shaykh*s: he or she must dress modestly, often in traditional style; refrain from swearing, drinking, smoking, laughing loudly, or using abusive language; and refrain, as well, from exaggerated expressions of joy or sadness, anger or lust. Initiates are also expected to keep their 'secret' with God (in other words, never to divulge religious experiences), avoid conflict and exercise 'control' regarding sex, food and speech. The same behavioural code is expected of women initiates. Roughly speaking, all adult females, as well as initiated men and women and religious *shaykhs*, conform to more or less the same strict code, whereas the rich, adult males and the uninitiated tend to follow more relaxed rules. It must be stressed, however, that these categories are not rigid and mutually exclusive: members of each of them tolerate and understand the positions of the others. Moreover, the Druze often take a united stand toward economic and political realities, as well as other matters that do not come directly under the control of religion.

Among the Druze, there seems to be a special relationship that binds the older generation, especially the religious *shaykhs*, to the younger: the grandparent/grandchild complex. Al-Amir al-Sayyid was the first to stress the importance of teaching children. As *shaykh al-mashāyikh*, he appointed *shaykhs* for this purpose and personally paid for the instruction of orphans throughout the region. Commenting on the scriptures, he writes:

> The child is a trust in his parents' hands, his pure heart is a precious jewel, free from all impression, ready to receive any imprint and lean in the direction towards which it is turned. From tender age he should be used [accustomed] to simplicity in food, clothing, and surroundings, and should be warned against the love of silver and gold.[24]

Throughout his or her lifetime, both the initiated and uninitiated are expected to conform to a rigorous moral code. In their disciplinary procedures, the Druze, like all "little communities,"[25] manipulate what Ibn Khaldun called *al-wāziʿ*—the internal deterrent, the conscience, the feeling of guilt and the fear of shame. This stands in direct opposition to *al-wāziʿ al-sultānī*, the 'sultanic deterrent,' that is, the use of coercion and force. Nowhere in the Druze code is there any reference to resort to the use of force or any semblance of it. In fact, the covenant that binds Druze to their faith stipulates that—at least in theory—each person must chose freely and not be influenced by coercion in any form.[26]

From birth to death, each Druze is exposed to various methods of social control that come under the rubrics of good upbringing and self-discipline. The key word here is 'control' for, throughout their lives, the Druze learn to control their speech, appetites, desires and bodily pleasures, refraining from showing emotion or sentiment in public and from laughing or eating excessively. It is unsurprising, then, that the Druze have given *al-ʿaql* (from *ʿaqala*, meaning to 'control', 'tie', 'block', or 'imprison') a divine universal presence, have invoked 'His' name in the title of their highest religious office, the *shaykh al-ʿaql,* and have called the initiated the *ʿuqqāl*—namely, those who control themselves. This means that, etymologically speaking, the title of *shaykh al-ʿaql* is more aptly applied to the *shaykh al-dīn* and vice versa. *Al-dīn* is derived from *dānā* (*yadīnū*), meaning to 'act', 'judge', or 'sanction'; it is action and sanction blended together in a single formulation, precisely what the office of *shaykh al-ʿaql* is.

At a very early age, the Druze learn how to correctly pronounce the Arabic phonemes *tha, dhāl, ṣāḍ, ḍāḍ, ẓah* and *qāf,* which, to my knowledge, no other Arab group from the Gulf to the Atlantic shores does. They often refrain from the use of obscene, blunt, erotic, or foul language in favour of more socially acceptable terms. Customarily, for example, they refer to lying (*kādhib*) as a 'slip of memory' and the toilet as the 'house of good manners'; faeces (*kharā*) become *hazā; ʿilli,* a vulgar exclamation meaning 'illness', becomes *ʿilki* ('chewing gum'); and *qird,* another vulgar term reflecting anger, becomes *qirsh* ('piastre'). Unlike the many Arab Muslims who swear by God and the Prophet in almost every sentence or the many Lebanese Christians who swear repeatedly by Christ and The Virgin Mary, the Druze rarely utter such oaths and, when they do, they swear by 'truth' or by their Druze honour (*sharaf*). Profanity involving religion, shrines, saints and sexual organs is usually avoided.

One of the basic tenets of the Druze religion, as preached by Hamza ibn ʿAli, is 'to speak the truth' (*ṣiḍq al-lisān*), which is always associated with *ḥifẓ al-ikhwān,* rendering aid and protection to brethren. In the present context, it should be noted that *ṣiḍq* has a double meaning: both speaking the truth and speaking correctly, that is, correct pronunciation.

As Abu-Izzeddin notes:

> In the Druze ethical system truthfulness (*ṣiḍq*) is the cardinal virtue. It is the first in the seven precepts which the Unitarians are commanded to observe. Hamza wrote: "Know that truthfulness is equivalent to belief and to the confession of the Unitarian Doctrine in all its perfection. Lying is polytheism, unbelief, and error."[27]

Ṣiḍq further means having truthful intentions and, as the Arabic saying affirms, 'intentions can be revealed only by deeds.' Historically, the Druze have given particular emphasis to truthfulness in weights and measures in the *sūq,* where buying and selling take place. It is said that al-Hakim bi-Amr Allah himself used to oversee the proper observance of *ḥisba* (accounting and accountability), which involved controlling prices, verifying the quality of manufactured commodities, checking weights and measures, and maintaining law and order in the marketplace.[28]

But how does this emphasis on truthfulness relate to the practice of *taqiyya*?

Taqiyya is perhaps one of the most misunderstood concepts in Druze dogma—even among some of the Druze themselves. It does not involve deceit, lying, or hiding ordinary bits of information. There are two operational meanings to *taqiyya*: as an integral part of the *tawḥīd* way of worship and as a means to conceal religious identity. The first meaning implies that an adherent should not share or divulge his or her private experience in the practice of religion: this should remain a secret shared only with God. The second relates strictly to religious identity in times of crisis, when fearing or threatened with persecution. In the second sense, *taqiyya* is traced to the Qurʾanic verse (16:106) concerning "[a]nyone who, after accepting faith in God, utters unbelief, except under compulsion, his heart remaining firm in belief. . .."

It is said that this verse was revealed after the suffering that befell Ammar ibn Yasir when forced, by the early Meccan opponents of Islam, to disparage the Prophet. Later, when Ammar apologized to Mohammad for his wrongdoing, the Prophet remarked, "Do not shed tears over it: if they were to repeat what they did to you, you repeat what you said to them."[29]

The element of secrecy in religious practice is partly *taqiyya* and partly dogma. However, *taqiyya* does not apply to market transactions. It would be inaccurate for a group of businessmen to accuse a Druze colleague of practicing *taqiyya* if he refused to divulge his stock market profits. It is similarly inaccurate to suggest that the Druze claim to an Arab origin is an instance of *taqiyya*, as Hitti does when insisting that they are more likely of Persian origin.[30] Hitti's contention is based upon the fact that the Druze faith makes use of several Persian loan words, such as *al-bār*, meaning 'God', and that some Druze family names were originally Persian, for instance, Arslan, meaning 'lion'. Of course, the presence of Persian loan words is unsurprising since the Druze *imām*, Hamza ibn ʿAli, was of Persian origin, from the town of Zawzan in Khurasan province. There are several words in the Qurʾan that are traceable to Persian, but this does not render the holy book a Persian text. Indeed, there is hardly a language which is free of loan words, especially from neighbouring countries like Arabia and Persia.

By the same token, Layish's usage of *taqiyya* to refer to the Druze calling a *khalwa* a *majlis* is actually an instance of the confusion of two words signifying two different religious functions.[31] Whereas a *majlis* can be used as a *khalwa*, a *khalwa* is never used as a *majlis*. The *khalwa* is smaller in size, calmer and quieter than the *majlis*; only the very pious use the *khalwa*, seeking spiritual experience. By contrast, the *majlis*, which may contain a *khalwa*, is potentially open to all Druze at all times, irrespective of their status, wealth, age, sex, or level of religiosity. Evidently, *khalwa* may refer to the physical structure, the rituals conducted in it, or the person or persons performing the rituals.

Whether practiced as a part of dogma or to conceal religious identity in times of real or perceived danger, *taqiyya* predisposes the Druze to be respectful and considerate of the customs, rituals and traditions of others. And in so doing, the Druze have merely conformed to the notion of 'political correctness even before the expression was composed.'

The Druze understanding of *taqiyya* is quite different from the Shiʿa understanding of it. According to the late Ayatollah Khomeini, *taqiyya* is practiced when the Shiʿa *ʿulamāʾ* are complacent about governments controlled by earthly rulers. He believed that government must be in the hands of the *ʿulamāʾ* for they are the 'heirs of prophets,' who rule according to the Islamic *sharīʿa*, and not by force, coercion, or the control of economic and social resources. He explains his position in this way:

> The resort to *taqiyya* is legitimate only if it is intended to safeguard oneself and others from the dangers resulting from the application of subsidiary religious rules. But if Islam, all Islam, is in danger, there will be no room for *taqiyya* or silence. If the circumstances of *taqiyya* require some of us to place ourselves in the service of the sultan, we should in this case refrain from doing so even if our lives are at stake. The practice of *taqiyya* must be addressed only to the conquest of Islam and the victory of the Muslims.[32]

In this connection, one must distinguish between the Druze *ajāwīd* and the Shiʿa *ʿulamāʾ*: whereas the *ajāwīd* withdraw from society as they advance in religious knowledge and experience, the *ʿulamāʾ*, by contrast, become more involved in societal and political affairs. Like Imam ʿAli and his descendants, they become leaders. The *ʿulamāʾ* in Iran assumed direct political control as soon as they succeeded in toppling the Shahinshah's regime, one of the strongest in the developing world at the time. Druze history has never witnessed a parallel event in which religious *shaykh*s took control of the government or the top political leadership in the community. True, the Druze have never had an independent state of their own but, if they ever did, it is certain that the religious and power élites would not be rivals for control of the government. The two categories operate in two essentially different spheres of action.

Control of appetite is another behaviour highly cherished in Druze society. This is part of the process of 'restraining (*tarwīḍ*) the animalistic desires' in man. Some, not all, believe that it is forbidden for a Druze to eat *mulūkhiyya,* a famous dish composed of a green vegetable cooked with garlic and coriander in broth and served with lamb or chicken, rice, chopped onions, vinegar and toasted bread. It is reported that al-Hakim bi-Amr Allah forbade it because people consumed it with a lusty appetite; moreover, it has the reputation for making people sleepy and may, therefore, interrupt the rhythm of worship. However, I have seen many Druze eat *mulūkhiyya* and heard one Druze tell another the following joke about restraining the appetites:

> A father sent his son to buy soap from a nearby grocery store. After a while, the son came back empty-handed. The father inquired, "Where is the soap?" The son answered, "My *nafs* desired halva! I told her: No! She told me: Yes! I repeated. She insisted. Then I told her: 'Oh, my *nafs,* I am at your disposal.'"

When I interviewed a Druze initiate, he stated, with a touch of pride, "It gives me great pleasure to want something and then deny it to myself." But a *shaykh* commented, "This attitude may lead to pride in oneself," adding, "A *shaykh* signs his name under the title of the humble (*al-haqīr*)."[33] This observation is consistent with the following passage, taken from the writings of Hamza ibn ʿAli, as quoted by Abu-Izzeddin:

> The appetitive soul is man's worst enemy. When desire, pride, anger, and hatred are given free play they become master and lead to destruction. To overcome them is an arduous struggle; it is the greater *jihād* [the smaller one being fighting to spread the word of God]. With the lower soul subdued man finds the way to God. Whoever abstains from indulgence in carnal passions is more exalted than the angels.[34]

Undoubtedly, there is a strong Sufi influence in these teachings. Concepts such as discipline, the greater *jihād,* mastery of the self, subduing the lower soul and abstinence in general have a Sufi resonance. It is firmly believed that al-Amir al-Sayyid underwent considerable Sufi discipline while studying and teaching in Damascus. At any rate, the Druze doctrine is replete with Sufi teachings.

The emphasis that the Druze place upon moral codes as instruments of control becomes clear when we compare their penal code with those of other Muslims who developed, throughout their history, ideologies and laws adapted to state structures and central authority and based upon force and coercion. Consider, for example, their differing approaches to adultery, murder and theft, as well as divorce. In other Muslim communities, adultery is punished by stoning or whipping, sometimes until death occurs, depending upon the kinship relationship between the adulterers and the circumstances. If adultery is committed between two persons who are forbidden to marry one another, such as brothers and sisters, uncles and nieces, mothers and stepsons, the guilty parties will be beheaded by the sword irrespective of whether or not either of them has been 'fortressed.' A fortressed male (*muḥaṣṣan* or *muḥṣan*) is a free man who has a permanent wife with whom he has had intercourse and can do so again whenever and however he desires—within the accepted rules of the *sharīʿa*. A fortressed female (*muḥaṣṣana* or *muḥṣana*) is married legally and has experienced intercourse with her husband. By comparison, unfortressed adulterers (such as a female virgin) will be whipped one hundred lashes if they commit adultery with someone that they are eligible to marry.[35] The same principle of resort to force and coercion can be detected in cases of murder or theft. The penalty for the murder of a Muslim is death by the sword. Theft is punished by amputation of the hand.

The Druze do consider adultery to be a very serious crime, but punish the adulterer by excommunication or isolation (*al-buʿda*). However, if the adultery proves to be an honour crime involving a women from the *ʿird* (incest) group, only the shedding of the adulterers' blood will suffice. If the woman is a sister or daughter, her brother or father may kill her and her lover in defence of the family honour. Incidents of adultery in Palestine and Golan are often referred to the Druze court. In one case on record, the adulterer was forced to leave his village and those who gave him shelter were excommunicated. In another case, a married man abducted another man's wife and fled with her from the village; when he wanted to return, his own father refused to receive him. Honour crimes involving murder are doubly shameful. Although killing in defence of honour or one's self is not a punishable crime, any preconceived murder, no matter the reason, is religiously condemned.

The Druze punish theft by excommunication or isolation until the thief repents in public. These different forms of shaming (*miʿyār*)—isolation, excommunication, public repentance, withholding the 'prayer of mercy'—are morally-based instruments of control that can be effective only in small communities in which diffuse, primary relationships prevail.

In complex, urban settings, these measures lose credibility and give way to standard laws based upon force and coercion.

As a 'little community' that has succeeded in coping, throughout its history, with oppression and persecution, the Druze display deep interest in each other's affairs. News about crime, marriages, divorces, births, deaths, travel, emigration, employment, appointments and what have you becomes public knowledge soon as the events occur. This is perhaps the reason why individuals try to protect their privacy by being secretive and cautious. Consider the following anecdote:

> A young, radical Druze in his mid-twenties spoke unfavourably in a rather closed circle of a very influential Druze *zaʿīm*. He accused the leader of being dictatorial, selfish, opportunistic and out of touch with modernity. Within hours, he learned that his parents [either of fear or out of respect] visited the very leader that he had attacked and offered their apologies. Even after several weeks had passed, the parents still refused to communicate with their radical son.[36]

'Stay in line' is the Druze motto for rearing children. Al-Amir al-Sayyid taught:

> The child is a trust in his parents' hands; the carnal soul is man's worst enemy, and that man must be in constant struggle with it, rebuking and chastising it, and not putting aside for one hour the whip of discipline.[37]

It has been demonstrated in more than one study that the Druze are more willing to submit to the control of their group than other ethnic communities. In an ethnically-mixed sample of 880 Palestinian high-school students aged between 16 and 17 years, the Druze respondents, along with Arab Muslim and Christian counterparts, scored high on items implying group control—collectivism, cohesiveness, homogeneity and cultural 'tightness'—and low on individualism, group competitiveness, heterogeneity and cultural 'looseness.' By contrast, Western-oriented Jews had the lowest score on the first set of variables and the highest on the second. Middle Eastern Jews fell somewhere in between.

On adaptability, in other words, the capacity and readiness to accept modern family dynamics, such as a preference for the nuclear family, freedom of choice concerning residence and family size, Western-oriented Jews had the highest scores and Arab Muslims the lowest. The Druze, Arab Christians and Middle-Eastern Jews fell in the middle, meaning that, while they were ready to modernize, they simultaneously respected their cultural heritage.[38]

Because the Druze in Upper Galilee are treated by the Israeli authorities as a separate, independent ethnicity, they have been regularly chosen for various social, cultural and psychological studies. In one such study, researchers tried to examine the Druze understanding of the concept of rights—freedom of speech, religion and reproduction—first, in non-conflict situations and, then, when confronted with other moral and social considerations. Ninety persons were selected for the study, 15 males and 15 females for each of three age groups: 13-year-olds, 17-year-olds and adults between 34 and 70 years of age. The young were still in school: the adults had 10 or more years of formal education.

Irrespective of age, sex, or level of education, all in the study group considered the three freedoms to be rights, but in the 'abstract,' that is, in non-conflict situations. Simultaneously, all had subordinated, albeit to varying degrees, these freedoms to parental or governmental authorities. The Druze showed more willingness to accept restrictions imposed upon them concerning family size than when it came to freedom of speech or religion. While accepting the authority of fathers and husbands over daughters and wives, they opposed fathers' interference with sons. Concerning freedom of religion, they showed deep resentment at the notion of government interference, except when it was intended to protect them from real or perceived danger[39]; I suppose that this is where *taqiyya* becomes relevant.

In a similar study on social authority conducted using a sample made up of 172 Druze children and 179 Jewish children, the respondents agreed on many issues apart from one: conflict between personal choice and obedience to authority. Whereas Jewish children showed a tendency to prefer personal choice, Druze children were more accepting of the necessity of obedience, giving way to parental control.[40]

From the point of view of direction of change, these findings are interesting. They show that the willingness of Druze to accept modernity is balanced by an attachment to tradition. High scores on traditional family variables—collective action, homogeneity and cultural cohesion—are counterbalanced by an acceptance of adaptability and a readiness to modernize. By the same token, the Druze consider the three freedoms of speech, religion and reproduction as rights, but subject them to moral and social constraints.

The same phenomenon appears in J. Harik's survey of 325 Druze high-school students in the Shuf in Lebanon. Whereas 83% of the respondents would have preferred more power for the Druze, 90% agreed, quite contradictorily, that confessional politics in Lebanon should end. About 80% said that they would like to see sectarian affiliation taken off identity cards, yet 83% affirmed that they would fight again for the salvation of the Druze community.[41] Perhaps there is some truth in the French saying: 'To be liberated you have to have roots.'

Obviously, while retaining a very strong ethnic identity, the Druze respond positively to some modernizing trends. Individuals are so overwhelmed by group loyalty that internal conflicts or confrontations between generations, sexes and, to some extent, classes have not taken place. I say 'to some extent' because there have been modified forms of class conflict in Jabal al-ʿArab, as evidenced by three peasant rebellions. However, these peasant uprisings were highly tempered by kinship, clanship and community-based ties.

NOTES

1 Périllier 1986: 37.

2 Hitti 1928: 2.

3 Ben-Dor 1979: 44.

4 Churchill 1994: 142-43.

5 Batatu 1999: 12-13.

6 Atashe 1995: 156-57.

7 Stendel 1996: 170.

8 Florsheim and Gutmann 1992: 163.

9 Published posthumously by the Druze Heritage Foundation, London in 2004.

10 Oppenheimer 1980: 621.

11 Interview with Hassan Hatum, the curator of the Suwaida museum, on 1 November 2000.

12 Yiftachel and Segal 1998: 483.

13 Stendel 1996: 40.

14 Junblat 1982: 53.

15 Timoviev 2000: 165-66.

16 Interview with Mamduh al-Atrash on 2 November 2000.

17 Abi-Khzam 1995: 14.

18 Qur'an 6:52.

19 Interview with Shaykh Ghalib Qays of Hasbayya on 22 October 2000.

20 Abi-Khzam 1995: 106-7.

21 Ibid.: 28.

22 Saliqa 1995: 28.

23 Al-Sughayyar 1984: 136; ʿAlamuddin 1998: 403.

[24] As quoted by Abu-Izzeddin 1993: 173.

[25] Redfield 1947.

[26] This is said by virtue of the fact that movement into or out of the Druze religious community is not permitted.

[27] As quoted by Abu-Izzeddin 1993: 122-23.

[28] Ibid.: 77.

[29] Nasr 1997: 18.

[30] Hitti 1928: 14.

[31] Layish 1982: 14.

[32] Khomeini 1979: 142-43.

[33] Interview with Shaykh Wahib al-Hudaifi in Hasbayya on 17 October 2000.

[34] Abu-Izzeddin 1993: 126.

[35] Yahfufi 1984: 159-64.

[36] Interview with Dr. Ra'uf Ghusayni in Reading on 22 July 2000.

[37] Abu-Izzeddin 1993: 172-77.

[38] Florian, Mikulincer and Weller 1993: 189-201.

[39] Turiel and Wainryb 1998: 375-95.

[40] Wainryb 1995: 397.

[41] Harik 1993: 41-62.

REFERENCES

Abi-Khzam, Anwar. *Islām al-Muwaḥḥidīn: Al-Madhhab al-Durzī fi waqiʿih al-Islāmī wal-falsafi wal-tashrīʿī.* Beirut: Dar al-Yamama, 1992.

Abu-Izzeddin, Nejla M. *The Druzes: A New Study of Their History, Faith and Society.* New York and Leiden: E. J. Brill, 1984.

ʿAlamuddin, Sulayman Salim. *Tadhakkar ya Marwān: Al-Madāris al-fikriyya wal-tayyārāt al-siyāsiyya wa-daʿwat al-Tawḥīd al-Durziyya.* Beirut: Dar Nawfal, 1989.

Atashe, Z. *Druze and Jews in Israel: A Shared Destiny?* Brighton, UK: Sussex Academic Press, 1995.

Batatu, Hanna. *Syria's Peasantry, the Descendants of Its Lesser Rural Notables, and Their Politics.* Princeton: Princeton University Press, 1999.

Ben-Dor, Gabriel. *The Druze in Israel: A Political Study: Political Innovation and Integration in a Middle Eastern Minority.* Jerusalem: Magnes Press, 1979.

Churchill, Charles Henry, Col. *The Druzes and the Maronites under the Turkish Rule from 1840 to 1860.* Reading, UK: Garnet Publishing, 1994 [first published in 1853].

Florian, V., M. Mikulincer, and A. Weller. "Does Culture Affect Perceived Family Dynamics? A Comparison of Arab and Jewish Adolescents in Israel." *Journal of Comparative Family Studies* 24, no. 2 (1993): 189-201.

Florsheim, Paul, and David Gutmann. "Mourning the Loss of Self as Father: A Longitudinal Study of Fatherhood among the Druze," *Psychiatry: Interpersonal and Biological Processes* 55, no. 2 (1992): 160-76.

Harik, Judith P. "Perceptions of Community and State among Lebanon's Druze Youth." *Middle East Journal* 47, no. 1 (1993): 41-62.

Hitti, Philip. *The Origins of the Druze People and Religion, with Extracts from Their Sacred Writings.* New York: Columbia University Press, 1928.

Junblat, Kamal. *I Speak for Lebanon.* London: Zed Press, 1982.

Khomeini, Ayatollah. *Al-Ḥukūma al-Islāmiyya.* Beirut: al-Muʾassasa al-ʿArabiyya, 1979.

Layish, Aharon. *Marriage, Divorce, and Succession in the Druze Family: A Study Based on Decisions of Druze Arbitrators and Religious Courts in Israel and the Golan Heights.* Leiden: Brill, 1982.

Nasr, Mursal. *Al-Muwaḥḥidūn al-Durūz fi al-Islām.* Beirut: al-Dar al-Islamiyya, 1997.

Oppenheimer, W. S. Jonathan. "We Are Born in Each Others' House: Communal and Patrilineal Ideologies in Druze Village Religion and Social Structure." *American Ethnologist* 7, no. 4 (1980): 621-36.

Périllier, Louis. *Les Druzes.* Paris: Editions Publisud, 1986.

Redfield, Robert. "The Folk Society." *American Journal of Sociology* 52 (1947): 293-308.

Saliqa, Ghalib. *Tarīkh Hasbayya wa-ma yalīha.* Sidon: al-Matbaʿa al-ʿAsriyya, 1995.

Stendel, Ori. *The Arabs in Israel.* Brighton, UK: Sussex Academic Press, 1996.

al-Sughayyar, Saʿid. *Banū Maʿruf fi al-tarīkh.* Al-Qrayya, Lebanon: Zainuddin Press, [1984].

Timoviev, I. *Kamal Junblat: Al-Rajul wal-ustūra.* Beirut: Dar al-Nahar, 2000.

Turiel, Elliot, and Cecilia Wainryb. "Concepts of Freedoms and Rights in a Traditionally Hierarchically Organized Society." *British Journal of Developmental Psychology* 16, no. 3 (1998): 375-95.

Wainryb, Cecilia. "Reasoning about Social Conflicts in Different Cultures: Druze and Jewish Children in Israel." *Child Development* 66, no. 2 (1995): 390-401.

Yahfufi, Sulaiman. *Damān al-jins fi al-Islām.* Beirut: al-Dar al-ʿAlamiyya, 1984.

Yiftachel, Oren, and M. D. Segal. "Jews and Druze in Israel: State Control and Ethnic Resistance." *Ethnic and Racial Studies* 21, no. 3 (1998): 476-504.

Bernadette Schenk

Druze Identity in the Middle East: Tendencies and Developments in Modern Druze Communities since the 1960s

The Druze are a Middle Eastern minority who have formed a 'closed' community since early times: conversion to their faith is impossible; marriage to a non-Druze is forbidden; religious teachings are kept secret; and adjustment to their various and often hostile surroundings involves *taqiyya,* that is, dissimulation, prudence and carefulness. Brutally persecuted in their native country, Egypt, the adherents to the Druze faith survived only in the mountainous regions of Syria and Palestine, as well as Mount Lebanon. Nevertheless, they remained exposed to manifold suspicions and persecutions nurtured, in particular, by their heterodox Muslim character. Although both the Mamluks and the Ottomans usually recognized them as Muslims, they have been repeatedly denounced as heretics and their affiliation to Islam questioned by the Sunni establishment. Since the disintegration of the Ottoman Empire and the subsequent rise of the nation-state in the Middle East, the Druze have also been accused of isolationism and separatism.

In this paper, I will focus upon the Druze search for their own identity, a process that can be traced back to the middle of the last century,[1] when it became necessary to their survival in a changing order of state and society. The debate on how to define Druze identity not only involves the relationship of the Druze to Islam and Arabism, but also the positions of Druze populations within various Middle Eastern nation-states. It is additionally connected with vehemently expressed demands for inner reform of their own patriarchal and undemocratic structures and for reassessment of the validity of traditional concepts of order. Against this background, one may describe today's Druze as a community (or communities) in transition, with the majority of Druze regarding this stage as a crucial crisis and landmark in their long history.

The crisis was revealed by the discussion surrounding ʿAbd Allah al-

Najjar's *Madhhab al-Durūz wa'l-tawḥīd,* which was published in 1965. Al-Najjar was the first Druze to give up the principle of *taqiyya* and to quote verbatim from the *Rasā'il al-ḥikma,* the holy scriptures of the Druze. Publication of his book led to an extensive and highly controversial debate among the Druze that reflected their difficult search for identity and illustrated the need for internal reform to cope with the impact of change within and outside of their communities.

This paper is based upon the results of two years of field research in Lebanon, Syria and Israel and includes both written and oral sources. The focus upon Lebanon's Druze community can be best explained by an internal Druze perspective: seeing their Lebanese counterparts as a sort of avant-garde, both Syrian and Israeli Druze say again and again that the 'key to understanding the Druze lies in Lebanon.' It is in Lebanon that the discourse on Druze identity is being conducted most passionately, bringing forth a flood of literature. And it is in Lebanon that the critique of traditional laws, such as the prohibition against marriage with non-Druze and the radical division of initiates from non-initiates, is particularly strong. This may be due to the Lebanese confessional system, which guarantees the Lebanese Druze the right to control and govern their own religious affairs. Because of this, the Syrian and Israeli Druze speak of the Lebanese Druze community as the one that is most 'ordered' (*munaẓẓama/murattaba*), which means that it has specific Druze institutions, organizations and other possibilities for self-expression. Besides the political and structural advantages that the Lebanese Druze enjoy, their community is considered to be the religious and intellectual centre of their faith, particularly for Druze communities in the diaspora. The Lebanese *rijāl al-dīn* or religious experts—and especially those from the circle of al-Bayyada, a spiritual and teaching centre in southern Lebanon—are regarded as the highest authorities on religious questions. The last decades have also seen the emergence in Lebanon of groups of young Druze intellectuals, in whose circles ideas of reform have grown and matured. Taken together, the relatively large numbers of *rijāl al-dīn* and well-educated, ultra-liberal Druze living in Lebanon explain why Syrian and Israeli Druze insist that the Lebanese community is the one most representative of extreme viewpoints. Israeli Druze visiting relatives in the Shuf during the Lebanese civil war were deeply shocked and angered by the laxity and liberalism with which their Lebanese brothers in faith approached Druze traditions. They had the impression that 'these were no longer Druze.'

Considering all of this, it is not surprising that the Druze reform and identity discourse first appeared in Lebanon in the 1960s and only later found its way to the Druze communities of Syria and Israel.

A comparison of the three Druze communities, however, shows that, in spite of these differences, there are similar tendencies and developments among them, even though they differ in intensity.

After analyzing the general background of the identity discourse, I will focus, first, upon its main characteristics and, second, upon a comparison of the Druze communities in Lebanon, Syria and Israel. Finally, I will try to show current trends and developments.

Background

The identity and reform discourse of the Druze was greatly influenced by social and economic developments during the last decades of the twentieth century. These included a weakening of family and village ties, growing migration from rural to urban centres and an increase in the number of commuters travelling to work in towns or cities. They also involved the appearance of women's movements and, most importantly, the emergence of a group of urban intellectuals who demanded that Druze religious and political leaders dismantle hoary traditions.[2] These factors greatly affected the general Druze population by creating doubts concerning the centuries-old practices of the faithful. In particular, the younger generation began questioning the values and rules of their own community. The following quotation (1980) from the Israeli Druze, Fayiz Azzam, substantiates this process, which set in motion the search for a Druze identity:

> The expansion of secular education and the concurrent undermining of the patriarchal system, an increase in media communication and daily contact between Druze and other communities both on a social plane as well as in areas of employment, army service, etc. have drawn the Druze closer together and have forced them to become introspective, asking the question: What really distinguishes the Druze from his non-Druze neighbor?[3]

Above and beyond this, a slow "subjective secularization,"[4] in other words, a gradual but constant decrease in religion's importance to human thought and action, has weakened the power and interpretation monopoly of the *rijāl al-dīn*. It has reduced the Druze religion to a mere realization of a common history and an insecure future.

The diaspora Druze are particularly challenged by the problems and dangers that arise from this loss of identity, as well as the potential breakdown of traditional communal structures. It is, therefore, unsurprising that the principal impulse for the reform of the Druze faith has come from Druze communities in North and South America. In an ironic, although amusing story, Lebanese Druze scholar Najib Alamuddin sums up the problem quite astutely:

> I well remember how, the first time I arrived in New York, an immigration officer, for reasons of his own, asked about my religion. "Druze," I replied. "Jews," he stated. "No, no, Druze," I repeated. "What sort of religion is this?" he asked. "It is a secret religion," I replied. He looked at me sternly, thinking I was making fun of him, and said: "Come, come, now. There are no secret religions. Tell me something about it." "Friend," I replied, "it is so secret that I know nothing about it myself."[5]

Deeply shaken by the scandal that followed the publication of ʿAbd Allah al-Najjar's book, Druze intellectuals in Lebanon and, somewhat later, their counterparts in Syria and Israel began a similar discussion.

The process upon which the Druze had now embarked cannot be seen as a unique phenomenon. The steady increase in urbanization, the breakdown of traditional order and the resulting reorientation of the younger generation had led to the rise of similar problems in other religious communities.[6] This was particularly true of those Muslim minorities that might be characterized as syncretistic.[7] Such communities are further distinguished by the strong influence that extreme Shiʿi beliefs have had on them, the initiation rites that adherents must undergo in order to obtain esoteric knowledge and the fact that each of them possesses a hereditary class of religious specialists. From a certain historical moment onward, group endogamy became predominant and initiation into the secret doctrine was restricted to those born into the community. Beyond that, members of all of these communities resorted to *taqiyya* to conceal their own religious identities.

Often called heretical and subjected to social and economic discrimination, these communities were particularly in danger of a slow and gradual assimilation into the religious mainstreams of their various countries. Such developments have been noted among the Turkish Alevites,[8] the Kizilbash Kurds in the Dersim region of Turkey,[9] the Ismaʿilis (who follow the Aga Khan),[10] the Ahl al-Haqq in Iraq and Iran[11] and, if only in the early stages, the ʿAlawis in Syria.[12]

Fearing the loss of their identities and the decline of their communities and rebelling against constant and unbearable stigmatization, the laymen within these minorities—members of the new secularized intelligentsia—finally began to act. In order to ensure the security and, indeed, existence of their various collectivities, they called for a "symbolic recreation of . . . [each] distinctive community through myth, ritual and a 'constructed tradition.'"[13] They sought basic changes in their centuries-old traditions by demanding that their communities be opened to converts and that their beliefs and laws, which had hitherto been orally transmitted, be fixed in printed texts. Such textual preservation was expected to make possible a general consensus of meaning: no longer would traditions be left open to local interpretations. This demand for a fixed text was paired with an often-articulated belief that a return to religious values could only be achieved by a leadership chosen on the basis of knowledge and aptitude, thus strengthening communal coherence.

Generally speaking, however, this process of renewal and reformation has developed differently in the various communities owing, in particular, to the different opportunities found in each to voice opinions and debate central theological questions.

Main characteristics of the identity discourse

The process of Druze self-assertion, combining both components of the reform movement—'a return to roots' and 'a new formulation of laws and traditions'—was the primary topic of those whom I interviewed and of literary publications in all three Druze communities. Members of each of these considered their own community to be undergoing a 'period of change or transition,' in which the foundations of the future were being laid. The existential question was: How might they meet the challenges of modern society and integrate themselves into their respective nation-states without losing their own identity and communal cohesion? The goal of this effort at self-preservation was, therefore, the assurance of a collective Druze identity and the reinforcement of its cohesion through a redefinition of its historical, political and religious position in state and society. It was hoped that this might guarantee the survival and functioning of the three communities in the years to come. Thus, the members of Druze circles are striving to revisit the roots of their heritage and to bring about a positive reappraisal of religious patterns of identification, as well as related social and cultural values. This attempt to define their own position has two objectives. *Inwardly*, it seeks to intensify a feeling of Druze separatism from their surroundings in order to preserve Druze identity and cohesion. *Outwardly*, it aims at a controlled integration into the nation-state by stressing common ground and avoiding any challenges to Arab/Muslim or national interests. The consequences may be described as a difficult 'walk on the wire' that attempts to find a balance between integration and separatism. On the one hand, the Druze want to take pride in the specific character of their own community. On the other, they wish to prove to the outside world that they are not seeking political or social isolation but, in fact, just the opposite.

As difficult as this position is, it reveals other typical aspects of the Druze identity discourse. I refer to its apologetic character, its almost complete rejection of differentiation and the impression that it gives of self-censorship, as well as its recourse to outside representations of the Druze faith in order to declare them to be prejudiced and discriminatory. In the opinion of the Druze, such polemics have stigmatized their community, isolating and separating them in the political sphere, while marking them as heretics in the religious sphere.

In their literature, the Druze seek to convey a cohesive self-portrait, one which is in complete harmony with Islam, underlines their Arab origin and reconfirms their entrenchment in the historical development of their various home countries. The tendency to stress the Islamic character of the Druze faith and to declare themselves to be 'true' Muslims may be interpreted as a reaction to the often-heard charge that the Druze are heretics and not really Muslims. At the same time, however, the Druze seek to ascribe to the Druze faith a specific character within the framework of Islam by interpreting the fundamental doctrine of Islam, *tawḥīd*, in a way that goes beyond the understanding of mainstream Islam. Furthermore, they stress the significance of virtue and morality and point to their belief in the transition of the soul (*taqammus*) as an expression of the righteousness and justice of God.

Yet, written and oral sources show certain discrepancies, one of which is the politically and theologically sensitive question of whether the Druze faith is an Islamic 'sect' (*madhhab*) or a separate religion in its own right (*dīn*). Whereas the literature unanimously insists upon the faith's Islamic character, the great majority of the Druze with whom I spoke explicitly called themselves Druze and not Muslims. Moreover, many Druze express the conviction that the Druze faith has its roots in Islam, but developed into an independent religion over the centuries.

These apologetics vary in private interviews, depending upon the informant, but are ever-present in the literature, even though there are subtle differences. Statements on the historical and political engagement of the Druze and calls for more political influence are rather combative. However, statements on religious questions, touching the very roots of Druze identity, appear to be defensive in nature and motivated by a desire to protect the community from external attack.

When we examine more recent Druze publications, the overwhelming majority can be seen to reappraise the community's history with a view to putting the common historical legacy into perspective for the present generation. This tendency may also be observed among other ethnic and national in-groups: a collective identity is sought through an emphasis on a collective history.[14] The attempt to define the community primarily through its history may, in the case of the Druze, arise from the fact that most adherents have no knowledge of the substance and meaning of their religion. Hence, it is difficult to find a common identity based upon religion. It is also less difficult for the readers of these works—and for their authors—to deal with Druze history than with the complexity of Druze dogma, for which there are few consistent documentary references.

These historical presentations may be reduced, for the most part, to three central ideas:

- The Druze are authentic and legitimate Arabs—not only by origin, but also by language, tradition and their support for the Arab cause.
- The Druze communities are deeply rooted in historical Syria and, therefore, an inseparable part of the Arab/Muslim world.
- The Druze are a minority without a 'minority-complex.' The Druze self-conception has not been formed by a tendency toward isolationism, but by the profound patriotic and historical attachments that members of the three communities have held for their respective homelands.

But who are the people involved in this identity and reform discourse? For the most part, the discussion is being carried out by highly schooled laymen and, with a few exceptions, by those women who received their education and attained social status outside of the Druze communities. Educated in the universities of Beirut or in Western countries, these individuals have become lawyers, engineers, teachers, or professors. If not academics, they are writers who call themselves businessmen or women when asked their occupation. They represent a new Druze social élite that expresses its decided views in interviews and in literary works. Owing to their intensive contact with the world outside of the Druze community, they are confronted not only with other social, political and religious views and values, but also with discrimination, slander and defamation.

The possible dangers of Druze criticism within the community, which might well lead to the estrangement of some of its members, are also recognized by the *rijāl al-dīn*. However, their reaction seems to be confined to bewailing fading moral values and what they see as the continuous spread of the cancer of nihilism. Consequently, they demand a more rigorous enforcement of Druze laws and values and energetic opposition to the aspirations of members of the younger generation who seek schooling outside of the community.

A comparison of Druze communities in Lebanon, Syria and Israel

In spite of the great differences in state and society in Lebanon, Syria and Israel, the Druze communities in all three countries face the same problems and are equally motivated to solve them. The most important parallel involves demands for internal structural reform in each of the individual communities. These reforms would finally reduce the uncontrolled political and/or religious power held by men who are not elected, but have largely attained their positions through traditional family means.

The often-repeated demands for inner reform come, first of all, from a new generation of young, well-educated Druze who are no longer willing to tolerate traditional patriarchal and undemocratic structures. Second, the deaths of members of the traditional leadership, especially the Lebanese *shaykh al-ʿaql,* Muhammad Abu Shaqra, in 1991, and the Israeli *raʾīs al-rūḥī,* Amin Tarif, in 1993, have created a political vacuum. Thus, in all three states, reforms are being asked of the highest religious authorities, the *mashyakhat al-ʿaql* in Lebanon and Syria and the *riʾāsa al-rūḥiyya* in Israel. Also on the agenda are the implementation of democratic controls over religious endowments (*awqāf*) as well as the revival of the communal council (*majlis al-madhhabī*) in Lebanon and the establishment of a religious council (*majlis dīnī* or *millī*) in Israel.

In *Israel,* after a lengthy dispute between the Tarif family and the Druze 'control' council (*lajnat al-mutabaʿa*), led by Asʿad Asʿad, a member of the Israeli Knesset, a compromise was reached in August 1997. The Tarifs, who had traditionally held political and religious power in the Druze community, had sought to retain their position and the political status quo by laying claim to the vacant office of the *riʾāsa al-rūḥiyya.*[15] The *lajnat al-mutabaʿa,* however, had aimed at the establishment of a new 'modern' order in the Druze community that would include the introduction of democratic structures into the *awqāf* administration and an elected *raʾīs al-rūḥī.* According to the terms of the compromise, a religious council (*majlis dīnī*) composed of 78 *rijāl al-dīn* was founded and Muwaffaq Tarif, a grandson of Amin Tarif who had been designated as his successor in his will,[16] was chosen as its spiritual leader for a five-year term. The other reform proposals were put on hold.

In *Syria,* the reform movement has concentrated upon reorganizing the *awqāf,* which have known no legal controls up until now and have been governed by custom (*ʿurf*), just as they are among Syria's other religious communities. The *awqāf* are controlled and managed by three *shuyūkh al-ʿaql* who have been unencumbered, in the past, by any necessity for transparency in their disbursements of the *awqāf's* financial resources. Since these are quite extensive, Druze intellectuals have stressed the need for a new structural concept. They have also called for the election of a single *shaykh al-ʿaql* for the entire community. This movement toward a merger of the *mashyakhat al-ʿaql,* however, is not as strong as the one toward a new *awqāf* structure because the *shuyūkh* theoretically represent the Druze community to the Syrian state and require, as in Lebanon, a document from the government according them official recognition (although, in reality, they have little political strength or influence).

In *Lebanon,* the conflict over choosing a successor to the deceased *shaykh al-ʿaql,* Muhammad Abu Shaqra, which began in October 1995, has not yet been resolved, despite many attempts to reach a consensus. Thus, the problem of the communal council (*majlis al-madhhabī*) and the democratization of the management of Druze endowments cannot yet be addressed.

Differences exist among the three Druze communities regarding their identity recourse. The Syrian and Lebanese Druze are strongly influenced by Arab nationalism and Sunni Islam, and strive to be accepted as 'genuine' Arabs and Muslims, whether from conviction or social pressure. In contrast, the majority of Israeli Druze are adamantly convinced that they constitute a distinct ethnic and religious community that has nothing in common with Muslims and that shares only a language with Arabs. This distinction was acknowledged, in their view, by the prophet Shuʿaib, whom the Israeli Druze revere as their founder. As the son-in-law of Moses, he further symbolizes the historic unity of the Jewish and Druze communities.

In Druze dogma, Shuʿaib is seen as the personification of *al-ʿaql al-kullī.* Nowhere in Syrian and Lebanese literature is he given further importance; in interviews and discussions with Syrian and Lebanese Druze, his name is never mentioned. When asked about this phenomenon, Israeli Druze argue that their Syrian and Lebanese brothers in faith practice *taqiyya* on this question, since they are forced to acknowledge Muhammad to be the greatest prophet. Only a minority of them, the most prominent being Samih al-Qasim, Salman Natur and Shaykh Jamal Muʿaddi, openly distance themselves from this position and insist upon their identity as Muslim Palestinians.

Al-Qasim, who claims to be a Palestinian, rather than a Druze, and who is a poet and the editor of the Arabic newspaper, *Kull al-ʿArab,* openly rejects the state of Israel. In an interview, he called Israel an "historic catastrophe" for the Druze. In his opinion, the political, social and economic position of the Druze in Israel is much weaker than in Lebanon and Syria. He admitted, however, that the Druze alliance with the Jews had been a "rational step," since it has protected them from expulsion and exile and suggested that, if the Palestinians had done the same, the political situation today might be very different.[17] Salman Natur, poet, writer and one of the founders of the Initiative Committee (*lajnat al-mubādara*), which has promoted the suspension of the law requiring Israeli Druze to serve in the military, also defines Druze identity as Arab/Palestinian.[18]

A comparison of interviews with Druze in the three countries shows that Israeli Druze seem to be the ones most resistant to reform movements seeking to open their community to the outside world or to allow their culture to absorb influences from it. The communities in Syria and Lebanon show a much greater willingness to accept basic changes in their traditional religious, social and political policies. This observation is based not only upon the impressions of foreign observers, but also upon the perceptions of Lebanese and Syrian Druze. They consider the Druze in Israel to form the most 'tightly-woven,' 'closed' and 'traditional' Druze community. The reasons for this can be found in the socio-political position of the Druze in Israel. Since Israel is a declared Jewish state, the Druze will never be able to identify with it completely. The officially propagated Zionism is hardly an ideology attractive to non-Jews. In addition, the Israeli government seeks to keep the distinctive identities of non-Jewish minorities within a framework that suits its politics. As a result, the desire of—or the social pressure from—non-Jewish communities for integration into Israeli society is very small, even if the Western-oriented life-style of many Israelis might tempt the younger generation of Druze.

In Lebanon and Syria, which possess predominately Arab/Muslim populations, the Druze have greater possibilities for social and political influence and advancement. This gives them, in turn, an incentive to overcome their minority status—albeit in a controlled and gradual manner. Moreover, one must not underestimate the attraction of secular ideologies, such as Arab nationalism and socialism, although these have lost much of their strength in recent years. For both of these reasons, the chances of positive integration into the social and political spheres are much greater in Lebanon and Syria than they are in Israel.

In spite of their ideological and political differences, members of the faith in all three countries confirmed in interviews that the Druze community is undergoing a process of change and transition. There are different views of the future and few people are optimistic. Most are afraid of religious decline and the loss of identity. They see themselves as being bound to developments in the Middle East, in particular, the Arab-Israeli conflict and the growing power of political Islam. Whereas the former increases the political and ideological divide between Lebanese and Syrian Druze and their coreligionists in Israel, members of all three communities view Islamic fundamentalism as a great danger to every Muslim minority in the region. They fear a climate of increasing intolerance and suppression and believe that it can only be averted by the secularization and democratization of the Middle East's social systems.

There is also great fear that the three communities may be driven into extinction by the breakdown of traditional communal ties, by the loss of Druze identity and through slow assimilation into the majority societies of their various countries. This process may be intensified owing to internal factors, such as the insurmountable differences between the initiated and the non-initiated and between the traditional élite and the new class of intellectuals. There are also the unresolved problems of urbanization and emigration, which destroy the tightly-bound village communities and may lead unborn generations to put down roots elsewhere. In the face of such dangers, some Druze may retreat into their own communities and sever their connections with the rest of the society, hence, depriving themselves of the possibility of influencing political decisions. The women, in particular, tend to observe that the low birth rate might be a decisive factor leading to the extinction of the Druze.

Only the *rijāl al-dīn*—with very few exceptions—have come forth with a collective opinion concerning the future of the Druze. They regard the weakening of Druze dogma and their religious and social traditions as the real danger. In their view, external threats to the faith have existed throughout the thousand years of the community's existence, yet have always been overcome. Therefore, there is no need to react overly now.

Outlook: Opening and closing

Any consideration of the struggle to define the historical, religious and political positions of the Druze gives rise to questions about current developments in the three Druze communities. Do those who strive for reform have a real chance against traditional movements, which still include the majority of Druze? Which is stronger—the desire for reform, which, by definition, brings a controlled opening to the outside world, or the wish to retain and strengthen traditional values, which may lead to the 'closing' of the communities?

Although ʿAbd Allah al-Najjar's book started an irreversible process in 1965—one that has not only influenced Druze self-identity, but also the structure of Druze communities—there will certainly be no fundamental changes or 'opening' to the outside world in the near future. This is despite the fact that the great majority of Druze are unsatisfied with the status quo and feel the need for radical reform. There are two major reasons why changes or 'opening' are impossible at the present time.

First, the current balance of religious and political power in the Middle East represents an important external obstacle to any 'opening' of the Druze community. In today's climate of deep intolerance owing to an increasingly strong and radical political Islam, only a small number of Druze favour a complete disclosure of Druze dogma, which the Sunni majority would most certainly deem blasphemous. Under these circumstances, it does not seem advisable to suspend *taqiyya* completely. One hears again and again that if the Druze lived in democratic societies, for instance, in the United States or Europe, there would be no danger in publishing texts revealing their religious beliefs and rituals—but most of them do not live outside of the Middle East. Hence, only a small minority agree that the Druze should disclose all and are prepared to take the consequences. A repeal of Druze laws banning publication of the dogma is only one of the three most important indicators of an 'opening' of the community, with the others involving similar repeals of laws banning outmarriage and conversion. Most Druze are equally ambivalent about all three of these subjects.

Another external obstacle involves the official politics and political structures of the different countries in which the Druze live. In particular, the Lebanese confessional system, which favours traditional structures, may be expected to impede the complete democratization of the Druze community, rather than support it. But, in Syria and Israel too, where governments have an interest in maintaining the status quo, the initiation of such a democratic process is unlikely to gain governmental support easily.

Second, obstacles within the communities themselves must also be overcome. Here I am referring to the objections of traditional leaders, who are only interested in retaining their political power, and—to an even greater extent—the passivity of the *rijāl al-dīn*, who refuse to support fundamental reforms of any kind. There are no reformers in sight who seem sufficiently qualified to lead the way. The *rijāl al-dīn*, who have the greatest knowledge of the faith, should and could be the initiators, but they refuse to take part in any discussion on reform and remain unreceptive to the idea. Many Druze favour the establishment of an assembly of *rijāl al-dīn* to deal with the question of necessary religious reforms, but such an endeavour seems hardly possible at the present time. As a consequence, the monopoly on religious knowledge, which the *rijāl al-dīn* still enjoy, will remain intact, despite the fact that the Druze today are in a better position to learn the details of their religion than they have been in the past.

Although the communities are unlikely to open themselves up to the outside world in the near future, we can be more optimistic about internal reforms and an internal 'opening' that may be on the horizon. Religious studies for Druze schoolchildren, special training for the *rijāl al-dīn* and the careful democratization of community structures are all under consideration. This process has been given added force by a new phenomenon—a rising Druze consciousness of the community's faith and roots. In Lebanon, this rise in consciousness has been a result of the long civil war, which was carried out along confessional lines: during the conflict, the religious affiliation appearing on one's identity card sometimes meant the difference between life and death. In Syria, Druze consciousness has increased owing to a high degree of disappointment with the failure of the socialist and pan-Arab ideals of the Baath Party. In Israel, this 'back to roots' movement, although weaker than in Lebanon and Syria, seems to have resulted from frustration at the unfulfilled promise of Prime Minister Levi Eshkol's 1967 expression ("You are as we") of Druze-Jewish brotherhood.

In the last decades, the publication of an immense amount of Druze literature has also encouraged this movement. This has finally provided the Druze layperson with the information needed to form his or her own opinions and to present them publicly.

IN THE LONG TERM, THEREFORE, well-educated laypeople may lead the way to new interpretations of the Druze religion and reorganizations of the three Druze communities. In the past, the rendering of religious doctrines involved what might be characterized as a "limited literality"[19]: the *rijāl al-dīn* were relatively free in their own individual interpretations of both oral and written religious traditions, often enhancing their words through their own personal charisma. This recent phenomenon of an "uncontrolled and individualistic scriptualization," however, when connected with free access to and interpretation of holy writings by lay people, might weaken the position of the *rijāl al-dīn,* since their views would be subject to open debate and discussion.

The overall consequences of the reform process initiated in 1966 by al-Najjar's book are not yet foreseeable. What can be said, however, is that it is irreversible. The tension between secrecy and revelation—between closing and opening—will continue to determine the Druze identity and reform discourse.

Notes

[1] What follows is based on my D.Phil. thesis, *Entwicklungen und Tendenzen in der zeitgenössischen drusischen Gemeinschaft des Libanon: Versuche einer historischen, politischen und religiösen Standortbestimmung* (Berlin, 2002).

[2] Urbanization has been considered to be the central force behind the breakdown of conventional conceptions of order in traditional societies. See, for example, Mordechai Nisan, *Minorities in the Middle East: A History of Struggle and Self-Expression* (Jefferson, 1991), 12; Thomas Scheffler, "Zwischen 'Balkanisierung' und Kommunalismus: Ethnisch-religiöse Konflikte im Nahen und Mittleren Osten," *Orient* 26 (1985), 192f.; Krisztina Kehl-Bodrogi, "Die 'Wiederfindung' des Alevitentums in der Türkei: Geschichtsmythos und kollektive Identität," *Orient* 34 (1993), 269; Reha Camuroglu, "Some Notes on the Contemporary Process of Restructuring Alivilik in Turkey," in *Syncretistic Religious Communities in the Near East. Collected Papers of the International Symposium "Alevism in Turkey and Comparable Syncretistic Religious Communities in the Near East in the Past and Present," Berlin, 14-17 April*, edited by Krisztina Kehl-Bodrogi, Barabara Kellner-Heinkele and Anke Otter Beaujean (Leiden, 1997), 25f.

[3] Fayiz Azzam, "Druze Identity—A Problem Demanding Solution," in *The Druze: A Religious Community in Transition*, edited by Nissim Dana (Jerusalem, 1980), 115.

[4] Peter Berger, as quoted by Francis Robinson in "Säkularisierung im Islam," in *Max Webers Sicht des Islam*, edited by Wolfgang Schluchter (Frankfurt, 1987), 258.

[5] Najib Alamuddin, *Turmoil: The Druzes, Lebanon and the Arab-Israeli Conflict* (London, 1993), 8.

[6] See the different studies in Kehl-Bodrogi, Kellner-Heinkele and Beaujean, eds., *Syncretistic Religious Communities.*

[7] See Carsten Colpe, "The Phenomenon of Syncretism and the Impact of Islam," in Kehl-Bodrogi, Kellner-Heinkele and Beaujean, eds., *Syncretistic Religious Communities*, 35-48.

[8] Karin Vorhoff, *Zwischen Glaube, Nation und neuer Gemeinschaft: Alevitische Identität in der Türkei der Gegenwart* (Berlin, 1995); Krisztina Kehl-Bodrogi, *Vom revolutionären Klassenkampf zum 'wahren' Islam: Transformationsprozesse im Alevitum in der Türkei nach 1980* (Berlin, 1992).

[9] Martin van Bruinessen, "'Aslini inkar eden haramzadedir!' The Debate on the Ethnic Identity of the Kurdish Alevis," in Kehl-Bodrogi, Kellner-Heinkele and Beaujean, eds., *Syncretistic Religious Communities,* 1-24; Martin van Bruinessen, "Kurds, Turks and the Alevi Revival in Turkey," *Middle East Report* (July-September 1996), 7-10.

[10] Werner Schmucker, "Sekten und Sondergruppen," in *Der Islam in der*

Gegenwart: Entwicklung und Ausbreitung, Staat, Politik und Recht, Kultur und Religion, edited by Werner Ende and Udo Steinbach (Munich, 1989), 509-517; Heinz Halm, *Die Schia* (Darmstadt, 1988), 224-32.

[11] Ziba Mir-Hosseini, "Breaking the Seal: The New Face of the Ahl-e Haqq," in Kehl-Bodrogi, Kellner-Heinkele and Beaujean, eds., *Syncretistic Religious Communities*, 175-94.

[12] Schmucker, "Sekten und Sondergruppen."

[13] Anthony Cohn, *The Symbolic Construction of Community* (London and New York, 1985), 37.

[14] See the different studies in *History and Ethnicity*, edited by Elizabeth Tonkin, M. McDonald and M. Chapman (London, 1989); Jürgen Straub, "Geschichten erzählen, Geschichten bilden: Grundzüge einer narrativen Psychologie historischer Sinnbildung," in *Erzählung, Identität und historisches Bewußtsein: Die psychologische Konstruktion von Zeit und Geschichte*, edited by J. Straub (Frankfurt, 1998), 128. Jan Assmann, *Das kulturelle Gedächtnis: Schrift, Erinnerung und politische Identität in frühen Hochkulturen* (Munich, 1999).

[15] With their legal recognition as a separate community, the Druze were given judicial autonomy in matters of personal status and *waqf*. This included the legal authority to establish their own independent religious leadership (*ri'āsa al-rūhhiyya*). The latter, by virtue of custom, went to the three leading families, the Khayr, Mu'addi and Tarif, with the paramountcy being held by the Tarifs, namely Amin Tarif. See Kais Firro, *The Druzes in the Jewish State: A Brief History* (Leiden, 1999), 161f. Until the present, there is no law, that regulates the investiture of the *ra'īs al-rūhī* (interview with Fayiz Azzam in Isfiyya, January 1997).

[16] For the contents of his will, see the newspaper, *Al-Sinara* (Nazareth), 10 August 1993.

[17] Interview in Nazareth, November 1996.

[18] Interview in Daliyat al-Karmil, October 1996.

[19] For this phenomenon, see Jack Goody, "Funktionen der Schrift in traditionalen Gesellschaften," in *Entstehen und Folgen der Schriftkultur*, edited by Jack Goody, I. Watt and K. Gough (Frankfurt, 1986), 42.

INTISAR AZZAM

Druze Women: Ideal and Reality

THIS ARTICLE IS PART OF an anthropological study in progress to investigate the dynamics of gender relations among the Druze of Lebanon and the formulating factors affecting the experience of Druze women in comparison to their status in the Druze scriptures and under the Lebanese Druze legislative codes.

As a Druze woman who gradually became more knowledgeable about the *Tawḥīd* perspective, I came to realize that its principles do not necessarily contradict those of modern life. I also realized, as I will argue here, that the efforts of Druze women to attain equality may most peaceably be accomplished through conscious knowledge of their authentic status in their scriptures. In order to investigate the factors that affect the experience of Druze women, while avoiding the pitfalls of comparing one's ideal with someone else's reality or one's reality with someone else's ideal, I decided that it was imperative to use the empirical method and to study the actual lives of Druze women. Qualitative research and comparative fieldwork are the best strategy for investigating stereotypes and generalizations about Druze women when their experiences can be diverse in relation not only to their status in the scriptures or Druze family law, but to their socio-economic status across time and place.

The starting point should be the acknowledgement that the experience of Druze women in Lebanon cannot be separated from that of Arab Muslim women in general nor the broader struggle in the Arab world for liberation, independence and progress. It is well known that the question of women's liberation in the Arab world is, as elsewhere, a sensitive one and that it has occupied diverse categories of investigators—including intellectuals, modernists and Islamists—and given rise to an ample literature. Many of these scholars allude to a correlation between women's liberation movements and political or national movements for liberation and independence in the

Arab and wider developing world. In a recent comprehensive review of a number of studies by both men and women dealing with the status and role of Arab women since 1889, the date of the publication of Qasim Amin's progressive work, *The Liberation of Women*, Muhammad al-Khatib demonstrates how the efforts of Arab women to improve their status rose and fell alongside schemes to advance and renew Arab societies—thriving in the mid-nineteenth century and in the early 1920s and the 1950s and 1960s of the twentieth century and receding during periods of social, political and economic stagnation (al-Khatib 1999, 1:5-7).

As mentioned above, the literature on women in Muslim societies is rich and abundant, but works focused specifically upon women in Druze communities are few and tenuous. In fact, extensive anthropological studies are not available. The present work was predominantly motivated, therefore, by this serious lacuna, as well as my own awareness of the cultural reality of being a Druze woman, a product of an historical process shrouded in ambiguity, misconception and misrepresentation. As a consequence, my objective has been to fill this gap in knowledge and to explore or illuminate alternative discourse concerning gender and human relations.

Because *al-Tawḥīd* is recognized as an offshoot of Islam, we cannot explore gender in it while bypassing gender in Islam, a subject that is highly charged not only at the popular level, but among scholars as well. While some consider gender in Muslim societies to be an exclusively religious issue and either praise or blame Islam for the status that women have under it, others insist that the accumulated ills of Muslim women and their liminal status or inferiority are more attributable to socio-economic forces and the abuse of religious belief than to religious belief itself (Mernisi 1987, 8 and 62). This paper is not intended to contrast these points of view nor the various ways in which women are treated in Muslim societies, although my broader study will include a brief historical perspective on patriarchy and gender in Islam as we cannot overlook the formative influence of Islam on the role of women and men in all past and present Muslim and Arab societies. Here, the formative influence of Islam on the experience of Druze women will gradually become apparent owing to the comparative nature of this inquiry.

Gender in the Druze scriptures

Throughout the Druze epistles, including *al-Sharīʿa al-Rūḥāniyya*,[1] women and men are mentioned jointly and asserted to be equal in all rights and obligations. Even in the four epistles addressed specifically to girls and women (8, 18, 83 and 84), it is specified and reiterated that women and men are equally accountable for their moral actions and behaviour, and both sexes are cautioned against deviance from *al-Tawḥīd*. Many argue that, in principle, this is the case in the Qurʾan as well (see Ahmad 1992; Makhlouf Obermeyer 1992; Shaaban 1998; and Jawad 1998). So can we say that, ideally at least, there is no difference between Islam and *al-Tawḥīd* when it comes to gender?

Essentially, the perception of difference stems from some interpretations of specific verses in the Qurʾan that have to do with marriage and its dissolution and others that involve the right to inherit and bequeath property without restriction. The Qurʾanic *ṣūra* entitled *Al-Nisāʾ* (Women) permits a form of polygamy known as polygyny (when a man has more than one wife at the same time) so long as the man treats all of his wives with absolute justice both in feelings and actions: "If you fear that you will not act justly toward the orphans, marry such women as seem good to you, two, three, four; but if you fear you will not be equitable, then only one" (Qurʾan 4:3). Some Islamists argue that the permissibility of polygyny here is situational and meant to protect the orphaned and widowed during times of war.[2] However, verse 129 of the same *ṣūra* asserts that it is impossible to satisfy the condition of absolute justice: "You will not be equitable between your wives, be you ever so eager" (Qurʾan 4:29). This assertion ultimately prompted the Fatimid caliph, al-Muʿizz, to be the first to ban polygamy, which occurred before the call to *Tawḥīd* in AD 1017 (Abu-Izzeddin 1984, 230). *Al-Tawḥīd* embraced the caliph's interpretation and banned polygamy, while promoting further pertinent egalitarian measures on gender relations through the prohibition of concubinage and temporary marriage (*zawāj al-mutʿa*), as well as any form of secret marriage.[3] In *al-Sharīʿa al-Rūḥāniyya*, it is unlawful for a man to have more than one wife at the same time or for either partner to indulge in any sexual behaviour outside of marriage. The charge of adultery requires two qualified witnesses and both the male and the female offender are punished (SR, 230-36). These conditions are unequivocably stated in *al-Sharīʿa al-Rūḥāniyya* and in Druze epistles 15, 25 and 83.

Gender equality is clearly confirmed in all that concerns marriage in *al-Tawḥīd*, which considers it to be a union between two consenting equals: a *Muwaḥḥid* and a *Muwaḥḥida* (SR, 238), who have the same obligation toward their union and the same right to end it if it becomes inharmonious. According to *al-Sharīʿa al-Rūḥāniyya*, a woman is not to be married without first being consulted, for she knows herself better than anyone else does; if she refuses an offer, she may not be forced to marry (SR, 235).

As for the dowry (*mahr* or *ṣidāq*), although a husband is obliged to pay one to his bride (SR, 235), the *Muwaḥḥidūn* are urged to minimize the amount because it does not constitute the worth of a wife nor her compensation upon the dissolution of an unsuccessful marriage. Regarding the first point, the worth of a wife, *al-Sharīʿa al-Rūḥāniyya* asserts that the best women among the *Muwaḥḥidūn* are the richest in wisdom, the most patient, and those who receive the least dowry (SR, 228-29). Regarding the second point, all of the rules regulating the marriage of the *Muwaḥḥidūn* are detailed in Epistle 25 (*Sharṭ al-imām*),[4] which epitomizes the principles of gender equality. In this epistle, Hamza stipulates that "if a *Muwaḥḥid* takes to himself a *Muwaḥḥida* as a wife, he shall treat her as his equal and share equally with her all that he possesses." In other words, the wife immediately becomes an equal partner, both socially and economically. Moreover, "should the husband decide on the dissolution of the marriage through no fault of the wife, she is entitled to half of what he possesses, including clothing, furniture, silver, gold, cattle and all that he has acquired."

Further evidence that the *mahr* is symbolic and does not constitute a wife's worth nor her compensation may be found in the fact that the same rules apply if it is the wife who decides to dissolve the marriage: "If separation becomes necessary and it is the wife who wishes to leave her husband, although it is known to the trustworthy in the community that he is fulfilling his obligations toward her, then the husband is entitled to half of what she owns" (Epistle 25). Hence, if either spouse, due to irreconcilable differences, is no longer content with the marriage and chooses to divorce, the marriage must be dissolved according to rules that apply equally to both men and women. The issue of irreconcilable differences and irremediable harmony is critical because the Druze view divorce as a last resort that should not be granted or approved unless trustworthy *thuqāt* (or 'arbiters') have exhausted all efforts to solve the dispute or bridge the gap between spouses. The dissolution is absolute, final and irrevocable no matter what the circumstances. *Al-Sharīʿa al-Rūḥāniyya* forbids the remarriage of former spouses to one another or even any form of interaction between them. Remarriage to one another is taboo and viewed as incest (SR, 240): in other words, the former wife becomes a virtual *mahram* (someone who is at a degree of consanguinity precluding marriage) to her former husband.[5] This is clearly intended to deter spouses from hasty decisions and from divorcing without good reason. Consequently, *al-Sharīʿa al-Rūḥāniyya* forbids the verbal repudiation of the spouse, namely, the unconditional right of the husband to dissolve the marriage without any justification or revision of his decision (SR, 164).

Indeed, repudiation is an action that is very degrading to the dignity of women. Many Muslim scholars also argue that it is contrary to the way that women are commended in the Qur'an, which urges esteem, kindness and courtesy toward them and respect for their rights (Jawad 1998, 77; Doi 1989, 7). The Qur'an, in several instances, commends mutual compassion between men and women, for example: "they [women] are your garments and you [men] are their garments"(Qur'an 2:187); "they [women] have rights similar to those over them [men] in kindness" (Qur'an 2:228); and "consort with them in kindness" (Qur'an 4:18). Unconditional verbal repudiation certainly does not reflect mutual compassion.

Another egalitarian principle in *al-Tawḥīd* is the right of men and women to own property and to dispose of it freely, without any restrictions, whether as a gift, grant, or bequest. Absolute freedom of endowment or testacy is asserted in recognition of the right of every individual to independent ownership, which entails freedom in the disposition of property. *Al-Sharīʿa al-Rūḥāniyya* makes the preparation of a will the duty of every property owner, male or female, as a reminder of the transience of life. According to *al-Sharīʿa al-Rūḥāniyya:* "It is not proper for a *Muwaḥḥid* or a *Muwaḥḥida* to spend a night without his/her written will next to his/her head" (SR, 188). Elsewhere it is written: "The grantor has no restrictions on whom he may endow his/her money.. . . And whatever is written in the will is sanctioned" (SR, 185). Also, "a person is absolutely free to bequeath whatever of his/her property to whomever" (SR, 189). For further clarification, it is asserted: "Heirs have no claim over anything that was given, or assigned to be given, by the testator to whomever he/she has chosen, when the endowment has been accepted" (SR, 186).

Although all *Muwaḥḥidūn* are urged to leave a will, if a person does die intestate, inheritance is transmitted in accordance with Hanafi doctrine. But the fact that the will releases the testator from the application of Hanafi doctrine has resulted in serious misconceptions about the legitimacy of making a will and has further led many people, including such scholars as Aharon Layish (1982), to accuse the Druze of paying lip service to Hanafi doctrine without making any real concessions. Layish, however, propagates the argument of J. N. D. Anderson,[6] which states that absolute freedom of testacy is a form of *kitmān* ('concealment') that is intended to neutralize Hanafi doctrine through *taqiyya*.[7] But informed Druze, such as religious judges and scholars, argue that the absolute freedom of testacy is in full accordance with the Qur'an. In his introduction to *Al-Waṣiyya wal-mirāth* (Testacy and inheritance), by the Druze judges, Murcel Nasr and Halim Taqi al-Din, Sami Makarem explains that this principle is in accordance with verse 180 of *ṣūra* 2, *Al-Baqara* (The cow), which is referred to as *āyat al-waṣiyya,* the verse of testacy (Nasr and Takieddine 1983, 9-12): "Prescribed for you when any of you is visited by death, and he leaves behind some goods, is to make testament in favor of his parents and kinsmen honourably—an obligation on the God-fearing. Then if any man changed it after hearing it; surely God is All-knowing" (Qur'an 2:180). In other words, verbal testacy is urged in case of unexpected illness or death. Makarem further clarifies that this verse is not refuted, as claimed, by verses 11-14 of *ṣūra* 4, *Al-Nisā'* (Women), which are known as the verses of heirs, *āyat al-mawārīth,* because the verses explain in detail the share given to each heir in all possible circumstances. The verses repetitively assert that these shares should be calculated and dispensed after payment of any bequest or debt.[8] Therefore, the legitimacy of testation is reaffirmed in the Qur'an in five instances and not refuted.

Hafaa Jawad, a Muslim scholar, also argues that making a will is in accordance with the Qur'an, contrary to the misconception of large segments of the Muslim public who believe that a person has no right to make a will. Jawad says that there are even some misguided jurists who argue, contrary to principles clearly articulated in the Qur'an, that Islam does not recommend the making of wills. "This negative attitude," she says, "... has confused ordinary Muslim people and has led many to abandon the idea of making wills" (Jawad 1998, 65-67). It seems obvious, then, that no lip service is being paid by Druze to the Hanafi doctrine.

In general, one can say that the basic difference between attitudes to gender in *al-Tawḥīd* and those in Islam stems from the interpretation of Qur'anic verses aimed at asserting the equality and the compassion that are promised to all human beings under Islam.

Unfortunately, despite the fact that the *Tawḥīd* scriptures establish and confirm fundamental principles of equality between men and women that are compatible with the demands of modern life, my fieldwork, which is still in process, reveals a serious gap between these egalitarian principles and the actual experience of Druze women in Lebanon. The following exemplifies several cases epitomizing the drift from these egalitarian principles.

Nawal, a bright young woman married for two years, continuously protested to her parents the arbitrary verbal and physical assaults of her husband on her. Her father accused her of instigating the conflict and of provoking her husband by "being too outspoken." She said:

> My father stands for my husband because they are two of a kind. They believe that a woman is born to be ordered and bullied around. He keeps

> telling me how I am just like my mother when they first got married and that, in time, I will learn to be quiet and will know my place, just like she did. My poor mother doesn't dare say anything other than "Be patient. Don't talk back at him when he has a tantrum. A man is not a man if he doesn't demonstrate a hot temper every once in a while!" What choices do I have if my own parents won't stand up for me! If my husband grants me a divorce—that is, *if*—I will be blamed for breaking up my marriage and ruining my own life. And you know how problematic a second marriage is for a Druze women—a divorcee, what a stigma! Only an old man with children would want a divorcee to take care of him and his children. But I swear to God, I will not shut up and whatever will be will be! For I've been told this is not in keeping with our religion.[9]

Nawal has a vague knowledge of her marital rights according to her religion, but other women in similar circumstances do not and are denied any opportunity to act. This usually seems to lead to frustration transformed into submission.

This drift from the essential egalitarian features of the Druze faith persists despite the promulgation of the Lebanese Druze Judicial Law in 1948, with provisions based upon the principles mentioned above and aimed at reinforcing them. According to Saji῾ al-A῾war, consultant for the Druze Supreme Court of Appeal in Lebanon, the Druze Judicial Law was highly esteemed by non-Druze judges at the time that it was passed, being viewed as compatible with the needs of the modern nuclear family and the advanced status of women. It was also considered to be suitable and ideal for all other sects in the country (al-A῾war 1983, 19). Yet, the disparity between the ideal and the real persists to this day.

I hope that my broader inquiry, when completed, will allow me to explain how and why certain ambiguous conditions and inegalitarian traditions evolved and persisted to acquire formal status in Druze social life as well as Druze legislative codes sanctifying and affirming certain patriarchal norms incompatible with the egalitarian principles expressed in Druze scripture. I also hope that my fieldwork, when completed, will bring forward and illuminate different facets of the human experience and infuse gender discourse with relevant concerns instead of dominant reductionist perspectives and prevailing representative assumptions.

Finally, I think that the *Tawḥīd* scriptures can be considered as a fundamentally progressive covenant in terms of establishing practical principles and rules for gender equality that are in line with the demands of modern life and those of most organizations and individuals striving for gender equality in Lebanon, as well as elsewhere in the world. In my opinion, change toward greater equality for women and more humanistic, just and fair gender practices can be achieved by way of conscious reassertion of the *Tawḥīd* doctrine, as well as modernization. I believe such an approach is incapable of alienating most of the Druze community, *ʿuqqāl* and *juhhāl,*[10] men and women, and especially the young, who aspire for equality but believe, according to my research, that religion can be a hindrance or impediment to gender equality, owing to the threat to their religious identity in a sectarian political structure where religious identity is an imperative, even when it is not a viable or fruitful choice.

NOTES

[1] The quotations from the Druze epistles, including *al-Sharīʿa al-Rūḥāniyya* (referred to here as SR) are my own translations from a manuscript copy of *Kutub al-ḥikma,* which contains 111 epistles in six books.

[2] For more details, see Siddiqi 1988, 116-17; cited also in Jawad 1998, 45 and 122.

[3] The Qur'an in several places permits men to seek sexual pleasure with slaves or "what their right hands possessed": see Qur'an 4:3, 24:5 and 33:50. It should be mentioned that slavery was prohibited to his followers and subjects after al-Hakim liberated all of his male and female slaves in AD 1013 (Abu-Izzeddin 1984, 79). The citations from the Qur'an in this paper are taken from the 3rd edition of M. H. Shakir's translation, *Al-Qur'ān al-Hakīm/Holy Qur'an,* published in New York in 1984 by Tarsil Tahrike Qur'an.

[4] Written by Hamza, the first of the five *ḥudūd* dignitaries who propagated the *Tawḥīd* faith.

[5] In *al-Tawḥīd,* a man is prohibited any of the following categories of females to whom he is a *maḥram*: his mother and grandmother; his daughters and granddaughters; his sisters, nieces and sister's granddaughters; his paternal and maternal aunts; his daughters-in-law and the daughters of his sons and grandsons; his wife's mother and grandmothers; his father's or grandfather's wife; and his wife's daughters and granddaughters.

[6] J. N. D. Anderson, *The Personal Law of the Druze* (1952), quoted in Layish 1982, 289.

[7] *Taqiyya* or conformity with prevailing practices as a way of concealing information from hostile outsiders is authorized in the Qur'an in cases of extreme necessity (Qur'an 5:15; 6:119 and 16:106). For more details, see Azzam 1997, 37-41 and Abu-Izzeddin 1984, 119.

[8] "To the male the like of the portion of two females, and if they be women

above two, then for them two thirds of what he leaves, but if she be one then to her a half; and to his parents to each one of the two the sixth of what he leaves; if he has children; but if he has no children, and his heirs are his parents, a third to his mother, or, if he has brothers, to his mother a sixth, *after any bequest he may bequeath, or any debt.* Your fathers and your sons—you know not which out of them is nearer in profit to you. So God apportions. Surely God is All-knowing, All-wise. And for you a half of what your wives leave, if they leave no children, then for you of what they leave a fourth, *after any bequest they may bequeath, or any debt.* And for them a fourth of what you leave, if you have no children; but if you have children, then for them of what you leave an eighth, *after any bequest you may bequeath, or any debt.* If a man or a woman have no heir direct, but have a brother or a sister, to each of the two a sixth; but if they are more numerous than that, they share equally a third, *after any bequest he may bequeath, or any debt not prejudicial*; a charge from God. God is All-knowing, All-clement" (Qur'an 4: 11-14; my italics).

[9] Translated from several conversations with Nawal (surname withheld) in al-Matn district of Lebanon in April 1999.

[10] The *ʿuqqāl* or *ajāwīd* are the devout religious members of the Druze community and the *juhhāl* or *jismānī* are those ignorant of the *Tawḥīd* path or not in conformity with the standards of religious behaviour.

BIBLIOGRAPHY

'Abduh, Muhammad. 1979. *Al-Islām wal-marʾa.* 3d ed. Compiled and introduced by Muhammad Amarah. Beirut: Al-Mu'assasa al-'Arabiyya lil-Dirasat wal-Nashir.

Abu-Izzeddin, Nejla M. 1984. *The Druzes: A New Study of Their History, Faith, and Society.* Leiden: E. J. Brill.

Ahmad, Leila. 1992. *Women and Gender in Islam.* New Haven: Yale University Press.

al-Aʿwar, Saji'. 1983. *Al-Aḥwāl asshakhṣiyya: Al-Durziyya ʿilman wa ijtihādan.* Beirut: By the author.

al-Khatib, Mohammad Kamal. 1999. *Qaḍiat al-Marʾa* [in three volumes, as part of *Qadāya wa Hiwarāt al-Nahda al-ʿArabiyya* "25"]. Damascus: Ministry of Culture.

Amin, Qasim. 1889 [1992]. *The Liberation of Women.* Translated by Samiha Sidhom Peterson. Cairo: American University of Cairo Press.

Azzam, Intisar. 1997. *Change for Continuity: The Druze in America.* Beirut: M. A. J. D. Enterprise Universitaire d'Etude et de Publication (S.A.R.L.).

Doi, Abdur Rahman. 1989. *Women in Shariah.* London: Taha Publishers Ltd.

Jawad, Hafaa. 1998. *The Rights of Women in Islam: An Authentic Approach.* London: Macmillan Press Ltd.

Layish, Aharon. 1982. *Marriage, Divorce and Succession in the Druze Family: A Study Based on Decisions of Druze Arbitrators and Religious Courts in Israel and the Golan Heights.* Leiden: E. J. Brill.

Makarem, Sami. 1974. *The Druze Faith.* Delmar, NY: Caravan Books.

Makhlouf Obermeyer, Carla. 1992. "Islam, Women and Politics: The Demography of Arab Countries." *Population and Development Review* 18, no. 1: 33-60.

Mernisi, Fatima. 1975. *The Veil and the Male Elite.* New York: Addison Wesley.

________. 1987. *Beyond the Veil: Male/Female Dynamics in Modern Muslim Society.* London: Al-Saqi Books.

Nasr, Murcel, and Halim Taqi al-Din. 1983. *Al-Waṣiya wal-mīrāth ʿind al-Muwaḥḥdīn al-Durūz.* 2d ed. Beirut: by the authors (distributed by Dar al-Hadatha).

Shaaban, Boutheina. 1998. "Persisting Contradictions: Muslim Women in Syria." In *Women in Muslim Societies,* edited by Herbert L. Bodman and Nayereh Tohidi. London: Lynne Rienner Publishers.

Siddiqi, Mohammad Mazharuddin. 1988. *Women in Islam.* New Delhi: Adam Publishers & Distributors.

LEILA FAWAZ

The Druze-British Connection in 1840-1860

IF THERE WERE ANY DOUBTS as to the special nature of the Druze-British relationship in nineteenth-century Lebanon, they were eliminated during the troubled decades of the 1840s, 1850s and 1860s. The crisis of 1860 fully revealed the depth and strength of the ties that the Druze had developed with the British. It is a well-known axiom that you can tell who your friends are in times of trouble; and, if this were applied to the Druze in their darkest hour, after the 1860-61 civil war in Greater Syria, then the British were indeed their friends. Yet, in the long run, did this connection make all that much of a difference to Druze destiny? This is what the present paper will consider.[1]

Elsewhere, I have argued that, although Christians had helped start the civil war of 1860, their ultimate defeat, accompanied by their terrible human and material losses, obscured that fact.[2] As they began to win the war and, certainly, after its end, the Druze in Mount Lebanon became the culprits in reinterpretations of what had happened. Such rewriting of history is typical of all periods, but particularly those involving bloodshed and civil war, as history is revised to suit the objectives of the victorious or of those in power—who are often, but not always, one and the same.

Yet, even in the immediate aftermath of the 1860 civil war, the Druze had their defenders. Among them were the British officials based in Syria, particularly Lord Dufferin, the Irish peer, then 34 years old, who would later hold important government posts, including that of viceroy to India. At the end of July 1860, he was appointed British commissioner to Syria in order to help Sir Henry Lytton Bulwer, British ambassador to the Porte, in the inquiry into the causes of the civil war. He arrived in Beirut on 2 September 1860.[3]

The Druze might also have had support from prominent local leaders, such as Emir ʿAbd al-Qadir, the Algerian hero who had resisted the French conquest of Algeria in the 1830s and 1840s and retired to Damascus in 1855. ʿAbd al-Qadir is better known as the man who saved thousands of Christians when, in July 1860, the conflict in Mount Lebanon spilled over into the interior and the Christian residents of the Bab Tuma quarter of Damascus were attacked.[4] Yet, ʿAbd al-Qadir had also remained in touch with Druze leaders and, with their help, ensured the safety of Damascene Christians who escaped to the coast and Beirut.[5] Just after the crisis of 1860, French officials, who praised ʿAbd al-Qadir most enthusiastically, nonetheless noted that he had advised Fuad Pasha, the Ottoman statesman sent to Syria in July 1860 as Ottoman envoy extraordinary and given an open-ended mission of restoring order in the province as he saw fit, to act cautiously against the Druze in the Hawran.[6]

To some extent, one might even argue that the Druze received some inadvertent support from an individual better known for his condemnation of their actions in 1860. Fuad Pasha criticized the Druze and wanted their leaders punished for their role in the civil war.[7] But he also kept reminding the European commissioners that the Christians had provoked the crisis and had some responsibility for it. His main agenda was to reaffirm Ottoman control over Syria and to restore the damaged reputation of the Ottoman government for its failure to prevent the events of 1860; as a consequence, he was angry at all local parties for bringing such shame on the government. However, since he also feared French ambitions in Syria and, like other high-level Ottoman officials, distrusted European meddling in Ottoman affairs, he wanted the European representatives to know that the Druze were not the only guilty parties in the civil war. His position gradually became clear to the French government's representatives in Syria, particularly Marquis General Charles de Beaufort d'Haupoul, commander-in-chief of France's 1860 expedition to Syria.[8]

Of all of the prominent people involved in the fate of the Druze community in the aftermath of the civil war, Lord Dufferin probably cared the most about the Druze cause. His motives were those of his government: support Istanbul and safeguard the 'sick man of Europe' from the ambitions of other Great Powers. In particular, Lord Dufferin wished to counteract the French who supported the Maronites and Catholics and who, in the name of saving local Christians, had sent a French expeditionary force to Syria in 1860-61. But Dufferin's motives seem also to have been more personal. He expressed great empathy for the Druze leaders and, more generally, the Druze nation for their sufferings after the civil war.

Dufferin championed the Druze cause from a position of strength, for he represented the British government at the height of its influence in

Istanbul and stood by Fuad Pasha on most matters related to the settlement of the crisis in Syria. He went further than Fuad Pasha both in blaming the Ottoman officials in Syria for what had happened and in exonerating the Druze for their role in the civil war. To the annoyance of French agents in Syria,[9] he ceaselessly argued with the Ottoman authorities, particularly Fuad Pasha, for clemency toward the Druze. With passion and skill, Dufferin made the case to the Ottomans, other Europeans and his own government that blame for the bloodshed in the mixed districts of Lebanon rested not so much with the Druze leaders or their followers as with hot-headed, mostly Maronite Christian leaders in Beirut and in Lebanon, and with their followers, as well as local Ottoman officers and irregular troops who deserved to be punished before the Druze. Despite their differences, he and Fuad Pasha did agree that Christian Maronites and others had been responsible for stirring up the province and he was, most of the time, Fuad Pasha's closest Western ally in the long process of restoring order, determining guilt, keeping French forces in check and planning the future of the Syrian province.

It is well known that European influence in the Middle East increased with the region's integration into the world economy, the spread of steamship navigation and the growth of Europe's power and presence in the eastern Mediterranean from the 1830s onward. European governments and their representatives in the Middle East became protectors of various local communities and the ones supported by the British were the Druze and the Jews.[10] Dufferin's support for the Druze was, therefore, consistent with British policy in previous decades, although it is safe to conclude that he applied this policy with a level of personal commitment and passion particular to his own convictions and concerns about them.

For the purposes of this paper, then, let us assume that ties between the Druze and the British were close during the 1840s-60s and that the British used their considerable political weight at that time to argue the Druze case in both Beirut and Istanbul, where the Ottoman and European high commissioners met from the summer of 1860 to the spring of 1861. Their discussions revolved around how to resolve the crisis and how to settle Lebanon's future.

To assess how great a difference British support for the Druze made for the latter's destiny in the difficult and troubled decades of the mid-nineteenth century, let us speed forward to century's end and look back at the 1840s and 1850s with hindsight to assess who emerged as winners and who emerged as losers from the turmoil that then existed.

Undoubtedly, the greatest winners were the Ottomans, although that might not seem evident at first sight—after all, the empire collapsed at the end of World War I and was replaced by successor states. Also, as far as the Ottoman rulers were concerned, the crisis in Syria caused direct foreign intervention in yet another of their Arab provinces. From their point of view, they had to put up with European involvement, particularly the French military presence in 1860-61. Moreover, the new system introduced in Mount Lebanon in 1861 and revised in 1864 made the Mountain autonomous under international guarantee, with a Christian governor working with the assistance of an elected council composed of representatives of all of the communities.

Still, although the new system for Mount Lebanon was not free from international oversight until the Great War—and for the last stretch of Ottoman history—the Ottomans seem to have achieved their Tanzimat goals of centralism and reform. At the very least, they firmed up their control over the Syrian province, including Mount Lebanon, to a greater extent than in previous centuries. Historically, the Mountain had been one of the most autonomous sub-regions of the Ottoman Empire's Arab provinces, an autonomy that it lost after 1860. The causes of that autonomy have been hotly debated, however, Kamal Salibi's masterful and revisionist study, *A House of Many Mansions*,[11] convincingly argues that the lords of Mount Lebanon were little more than glorified tax collectors and that part of the region's autonomy was due, not so much to their spirit or their strength, as traditional interpretations of Lebanese history claim, but to nothing more than Ottoman indifference. For the Ottoman overlords, Mount Lebanon was little more than a side show.

Whatever the reasons behind the autonomy of Mount Lebanon in the preceding centuries of Ottoman rule, and despite European oversight, the Mountain was more firmly incorporated into the centralizing schemes of the Tanzimat after the 1860 crisis. Ottoman control was now imposed over a united Mountain under a directly appointed *mutaṣarrif* who cooperated closely with local community leaders. During World War I, the Mountain was placed under Ottoman military authority and that could not have happened without the decades-long process of integration into the Ottoman administration.

This is not to say that Mount Lebanon was hampered from developing its own distinctiveness within an Ottoman context—far from it. In his excellent study of the *Mutaṣarrifiyya* period of 1861-1920, Engin Akarli warns against reducing the history of a people to the external influences on them and he shows how an Ottoman leadership set on building a stable governmental order established centralized executive, fiscal and judicial branches and a centralized security force, as well as municipal administrations serving the towns. As he put it, "a sense of Lebanese-ness" emerged among the residents of the *Mutaṣarrifiyya* with the help of Ottoman statesmen and the local political leadership. The distinctive society of Mount Lebanon evolved even as the region was brought within the sphere of more direct Ottoman influence.[12]

If the greatest winners during the last period of Ottoman Lebanon seem to have been the Ottomans, the greatest losers were the Druze. This proud and ancient people, whose ruling dynasties and families had shaped Lebanese history (as the works of Abdul-Rahim Abu-Husayn and others show us so well[13]), were now at their lowest ebb. In the immediate aftermath of the civil war, although they had won militarily—and perhaps because of it—they had to cope with accusations that they were to blame for all that had happened. The Ottomans confused them with mixed messages: sometimes they pursued the Druze to punish them, which drove them to seek refuge in the Hawran and in other places where they felt safe and, at other times, the Ottomans used them or seemed to cooperate with them in order to enforce order in the Mountain.[14] After a time, it became clear that, possibly because of the pressure posed by the French expeditionary force and the wish to keep control in Ottoman hands, they would be subjected to humiliations never before experienced by them as a people.

These humiliations included military expeditions against the Druze; lists of perpetrators drawn by Christians, at the request of the government; and extraordinary tribunals set up at Mukhtara and Beirut to judge the accused Druze. Members of the Druze community were punished, occasionally harshly. A few were sentenced to death, although none were executed; others were sentenced to temporary exile for one, two, six, or twelve years. Their punishment was seen as too light by French agents and others, who also complained that, however harsh or lenient the punishment was, it was rarely imposed. But, to the Druze, the process and, sometimes, the result were very difficult to endure. Druze property was also confiscated, including that of Saʿid Janbalat, the richest of their leaders. Druze grain and produce were seized for distribution to Christians and the government also ordered the Druze to share other food supplies. All Druze and Muslim villages had to provide wood to Christians. In the Biqaʿ region, Druze mules were requisitioned for the use of Christians and their food depots seized. By the calculations of the Ottomans, subsequent to Fuad Pasha's arrival in Syria in the summer of 1860, Druze losses came to 20 million piastres or some 160,000 English pounds.[15]

By the spring of 1861, the Druze had suffered a great deal. Fuad Pasha wrote to Beaufort saying that the Druze were "under great accusation and pursued by the law," showed a "submissive attitude" and that they had become the object of "what I can say is a natural" Christian resentment. Yet, obviously, Fuad Pasha did not like how far the retaliation against the Druze had gone. He observed that the Druze were attacked daily. He added that when the Ottoman authorities were called upon to stop these attacks, they were accused of protecting the Druze at the expense of Christians. In fact, continued the Pasha, the authorities had to ensure the protection of all of the population and, if they seemed to favour one segment of it, it was simply because the Druze were being victimized. Referring to the Druze, Fuad Pasha commented:

> Everywhere they are hounded and the object of personal revenge. Druze peasants can neither circulate freely nor plough their fields without being attacked. Not a week goes by without assassinations or wounds being reported to the authorities.[16]

The worst loss for the Druze, however, was not tangible. The Druze are a proud and honourable people and the aftermath of the civil war caused them terrible pain and embarrassment. As a nation, the Druze had been judged and humiliated. No price tag can be put upon the emotions that they felt at having their fate discussed and determined by outsiders and at seeing their leaders imprisoned and sentenced—even if and when their sentences were commuted or not carried out.

In the long run, the Druze recovered, of course, but it was not they who emerged as the principal beneficiaries of the political and economic transformations that occurred during the long nineteenth century: the victors were the Christians. The process of opening Syria up to European commerce and to mostly local Christian minorities—a process unleashed during the Egyptian occupation of the 1830s—continued after the Ottomans took the province back between 1840 and the end of the empire. The Tanzimat edicts of 1839 and 1856 were notable landmarks in this process of opening to the West, but the humiliation of the Druze in 1860 also highlighted the new power of the Christians, particularly the Maronites. Despite the antipathy felt by Ottoman administrators toward France, which had supported their rival, Muhammad ʿAli Pasha of Egypt, in the 1830s and which had hastened to send a French expeditionary force to Syria after the civil war of 1860, and despite Ottoman reliance on the British to keep the French in check at critical points during the negotiations that followed the turbulence in the province of Syria, it was the

Christians who came out on top of all of the other communities.

Maronite ascendancy had begun at least a century earlier, as historians such as Kamal Ṣalibi, Albert Hourani, Dominique Chevallier and Antoine Abdel-Nour have shown. But it was most clearly evident after the crisis of 1860 in the city of Beirut, where commerce became increasingly concentrated, and in Mount Lebanon, where stability had been restored. The irony that the party defeated in 1860 ended up with most of the spoils in the peaceful decades that followed could not have been lost on the other local communities, including the Druze. In addition, staunch French protection of the Christians and, more particularly, of the Maronites and the growth of trade and construction projects involving the French, ensured that the Maronites cashed in handsomely on the new prosperity in this part of the eastern Mediterranean.

The road had been paved for Lebanon's post-World War I political domination by the Christians, in general, and the Maronites, in particular. In this sense, confessional politics in Lebanon after 1920 were the culmination of a long process dating back to Ottoman institutional changes during the periods of the Double Qaimmaqamate (1843-1861) and the *Mutaṣarrifiyya*.[17]

In the light of these observations, how useful was the special relationship the Druze had with the greatest European power of the nineteenth century? When we look back from the distance of a half century or so, it does not seem to have much profited the Druze. True, it attenuated the worst of the Ottoman government's retribution in 1860, but it could reverse neither the impact of the civil war nor the changing equilibrium—demographically, economically and politically—among Lebanon's main communities. It could not do so because processes at work since at least the eighteenth century had affected the dynamic among the communities, with the aftermath of the civil war of 1860 simply adding a nail to the coffin of Druze political domination.

Yet, no one could or did take away from the Druze their greatest asset: their long history of leadership, solidarity and dignity. They had played a pivotal role in the formation of Lebanese identity and, in the twentieth century, were the first community to understand that their communal identity would not be threatened by ideologies that transcended it. All of this, the Druze owed to themselves, not to the British supporters that they had acquired along the way. In the long view of history, British support for the Druze was interesting and, perhaps, flattering, but it ultimately had less impact than their own handling of their destiny as a community that is extremely distinct, yet open to broader ideologies and visions of identity.

NOTES

[1] 'Syria,' 'Syrian region,' 'Mount Lebanon' and 'Lebanon' are used here as they were in the nineteenth century and as defined in Kamal S. Salibi, *The Modern History of Lebanon* (London: Weidenfeld and Nicolson, 1965), xi-xii; and in Albert Hourani, *A History of the Arab Peoples* (Cambridge, MA: Harvard University Press, 1991), 91. 'Syria' and the 'Syrian region' refer to the territory stretching from the Taurus mountains in the north to the Sinai peninsula in the south and from the Mediterranean in the west to the Syrian desert in the east, a territory that had been under Ottoman rule since 1516. 'Lebanon,' 'Mount Lebanon' and 'the Mountain' refer to Ottoman Mount Lebanon.

[2] Leila Tarazi Fawaz, *An Occasion for War: Civil Conflict in Lebanon and Damascus in 1860* (Berkeley, CA: University of California Press, 1994). For an understanding of the 1860 conflict in Lebanon, also consult Kamal S. Salibi's works on Lebanon; Caesar E. Farah, *The Politics of Intervention in Ottoman Lebanon, 1830-1861* (London: Centre for Lebanese Studies in association with I. B. Tauris, 2000); and Ussama Makdisi, *The Culture of Sectarianism: Community, History, and Violence in Nineteenth-Century Ottoman Lebanon* (Berkeley, CA: University of California Press, 2000).

[3] London, Public Record Office, Foreign Office Archives, Series Foreign Office (henceforth abbreviated to F. O.) 78/1519, Moore-Bulwer, no. 65, 3 September 1860.

[4] Paris, Archives du ministère des affaires étrangères, Série: Correspondance politique de l'origine à 1871, Turquie, Consulat divers: Correspondance des consuls, Damas (herewith abbreviated to A. E., CPC/D), vol. 6, Outrey-Thouvenel, 28 July 1860, in which Outrey wrote about Emir ʿAbd al-Qadir: "Everyone acknowledges today that he saved 12 to 13,000 people from certain death."

[5] A. E., CPC/D/6, Outrey-Thouvenel, 28 July 1860, for example, reported that ʿAbd al-Qadir arranged with the French consul in Damascus for an escort of Algerians and Druze to take a first group of 500 to 600 Christians from Damascus to Beirut.

[6] Vincennes, Ministère de la défense, Archives militaires, Expédition de Syrie, 1860-1861 (henceforth abbreviated to V.), G4/1, Beaufort-Randon, no. 36, 10 February 1861.

[7] Fawaz, *An Occasion for War*, chapter 7; Makdisi, *The Culture of Sectarianism*, chapter 8.

[8] As examples, see V., Beaufort-Randon, no. 2, 22 August 1860, in which Beaufort complains about Fuad Pasha's failure to take any action against the Druze; and G4/5, Beaufort-Randon, no. 7, 21 September 1860, in which Beaufort complains about Fuad Pasha's slow pace in taking action against the Druze and

charges that he is looking for new ways to delay punitive measures. Even when Fuad Pasha prepared battalions and sent them out against the Druze, the French officials doubted his intentions to punish them properly. Again, in V., G4/1, Beaufort-Randon, no. 21, 19 November 1860, Beaufort notes that, in the north of Mount Lebanon, Fuad Pasha had asked the Christians to pay a tax, but had not requested it from the Druze, who had not paid the tax in years; and in V., G4/1, Beaufort-Randon, no. 39, 25 February 1861, Beaufort writes that Fuad Pasha had all sorts of ways for stalling the punishment of the Druze.

[9] V., G4/1, Beaufort-Randon, no. 41, 10 March 1861, reports that Dufferin, in order to gain time and try once more to save the Druze leader, Saʿid Janbalat, and the condemned Druze chiefs, had insisted that the sentences not be carried out before those of the Turkish agents were, as the International Commission was asking for more severe sentences for the latter.

[10] Roger Owen, *The Middle East in the World Economy* (London: Methuen, 1981); Abdul-Karim Rafeq, *Buhūth fi al-tārīkh al-iqtisadī wa'l-ijtimāʿi li-bilād al-Shām fi'l ʿasr al-hadīth* (Damascus, 1974).

[11] Kamal S. Salibi, *A House of Many Mansions: The History of Lebanon Reconsidered* (Berkeley, CA: University of California Press, 1988).

[12] Engin Deniz Akarli, *The Long Peace: Ottoman Lebanon, 1861-1920* (London: I. B. Tauris, 1993).

[13] See the works of Abdul-Rahim Abu-Husayn, including *Provincial Leaderships in Syria, 1575-1650* (Beirut: American University of Beirut Press, 1985) and "Problems in the Ottoman Administration in Syria during the 16th and 17th Centuries: The Case of the Sanjak of Sidon-Beirut," *International Journal of Middle East Studies* 24 (1992): 665-75.

[14] V., G4/1, Beaufort-Randon, 11 October 1860; V., G4/1, no. 17, Beaufort-Randon, 20 October 1860; V., G4/1, Osmont-Randon, no. 8, 16 August 1861; V., G4/5, Beaufort-Randon, no. 3, 27 August 1860; V., G4/5, Beaufort-Randon, no. 6, 12 September 1860; V., G4/5, Beaufort-Randon, no. 7, 21 September 1860; and V., G4/1, Beaufort-Randon, 11 October 1860.

[15] Fawaz, *An Occasion for War*, 169, 180ff.; F. O. 195/660, Fraser-Bulwer, no. 42, 10 August 1861; ibid., Fraser-Bulwer, no. 66, 4 November 1861; A. E., CPC/D/6, Outrey-Thouvenel, 28 July 1860.

[16] V., G4/1, Fuad Pasha-Beaufort, 17 March 1861, in Beaufort-Randon, no. 44, 24 March 1861 (my translation).

[17] Albert Hourani, *Syria and Lebanon: A Political Essay* (Beirut: Librairie du Liban, 1968); Roger Owen, "The Political Economy of Grand Liban, 1920-1970," in *Essays on the Crisis in Lebanon*, edited by Roger Owen (London: Ithaca Press, 1976), 23-32. For the role of the *Mutaṣarrifiyya* in building institutions that brought communities closer together, consult Akarli, *The Long Peace*.

ABDUL-RAHIM ABU-HUSAYN AND ENGIN D. AKARLI

THE SUBORDINATION OF THE HAWRAN DRUZE IN 1910: THE OTTOMAN PERSPECTIVE

THE 1910 DRUZE UPRISING in the Hawran was not the first event of its kind to take place in the Jabal, as the area inhabited by the Druze is commonly called, but the last in a long series of similar incidents that had characterized relations between the Ottoman authorities and the Jabal's Druze population, as well as their bedouin and peasant neighbours, since the middle of the nineteenth century. This particular instance of insubordination acquired extraordinary importance because of a remarkable juxtaposition of circumstances preceding and following the rebellion, although essentially unrelated to it.

The significance attached to the uprising in the literature is primarily due to the fact that it took place after the constitutional revolution of 1908 and an abortive counter-revolution that followed it in 1909. The constitutional revolution added an important dimension to the process of Ottoman modernization. By the time that it occurred, the physical or material modernization that had started in the mid-nineteenth century had already reached the Jabal: new schools had been opened, courts established, the administration reorganized and railway and telegraph lines extended to the area. The 1908 revolution instilled a political dimension into the modernization program in the form of constitutional and parliamentary government and politics—a political modernization that would also reach the Jabal, which subsequently participated in elections and sent representatives to the Ottoman parliament. Two ensuing events also contributed to later scholarly misinterpretations of the significance of the1910 uprising: the Arab Revolt of 1916 and the Great Syrian Revolt of 1925. The Jabal and its leadership also occupied central positions in both of these insurrections leading many scholars to see connections between all three events.

In the light of these three defining moments, many historians have tended to interpret the 1910 Druze rebellion in terms of the broader issue of deteriorating Arab-Turkish relations as they evolved under the Young

Turks, who dominated Ottoman politics in the constitutional era, and of a comprehensive anti-Arab policy instituted by the Committee of Union and Progress (CUP) in Arabia, Syria and Iraq. Thus, the local causes and nature of the Hawran episode within the context of a modernized Ottoman state were blurred in favour of more grandiose nationalist projects, whether pan-Arab or Syrian nationalist in nature.

There is no doubt that the Ottoman state of 1910 was much more modern, both materially and politically, than it had been in the second half of the nineteenth century. Nor can it be denied that its action against the Druze of the Hawran, as against similar insurgents elsewhere in Ottoman territory, was, to some extent, a by-product of this modernity. One directly relevant aspect of this modernization was legislative: at the time of the uprising, parliament had just passed, in May 1909, the "Law on Vagabonds and Suspected Criminals."[1] Moreover, the Ottoman state's political modernization gave its actions against the Druze additional legitimacy in certain quarters of Arab public opinion, denying the Hawran Druze some of the natural sympathy that they might have expected from other Syrians and even fellow Druze elsewhere, while its material or technological modernity gave it the means to deal effectively with Druze insubordination and to institute measures that brought the community under tighter control.

Contemporary documentation of the events of 1910 is abundant and detailed; the Arabic press of Damascus, Beirut and Cairo and the Turkish press of Istanbul covered the Ottoman military campaign against the Druze during that summer. An equally important but underused source (in relation to the Hawran part of the campaign) is the official Ottoman documentation of the episode which, in some ways, portrays a modern state in action, in form as much as substance.[2]

This documentation consists mainly of reports, instructions, or inquiries sent, in large part, through the telegraph service and originating in the Hawran, Damascus, or Istanbul (generally but not exclusively), which were addressed to the provincial or central government. A substantial portion of this documentation consists, as well, of exchanges between different Ottoman ministries in Istanbul, particularly, the ministries of the interior, justice and war.

Yet, as Eugene Rogan has demonstrated,[3] telegraphy as a manifestation of modernity was not only an "infrastructure of power" in the service of the state, but also an "instrument of voice" or resistance. So in addition to messages emanating from the central government or local officials, which make up the bulk of the correspondence relating to the events of 1910, the surviving telegrams also include others sent by the Hawran Druze to petition, protest innocence and profess loyalty and submission or to make specific requests.

In this paper, we will present examples of this documentary evidence pertaining to: the immediate causes of the Ottoman military campaign against the Hawran Druze; military operations and acts of rebellion by the insurgents; military court sentences and Druze complaints, objections and requests in this regard; post-campaign relief efforts undertaken by the government; and the official Ottoman view of the 1910 events in the Hawran as reflected in the conclusions of an official commission of inquiry into the immediate and long-term causes of the 1910 uprising, in particular, and the state of chronic lawlessness among the Druze of Hawran, in general, as well as the recommendations put forward to resolve these problems. Hence, this paper is not an exhaustive study of either the Ottoman documentary sources or the subject of Druze insubordination and Ottoman countermeasures; rather, it is intended to reveal some elements of the view from the centre, a view that has largely been ignored, especially by Arab historians of modern Syria.

Narrative

The Ottoman military action against the Hawran Druze in 1910 was not in response to any specific action by the latter against the Ottoman state—merely the sense that instability and disorder contravene the idea of an orderly state and, hence, may not be tolerated, which was the Ottoman position.

According to Ottoman documents, the direct cause of the campaign was a series of attacks and counter-attacks involving the Druze community in the Hawran and a leading Sunni family there, the Miqdads. In the course of a Druze attack on Busra Eski Sham, an officer and a soldier in the Ottoman army were killed, as well as 11 other people. The Druze leader, Hilal al-Atrash, also died, along with five of his men. The raids and counter-raids culminated in a Druze attack on the villages of Jasim and Maʿarba, which resulted in the deaths of 59 people, among them 12 women, three children and six non-Muslims. The cost of the material damage to a number of villages involved in the conflict, including destruction by fire and looting, was estimated to reach 50,000 Ottoman pounds—a figure that the governor of Syria considered to be exaggerated.[4] All of this happened in the spring and early summer of 1909. According to the same documents, the Ottoman response was delayed until the summer of 1910 owing to the counter-revolution in Istanbul in the spring of 1909 and the insurrection in Albania, both of which made the immediate dispatch of Ottoman troops to the Hawran impossible.[5]

It should be noted here that the Ottoman documents are much more elaborate in detailing the events leading up to the campaign of 1910 than contemporary and near contemporary Arab literature on the subject. This demonstrates the effective use, at the time, of modern means of communications by the local authorities, making it possible for them to report frequently to Istanbul on developments deemed to be important.

On 2 August 1910, the central government decided to send a huge military force comprising infantry and cavalry armed with heavy artillery and heavy machine guns to the Hawran under the command of Faruqi Sami Pasha. By 20 August, Sami Pasha had disembarked at Haifa with the major part of the designated force: the remainder of his troops arrived shortly afterwards. The Ottoman government appears to have been monitoring local reaction to the arrival of its troops in Syria, for a telegram indicates that "while the army of the constitutional order was camping in Darʿa, the Syrian newspapers spoke, in articles authored by their leading journalists, of this strong and awe-inspiring army. [Even] before the commencement of operations, these articles had the effect of dampening the morale of the Druze to a great measure."[6]

The Ottoman troops proceeded to occupy Suwayda and, according to Ottoman documents, met with no resistance. Sami Pasha then issued an ultimatum to the people of the town, allowing them a reasonable time to submit. Subsequently, on 29 September 1910, martial law was declared in the whole of the Hawran, with a copy of the declaration sent to the ministry of the interior on the same day.[7] In the meantime, telegrams were exchanged between Sami Pasha, the ministry of war, the ministry of the interior and the governor of Syria concerning the provisions that would be needed to conduct the military operations in the Hawran, especially camels. All of these supplies were made available for the army's use by the time that martial law was declared.

Thus supplied, Sami Pasha moved on to subdue the Druze. It would be tedious to recount the military operations in any detail, so we will only give examples of Ottoman punitive actions and acts of Druze resistance by way of illustration. These cases in point are taken from the progress reports sent by Sami Pasha to the ministry of war and by the governor of Syria, Ismaʿil Pasha, to the ministry of the interior.

Such progress reports were sent almost on a daily basis throughout October; they became less frequent in November as Ottoman control over the region increased. Ottoman punitive actions included the destruction and burning of Druze villages, such as the village of Sijn, which was completely destroyed, and the village of Buraykah, which was burned down; this was in addition to regular Ottoman operations, which involved the bombardment of Druze villages, such as Qanawat, Mafʿala, Mardak, al-Kafr, Harran and ʿAfifah, and gun battles with Druze fighters. Druze acts of resistance included the severing of telegraph lines, especially the one between ʿAhira, Suwayda and Busra al-Harir, which was cut more than once; on one occasion, in early October 1910, this left Sami Pasha and his army without access to communications for about a week. The Druze also managed to cut off water supplies to a number of army positions and attacked military convoys, particularly those that were transporting confiscated weapons. In the end, they withdrew to their traditional retreat in the Laja. But none of these tactics availed them in the face of a modern army.

In the second half of October, Druze fugitives in the Laja started to give themselves up, including the rebel chief, Yahya ʿAmir. Toward the end of October, the governor of Syria and Sami Pasha began reporting to Istanbul on the number of weapons seized from the Druze. A message sent on 23 October 1910 indicates that the weapons confiscated at one location (the qaimmaqamate of Suwayda) amounted to 3000 guns plus 40,000 bullets. At about the same time, the Ottoman army officially initiated the universal disarmament of the villages of the Jabal and a census of the population. Immediately thereafter military conscription commenced in the two districts of Suwayda and ʿAhira and in 16 other centres. The intention was to undertake similar measures in all of the Druze parts of the Jabal. By 3 November 1910, the governor of Syria was reporting that 300 Druze were already on their way to Damascus as conscripts.

Sami Pasha reported Ottoman casualties during the operations in the north and south as totalling only 34 dead, including a captain (*yüzbashi*), and 89 wounded; he speculated that Druze losses were much greater.[8] The Ottomans estimated that the number of Druze killed in Mafʿala alone (in the north-east) exceeded 400 men. Another report, dated 8 October, put the number of Druze dead in operations in the north and south at more than 2000.[9]

Meanwhile, a number of Druze chiefs and rebels had been arrested and stood trial before a military court in Damascus. Some of them were sentenced to death, still others received prison sentences to be served in the Hawran, Damascus, or Istanbul, and a large number were exiled to different locations in Anatolia and Rumelia, including the island of Rhodes. Yahya al-Atrash, who surrendered to Sami Pasha, had his death sentence commuted to exile to Rhodes. Some other Rumelian destinations for the exiles were

Monastir, Skopji and Janina (Yaniya), while the Anatolian ones included the provinces of Kastamonu, Ankara, Sivas and Bolu. The exiled or imprisoned came from all parts of the Jabal—from Harran, ʿAhira, Qrayya, Dinbayh, Majdal Shams, ʿAraman, Salkhad, Shquf, Baqʿata, Masamiyya, Shaqa, Yakne, Ghurba, Suwayhira, Lahta, Junayna and many other villages.

Exiling these Druze to different parts of the Ottoman territory was intended as a punishment for them. But it also proved to be a major headache for the central Ottoman government as well as a problem for the reluctant host provinces. In some cases, the province to which a particular person was to be exiled rejected him because of the danger that he might pose to the security of his proposed destination. For instance, the province of Monastir refused to receive Murshid ibn Yunus from the village of Harran (in the *kaza* of ʿAhira in Hawran) owing to his long criminal record, his rebellious deeds and the limited number of policemen available to keep watch over his activities. According to a letter by the governor of Monastir, "his exile here entails some risk." The ministry of the interior had to look for an alternative destination that would take him and telegrams were exchanged between the ministry and the capitals of different provinces in Anatolia and Rumelia, as well as Damascus. He was ultimately accepted by Janina.

Further concerns arose in connection with Druze exiles to other provinces. Some exiles did not like their proposed destinations and petitioned that they be sent elsewhere; for example, 11 people who were supposed to be exiled to Sivas asked that Ankara be chosen instead. In most cases, their petitions were approved.[10]

The government had also to provide a living allowance for most of the exiles. The ministry of the interior received requests from local authorities asking that per diems be paid to their "guests." The governor of Janina (Yaniya) recommended that the Druze sent there be paid five piastres each day as living expenses from the time of their arrival, arguing that keeping them in a foreign land, where they had no dwellings and no way of earning their livings as farmers, rendered their condition miserable and was incompatible with notions of justice.[11] Making the same request on behalf of his exiles, the governor of Kosovo argued that the condition of his two "guests" did not befit the dignity of the state.[12] Similar concerns were also voiced about the living conditions of exiles in the provinces of Kastamonu, Ankara, Konya, Sivas and Bolu.

In June 1911, Sultan Mehmet V visited Kosovo and an amnesty was issued for Albanians who had been involved in the insurrection there. This raised Druze hopes that they might similarly be pardoned and Druze prisoners in Istanbul, as well as the Druze in the Hawran, seized the occasion to present petitions. In some cases, these petitions were submitted to the sultan while he was still in Prishtina, with copies sent by telegraph to the grand vizier. One such petition, signed by Sayyid Ahmad on behalf of 19 prisoners in Istanbul, simply begs the sultan's pardon in keeping with his act of mercy toward the Albanian rebels. The version sent to the sultan reads as follows:

> As His Majesty's mercy reached the political prisoners and fugitives in Rumelia [that is, Albanian rebels who were pardoned], we, the political exiles of Hawran, whose hearts and minds are attached to His Majesty's threshold, have dared to appeal for his pardon.[13]

In the petition addressed to the grand vizier, Sayyid Ahmad pleads ignorance, professes loyalty and requests his intercession for the prisoners' release.[14]

Another petition, signed by Kanj Salih on behalf of seven political prisoners in Istanbul, complains of the local authorities' arbitrariness and reads as follows:

> We are of the people of Majdal Shams, who had absolutely nothing to do with the Hawran events. We were the victims of the *qāi'mmaqām's* injustice. Since our exile was contrary to law and justice and would not have had your approval, we have dared to submit our petition to the exalted Caliphate to request that the favour of our lord (*mawlāna*), the caliph, be extended to us as it was extended to the people of Rumelia and as there remains no other recourse to us except His Majesty's mercy.[15]

Other petitions emanating from the Jabal made the case for Druze loyalty to the Ottoman state. One such petition, written in Arabic and signed by Husayn Tarabay on behalf of all of the Druze of the Hawran (*ʿumūm Durūz Ḥawrān*), was submitted to the grand vizier. It contained the following words:

> After prayers to God to bestow victory and support at all times to the Ottoman state, we, all of the Druze of the Hawran, wish to express to the grand vizierate our willingness to sacrifice our lives and the lives of our sons to protect the pure Ottoman homeland from the pollution (*talwīth*) of enemies and to defend its sacred honour against aggressive enemies' actions. We beg you to intercede with our lord (*mawlāna*), the caliph, so

> that he may issue a general amnesty for those who were convicted in the military court of the Hawran. We declare our readiness to be one hand to raise the sword of *jihād* under the victorious Ottoman banner.[16]

Similar petitions bearing hundreds of signatures and imploring the ministry of the interior to release the imprisoned and to return the exiles home were also sent from the Jabal to Istanbul. But the authorities in the province of Syria were not impressed and appear to have been less forgiving than the central government. It may also be that the government in Istanbul was getting weary of the problems associated with the Hawran exiles, while the province of Syria was concerned with the revival of the rebellion if they came back home. Thus, when the ministry of the interior wrote to the province of Syria soliciting the governor's opinion concerning these petitions, the latter wrote back saying: "It has been proven by experience that there is no advantage to be gained by pardoning the convicted; it has always, in the case of the Druze, resulted in the contrary."[17]

The authorities in the Ottoman provinces where the Druze had been exiled were apparently weary of their Druze charges and inevitably supported their petitions for pardon on the grounds of their good behaviour; in fact, they actually pressed Istanbul to grant these pardons in the hope of getting rid of their 'guests.'[18] However, the province of Syria consistently opposed these requests, arguing that the presence of the Druze insurgents in the Jabal would cause disturbances.

While petitioning for financial assistance or pardon, some of the Druze exiles and prisoners were also busy planning their escapes and many of them managed to flee their places of exile or imprisonment. Cases of escapes, especially of exiles, were numerous. In one notable instance, a group of Druze exiles addressed a petition to the ministry of justice that argued their loyalty to the Ottoman state and the incompatibility of their exile with the constitutional order and submitted it on 20 August 1911. On the back of the petition, some high-ranking Ottoman official has written that he met with the petitioners and recommends that they be pardoned or given financial assistance. By 11 September 1911, however, the province holding them reports that the petitioners had escaped. The ministry of the interior issued a circular telegram ordering the authorities of all Anatolian provinces and Syrian provinces to have them arrested if they showed up.[19]

Government relief efforts: The failure of a modern state

Having demonstrated their military prowess in dealing with the Hawran Druze, the Ottomans also made a bid to win them over by showing them the benefits to be derived from loyalty to the state. On 7 August 1910, the governor of Syria sent a telegram to the ministry of the interior requesting the transfer of 100,000 piastres for distribution to the people of the villages that had been subjected to Druze attacks. In his message, the governor stated that the people were about to perish from hunger and asked permission to dispense immediately (on the same day) the sum of money that he was requesting.[20] Before the day was over, the ministry of the interior had referred the matter to the grand vizierate.[21] Meanwhile, it instructed the governor not to allow anyone to suffer from lack of food and to raise temporarily four to five thousand piastres from the municipality of Damascus or some such source (which would be reimbursed from the total sum that he had requested) while his request was being processed in Istanbul. The matter was placed on the agenda of the 8 August 1910 meeting of the council of ministers, which ultimately decided to make the needed funds available as a loan from a secret treasury fund (*hesapi mestur*) to be repaid by the beneficiaries at a later date.[22] Three days later, the ministry of the interior followed up on the matter, sending an urgent memo to the ministry of finance requesting that the sum be transferred by telegraph. The province of Syria was informed of this development.[23]

On 22 August, the governor of Syria again contacted the ministry of the interior to inform it that the sum had not yet been transferred and that permission to dispense money to the victims had still not been granted. The governor warned the ministry that the situation would further deteriorate and of dire consequences if permission was not granted promptly. Two days later, the ministry of the interior sent an urgent memo to the ministry of finance emphatically requesting it to authorize immediately the transfer and disbursement by telegram and to keep the ministry of the interior informed. But once more the money was not sent.

On 20 November, the governor of Syria cabled the ministry of the interior for a third time, urging that the money be made available before the onset of the agricultural season; the same appeal was made on 24 November. Two days later, the ministry of the interior again wrote to the ministry of finance, which responded on 11 December saying that that the money could not be dispensed from the secret fund as there was no money available in the budget. If payment of the sum was absolutely necessary, the message continued, the Sublime Porte would have to decide where the money would come from and instruct the ministry accordingly. Since nothing had been done, the ministry of the interior wrote to the grand vizierate to explain the situation on the ground in the Hawran as well as the administrative impasse.[24]

No one in the Hawran died of hunger, but it is significant that the Ottoman state, modern or not, was unable to come up with 100,000 piastres. The attempt of the government to fulfil its role as a provider had failed.

Investigation and findings

As this paper deals with the Ottoman perspective on the 1910 events in the Hawran, we would like to conclude by presenting and commenting upon the findings of a special commission of inquiry that was dispatched to look into alleged misconduct by Ottoman officers and administrators in the Hawran and Karak. These findings, as we will explain below, represent more than just the official view.

The commission consisted of the inspector general of the ministry of the interior and the first assistant attorney-general in the ministry of justice. Its formation and dispatch were in response to a report submitted by three Syrian deputies, Rushdi al-Shamʿa, Tawfiq al-Majali and Shukri al-ʿAsali, in which they alleged that acts of injustice and oppression had been perpetrated by Ottoman forces in the course of military operations conducted in the Hawran and Karak. We are limiting our remarks here to the section of the report that deals directly with the question of the Hawran Druze.

The report on the Hawran Druze makes the following observations by way of background:

1 The Hawran or Druze question had plagued the state for the last quarter century and was like an abscess in the body of the state or a volcano that might erupt at any time.
2 The Druze felt secure in their rugged region and the adjacent Laja and Safa, to which they might flee if the need arose, and acted in complete disregard of judicial, military and fiscal regulations. As their numbers increased, they expanded their territory by seizing the lands of their non-Druze neighbours in the Hawran.
3 Druze taxes from 1900-1910 amounted to 5,800,000 piastres, but the state could only collect less than 800,000 piastres.
4 Despite the fact that Druze were responsible for 50% of the crimes committed in Damascus, Wadi al-ʿAjam and al-Nabak, there were no Druze in prison and no Druze figured in any court records.
5 No Druze had been conscripted thus far.

The authors of the report conclude this section by stating that the Druze had long taken full advantages of their rights as Ottoman subjects, but had never fully met their fiscal or military obligations. They also refused to allow the law of the state to be applied to them. In short, they were a small rebellious group whose insubordination explained the repeated military action taken against them in Jabal Hawran. The state was also concerned because the Druze, who "are accustomed to disregarding the rights and lives of others, have turned this behaviour into an article of faith." By way of explaining this last point, the report goes on to state that, for the past century and a half, the Druze had been enlarging their landholdings to the west through aggression and forcible seizure that targeted their non-Druze Hawrani neighbours.

The report then recounts acts of Druze aggression against their neighbours from 1883 until 1910. These involved killing people and destroying and burning down villages in order to gain control of the land. Next, the report summarizes Ottoman disciplinary action taken in response to each major Druze act of "aggression," including the latest campaign under the leadership of Sami Pasha. This part of the report concludes by stating that, although there are individual criminal acts that are directly linked with the latest outbreak of Druze violence, the commission of inquiry has obtained strong evidence indicating that the decisive factor was the Druze desire to seize lands and increase their influence. This state of affairs constituted a sad social fact.

To substantiate their conclusion, the authors of the report turned to history. According to them, Druze aggression had resulted in whole villages becoming the property of the Druze. For example, the villages of Mafʿala, Kafar and Sahwat al-Balat, which were Druze villages at the time of writing, had belonged to the families of Mafʿala, Kafarina and Sahawina one hundred years before. The commission had learned this from the few surviving members of these families still living in the Hawran, but in impoverished circumstances. The report then lists other villages (Walfa, Sijin, Dara and Dubar Naʿla) which, forty years earlier, had belonged to the Zuʿbi family, and the villages of al-Zaban, Umm al-Rumman, ʿAnaz, Khirbat ʿAwwad and Mughayr, which had once been controlled by Christians and Sunni Muslims. It notes that the first group of villages and the major part of the second group had since come under Druze control. The authors argue that the Druze could have moved in an easterly direction, where the land was uninhabited and unclaimed, but had chosen to expand to the west, illegally seizing other peoples' lands. According to the report, one reason for this westward drive was possibly an attempt, by the Hawran Druze, to link Mount Hermon, Safad and Hasbayya to the Shuf, thus, establishing territorial unity in addition to the sectarian unity that already existed between the two regions.

Ottoman concern about the unity of cause between the Hawran and Shuf Druze had already been raised during the initial days of the 1910 campaign. In early August, the governor of Syria had reported that some Druze from Mount Lebanon were going to the Hawran. In response, the ministry of the interior had instructed the province of Syria and the *Mutaṣarrifiyya* of Mount Lebanon to take the necessary measures to stop the current movement of Druze from Mount Lebanon to the Hawran and to make it impossible for them to do so in the future. Both responded that such measures had been taken and that the Lebanese Druze had been strongly warned to refrain from joining the Hawrani Druze.[25] In this connection, the authors note that permitting this strategic region, which borders the Arabian Desert, to remain in a state of instability was extremely dangerous.

The recommendations made by the commission at the end of its report are rather vague and general and do not necessarily apply to the Druze in particular. The commission counsels the government to consider ways to end the state of affairs that it describes as a social danger to the Hawran. In more concrete terms, it recommends housing projects to accommodate nomadic tribes (a suggestion which does not apply to the Druze), the extension and improvement of education and agriculture, and the completion of the construction policy (*iʿmār*) started by Sami Pasha.[26]

Some observations need to be made concerning this report.

First, although it was submitted on 12 February 1912, it is an exact duplicate, barring the recommendations, of a report submitted by Fehim Bey, the *mutaṣarrif* of the Hawran, to the ministry of the interior on 16 November 1910. Fehim Bey's own recommendations had been even vaguer: namely, the establishment of certain civilian institutions that would be determined once the outcome of the military operation was known.[27] In the case of Karak, the commission had actually gone there and had conducted on-site investigations that included interviews with local people and officials: its findings had accused some Ottoman officials and officers of negligence or unlawful action against citizens. But, in the case of the Hawran, the commission evidently found it sufficient to copy the *mutaṣarrif's* earlier report, which must have been available to it.

The reports of the commission, the *mutaṣarrif* and the governor echoed sentiments, opinions, arguments and even words and phrases expressed previously by at least one Damascene. At an early point during Sami Pasha's 1910 campaign, the prominent Damascene journalist, Muhammad Kurd ʿAli, wrote an article in his weekly, *Al-Muqtabas* which, in some parts, is the same as the official reports cited above; in other parts, it differs only slightly in language and content. This leads us to conclude that the authors of these reports had done little more than edit this Damascene text to suit their purposes.[28]

Second, although these texts and others from the same period are undoubtedly hostile toward the Druze, their discourse indicates a significant change in attitudes since the sixteenth, seventeenth and eighteenth centuries. In earlier texts, the Druze (in the Lebanon, as there was no Druze presence in the Hawran at the time) are denounced not only as rebels who refuse to pay taxes and cause upheaval, but also as heretics who should be eradicated. In the twentieth-century texts, the denunciation is still very strong, but is entirely based upon secular grounds. In attitudes toward the Druze, political and social considerations had replaced religious ones, just as the intellectuals/journalists of Damascus and their editorials had replaced the *ʿulamaʾ* of Damascus and their *fatwa*s.

NOTES

[1] For a brief description of the articles of this law, see Stanford Shaw and Ezel Karal Shaw, *History of the Ottoman Empire and Modern Turkey* (Cambridge, 1977), 2:285-86.

[2] On the local Syrian view of the 1910 Ottoman campaign in Hawran, see S. Seikaly, "Pacification of Hawran (1910): The View from Within," *Archiv Orientalni,* Supplementa 8 (1998), 367-76.

[3] Eugene Rogan, "Instant Communication: The Impact of the Telegraph in Ottoman Syria," in *The Syrian Lands: Processes of Integration and Fragmentation,* edited by T. Philipp and B. Schaebler (Stuttgart, 1998), 113-28.

[4] Dahiliye Nezareti Siyasi Evraki (hereafter DH. SYS.) 28/1-8, lef 11, 12.

[5] DH. SYS. 28/1-9, lef 11, telegram of Fehim Bey, the *mutaṣarrif* of the Hawran, to the interior ministry; also DH. SYS. 28/1-9, lef 12-15, Fehim Bey's response to a telegram from the ministry of the interior requesting that details be supplied to the ministry on the Hawran events and their causes, along with the measures taken, in order to complete the file at the ministry; some of the papers relating to these events had apparently been burnt in the fire of Istanbul. Both documents are dated 11 February 1911. Also important is the telegram of Fehim Bey, dated 16 November 1910, to the ministry of the interior, DH. SYS. 28/1-9, lef 47-51.

[6] Telegram from the governor of Syria to the ministry of the interior, dated 16 November 1910, DH. SYS. 28/1-9, lef 33-37.

[7] Telegram from the governor of Syria, Ismail Pasha, to the ministry of the interior, DH. SYS. 28/1-9, lef 69.

[8] DH. SYS. 28/1-9, lef 64.

[9] Report of Ismail Pasha to the ministry of the interior, dated 8 October 1910, DH. SYS. 28/1-9, lef 75.

[10] DH. SYS. 86/4-3, lef 22, petition addressed to the ministry of the interior, dated 11 June 1911.

[11] DH. SYS. 86/4-3, lef 45, dated 2 January 1912; DH. SYS. 86/4-3, lef 12, dated 25 October 1911.

[12] DH. SYS. 86/4-3, lef 44, telegram from the province of Kosovo to the ministry of the interior, dated 27 November 1911.

[13] DH. SYS. 86/4-3, lef 54.

[14] DH. SYS. 86/4-3, lef 56.

[15] DH. SYS. 86/4-3, lef 55.

[16] DH. SYS. 86/4-3, lef 49, dated 22 October 1911.

[17] DH. SYS. 86/4-3, lef 60, letter from the governor of Syria to the ministry of the interior, dated 13 September 1911.

[18] DH. SYS. 86/4-3, lef 96, telegram from the ministry of the interior to the province of Syria, dated 25 June 1912.

[19] DH. SYS. 86/4-3, lef 31, 62, 92, 91, 32, 31, 30.

[20] DH. SYS. 28/1-8, lef 21, 17.

[21] DH. SYS. 28/1-8, lef 19.

[22] DH. SYS. 28/1-8, lef 26.

[23] DH. SYS. 28/1-8, lef 25, 27.

[24] DH. SYS. 28/1-8, lef 28, 8, 15, 14, 7, 6.

[25] DH. SYS. 28/1-8, lef 31, dated 18 August 1910; lef 30, dated 22 August 1910.

[26] DH. SYS. 28/1-9, lef 6, 9.

[27] DH. SYS. 28/1-9, lef 47-51; another version of the same is contained in the report of the governor of Syria to the ministry of the interior, DH. SYS. 28/1-9, lef 12-15.

[28] For more details on the negative attitude of the Syrian press toward the Hawran Druze, see Seikaly 1998. The article cited appeared in *Al-Muqtabas*, vol. 5, 1910.

KAMAL SALIBI

Jebel Druze as Seen by Rustum Haydar

ON 10 AUGUST 1918, eleven members of the secret Arab nationalist society *Al-Fatāt*, one of them a medical doctor, fled Damascus by night in somewhat unconvincing bedouin disguise to join Feisal and the forces of the Arab Revolt at Abul-Lasan, in the southern reaches of Transjordan. Among them was Muhammad Rustum Haydar (better known as Rustum Haydar), the son of a Shiʿi Muslim notable from Baalbek, who had studied at the Ottoman Imperial College in Istanbul and then at the Sorbonne and the School of Political Science in Paris, where he and two of his friends had founded *Al-Fatāt* in 1911. Rustum later became a leading political figure in Iraq, where a cashiered commissioner of police shot him to death in 1940.

At the time that Rustum and his companions left Damascus to join Feisal, he was 29 years old; and he apparently thought it important, from that moment, to begin a diary which he kept up, with some interruptions, until 25 March 1921. This diary, which he apparently kept strictly to himself, was discovered among his effects by one of his younger brothers following his assassination and was only published, with an introduction and notes, in 1988 (see Najdat Fathi Safwat, ed., *Mudhakkarāt Rustum Haydar*, published in Beirut by Al-Dar al-ʿArabiyya li-'l-Mawsuʿat, which is the source for this article). Replete with tantalizing information on the years which witnessed the formation of the modern Arab world, the diary reveals a man of superior intellect and unusual breadth of culture. Among the things that it preserves is a picture of Jebel Druze in 1918, where Rustum Haydar and his party stopped for twelve days for talks with leading local *shaykh*s before proceeding across the desert to Abul-Lasan.

With the British army under Edmund Allenby already in Jerusalem, the Sharifian forces at Abul-Lasan were awaiting their signal to join in the final offensive against the Ottomans in Syria who, by the summer of 1918, had re-deployed their forces for the defence of Damascus. This left Jebel

Druze as a sort of no-man's-land to which Damascus maintained access, but over which it exercised no effective control—a "Small Britain" (*Brītāniya al-Ṣughrā*), as one friend of Rustum called it in a sly reference to the old love affair between the Druze and Great Britain. Hence, it was a refuge where anyone fleeing the Ottomans, including Armenian fugitives (19, 140), might feel safe (135).

Hardly a decade earlier, the determination of the Ottoman government to tighten its grip upon the southern fringes of Syria had provoked a Druze uprising in the Jebel. A large expedition had been sent in 1910 to suppress this uprising and its leaders had been brought before military tribunals, which dealt death sentences to some (six men in all) and prison sentences to others. The harshness of these measures had left behind bitter feelings, but had restored Ottoman control over the area for a time.

By 1918, however, the Jebel, though still nominally under Ottoman rule, had become a world unto itself. During his sojourn there, Rustum Haydar remarked that "[an Ottoman] gendarme in the Jebel has the value of a stonemason among the bedouin" (130). Support for Feisal's father, the Sharif of Mecca, was very strong among the local Druze (130), as was anti-Turkish feeling, all the more so among the leading *shaykhs* whose own fathers had been executed by the Ottomans following the 1910 expedition, some of whom Rustum was to meet. Chief among them was the famed Sultan al-Atrash, who was no more than nineteen years old when his father, Dhawqan, was hanged. Now, at 27, he seemed to Rustum to be "the quintessence of the Jebel (*khulāṣat al-Jabal*)": the personification of its boundless hospitality, its valour and the aura of grandeur and dignity that it exuded (128, 142).

Rustum reports that Sultan al-Atrash referred to the Turks as "gypsies (*nawār*)" in his presence, not deigning to utter their proper name (137). Yet, he notes that the Druze of the Jebel, being politically shrewd (*adhkiyā'*), did not all share in the same political alliances. While some showed support for the Sharif, others continued to proclaim their loyalty to the Ottoman government. "Perhaps this division [of opinion] among them is required," says Rustum, "so that should fortune turn against one of the two warring sides, one party among them would be on the side of the [winner] to defend the other and so protect the community as a whole" (134).

Speaking of the customs and manners of the Druze of the Jebel at the time, Rustum observes that "they only differ from the nomadic bedouin in having agriculture and houses of stone; otherwise, the difference between them and the roaming tribes in their way of life, the food they eat and their dress is very slight" (141). He further notes that the speech of the local Druze was closer to that of the bedouins than to that of the sedentary Arabs (*haḍariyya*) and that this similarity became more pronounced as one moved southward in the Jebel, where the Druze intermingled with the bedouins to a greater degree; here or there, he found the Druze to be more articulate (*afsaḥ*) in their speech than the people of Damascus and its environs (134). The same was true of the Christians living among them—descendants of the many Christians who had sought refuge in the Jebel during the events of 1860 (probably from the villages of neighbouring Hawran)—who spoke, dressed and behaved much as the Druze did (183).

The Jebel appeared to Rustum as an impregnable fortress whose inhabitants may have differed amongst themselves, but were united in the face of external danger. "This is," he notes, "a natural phenomenon, for had they faced external dangers with divided ranks, they would not have preserved their separate existence (*kayān*), considering the [many] enemies that surround them: Hawranis, bedouins, Ruwala" (134). Their country being basaltic, all of their houses were built of black stone. The land was rugged and extremely stony, although sometimes interrupted with stretches of greenery which caught the eye; and the roads were bad. Travelling these roads from one village or town to the next, Rustum and his companions occasionally stopped to admire a cluster of oak trees, the ruins of a Roman temple (121-22), or the shrine of a local saint (122, 137).

Rustum was struck by the cordial hospitality of the Druze and has much to say about their social behaviour and the circumstances of their life:

> When a guest arrives in a village to stay in the guest-house, they take his horse and tether it, spread out a mattress for him to sit on, then offer him coffee. It is not customary among the Druze to start conversing with travellers before they have rested awhile. The master of the house remains standing [all of the time] to show respect for the guest and to carry out the duties of hospitality (*al-qirā*); he moves in and out, welcoming the guests every time he re-enters, saying, *Ahlan wa sahlan*. This welcome is repeated many times... . The coffee is offered [using] one cup or two, or. . . [at most] three, the same cup touching the lips of ten or twenty people without being washed (129-130)... . [I] awoke [one] morning to find a louse on my head-cloth; in fact, I never awoke once without seeing such disgusting insects: something one has to tolerate, the guest-houses being crowded with people of every sort (*mim-man habba wa dabb*) (124)... . Had it not been for the excellent climate and the sunshine that kills vermin (*al-ḥayawānāt al-danī'a*), disease in the Jebel would have been rampant... (130).

Rustum and his friends thought at first that a guest was expected to pay for the services of a guest-house or, at least, to make a move in this direction. As guests of Shaykh Salim al-Halabi at Khalkhala, which was their first stop in the Jebel, they offered to compensate him for his lavish hospitality, but "he would accept nothing," says Rustum, "not even [tips] for the servants" (121).

> Women work inside the house and outside, most importantly, in carrying water, there being hardly any springs in the villages: their dependence is on pools gathering [rainwater] from mountain streams (*suyūl*) [and] large ponds, some ancient, others new, some for watering animals, others for drinking. All of the water, however, is foul: it smells and tastes rank and is [also] murky. It is placed in large jars inside homes, with a large copper bowl [nearby] from [which] five or six people can drink [without refilling it] and from which everyone drinks water out of the jars (130).

> A Druze does not take more than one [wife]. If she dies or he leaves her, he [can] take another, but he cannot have two at the same time. A woman's lot [in the Jebel] is much like that of the Eastern woman in general (130).... [A man] came and told [my friend] the doctor: "There is a girl who [needs to have] her eyes cleaned." Then, her father came and said to him: "Begging your pardon, a female (*Ḥashāk, intāya*). . ." (129).

> There is no veiling [of women] except in the larger towns and acquaintance between a man and a woman is easy, so that a young man marries knowing [whom he is marrying], unlike the city man who only gets to see the face of his life partner on the first night. This may be one of the main reasons why divorce is rare in the Jebel (144).... Divorce only takes place for good reason, [in which case] a man need only tell his wife, "Go find the house of your parents (*fattishi ʿalā bayt ahlik*)," and she packs up and leaves, never to return, [Druze] divorce being absolute and final. The children remain with the father; but if the [divorced] wife, be she a stranger or a relative, has no kin other than her children, the man [divorcing her] assigns her a place to live in (*ghurfa*) close to his house and attend to her needs. If she has no children, he lets her go her way (*yulqi hablaha ʿalā gharībiha*).... A man may not divorce more than three times; otherwise, everybody would brand him a lecher (*fāsiq*). . . (147).

> Men and women only meet in one place if they are relatives. A woman has to defer to her husband's opinion and the father, brother, or uncle main-

> tains great authority over her, beating her and scolding her (*yahibūnaha*, apparently for *yuhibūnaha*) when [they deem it] necessary. Should she behave dishonourably (*idhā kharajat ʿan dāʾirat al-adab*), they kill her (147).

On the religious life of the Druze of the Jebel and their traditions for settling problems and disputes and dealing with crimes and felonies, Rustum has the following to say:

> Initiate men (*al-rijāl al-ʿuqqāl*) meet in the religious retreat (*khulwa*) every evening and there is a general meeting on Friday evening attended by initiates and non-initiates (*juhhāl*), the women having a special place adjoining the men's from which they can hear the sermons. Children may not attend these sermons, nor can outsiders (*ajānib*)... . The Druze are strongly attached to their [religious] beliefs, which strengthen their solidarity (*wiḥdatahum*) (147).

> Judgements are passed by the *shaykh* and the council of *shaykh*s (*majlis al-shuyūkh*). They meet in the home (*maḥall*) of the *shaykh* and pass the judgement. A murderer is expelled from the village along with [all of] the members of his family; then, the *shaykh*s intercede and some [members of the family] return [to the village], but only rarely do the brothers [of the murderer return]. After paying the blood money (30,000 piastres), the murderer [himself] may return home. If the murderer is poor, he appeals to the *shaykh*s and to rich men, and they may help him pay the blood money if they so choose. In any case, the *shaykh*s try to eliminate enmities among the people. The [members of the] family of a murdered person are at liberty to take their revenge on any relative of the murderer to whom they happen to be hostile... . [Such blood revenge] halts while mediation is in progress. A thief is fined and expelled [from the village] and can only return if he repents—and this [only] after a period of time. The sentences are absolute [and] thefts are rare. I used to go out [of a guest-house] and leave a lot of money [behind] and none of it was [ever] stolen. There is no government in the Jebel except for the *shaykh* and the council of *shaykh*s (147-148).

Rustum describes the Druze of the Jebel as a proud people who "love glory (*yuḥibb[ūn] al-ʿazama*)" (127). "What distinguishes the Jebel," he says, "is the courage of its people; their hospitality; [and] their great passion for arms..." (130). He notes how children are trained handle firearms from an early age. "Nayif, the son of Shaykh Husayn Bey [al-Atrash]," he reports, "carried a revolver at his side; he was [only] ten [years old], [yet] spoke of firearms with great expertise" (127). What further impressed Rustum was the manner in which a young Druze carried himself in the presence of older people. "A Druze youth," he remarks, "is bold and fearless: when he enters a place, he salutes with a loud voice, as if he wants to say something; then he salutes again and takes a seat, his eyes glowing with intelligence and alertness" (125).

The Jebel had no schools in 1918, which Rustum thought a pity, given the natural intelligence of its people. "Chivalry, courage and hospitality are beautiful traits," he remarks, "but remain to no avail without knowledge (*ʿilm*). An American women started some primary schools (*katatīb*) [in the area], but they were closed down after the war broke out." Sultan al-Atrash blamed the absence of education (*al-maʿārif*) on the government: "The Jebel has suffered what it has suffered," he told Rustum, "How can it advance and think of learning (*al-ʿūlum*) after all of the misfortunes that it has undergone?" (137-38).

On the state of public health in the Jebel, Rustum has little to say, except for briefly noting the services rendered by some Protestant medical missionaries in the area (134). However, he does dwell at some length on economic conditions in the Jebel:

> The war has brought great prosperity to the Jebel, which has become the main [Syrian] market for pedigree horses and high quality firearms. Wealth has increased to an extent never known before... . Rice, of which nothing remains in Damascus, is found in most houses [here], as is sugar (130).
>
> The Druze before the war was poor, living by the day, and the rich man in the Jebel used to spend what came to him; before year's end, even the great *shaykh*s would be in debt to their agents (*ʿumalāʾ*) in Damascus. Those [agents] used to send them all that they asked for at 25 percent interest and, at the end of the year, would import their crops and sell them, deducting the debt [plus] a ten percent commission and sending the balance to them, should anything remain. Thus, the Jebel used to plow and cultivate (*yaflaḥ wa yazraʿ*) to benefit the grain merchants (*bawwabkiyya;* literally, 'doorkeepers') of Damascus. Now, the situation has changed. The *mudd* [half bushel] of wheat sells for a [gold] pound instead of ten piastres and the Druze *shaykh* is a prince with no debts; he has become the richest of the rich. Of wheat alone, Sultan Bey [al-Atrash] can sell 8000 *mudd*s [a year], not to speak of barley and pulse. His [annual] income [from crop sales] is estimated at 15,000 [gold] pounds: an enormous fortune (141).

Sultan al-Atrash derived additional income from other enterprises. At ʿAyn Nimrah, for instance, he owned a highly profitable steam-powered mill (*maṭḥana tataḥarrak ʿalā al-faḥm* or 'a mill moving on coal') seen by Rustum and his friends (142), "which could grind sixty to eighty *shunbul*s [eight *mudd*s] of wheat a day at the rate of three and a half *majidiyya*s [twenty-piastre silver pieces] for every *shunbūl*."

Rustum notices that this new wealth had not changed the simple style of life of the Jebel's notables (141). In one place, however, he gives a detailed account of the furniture in the reception-room (*qāʿa*) in Husayn al-Atrash's home, which reflected, he believed, the intrusion of some Damascene influence:

> Its ceiling was painted, like the ceilings of Damascus; [the floor] was spread with carpets. On the side facing the door (*ṣadr*) were four mattresses upon which we sat; in the corners of the room at either side of the door were a [wooden] chest inlaid with mother-of-pearl and a cabinet of carved walnut inlaid with seashells: [both were] made in Damascus. On the walls [were] a number of rifles and a shelf [displaying] plates, [bottles of] syrup, tea-glasses and coloured glasses, [as well as] some photographs of famous Druze [figures]. Added to this were three brooms coloured green and red, a mirror, three bamboo chairs, straw trays for serving food [and] a chandelier... . There was [also] an alcove (*yuk*) [on one side of the room] to store the beds (126).

Foodstuffs in the Jebel came from the resources of the land and the nearby desert. Rustum Haydar frequently mentions the ingredients of meals to which he and his fellow guests were treated. For breakfast and morning snacks, they were served milk, cheese, ghee and honey in any combination, with bread and tea; for lunch or dinner, a *mansaf* of rice and boiled lamb steeped in melted ghee and eaten with the fingers or a *fatta* of bread, yoghurt, ghee and boiled lamb, also eaten with the fingers; for mid-afternoon snacks: eggs, yoghurt, cheese and fried eggplant; as salad at any time: tomatoes and cucumbers (the dark green *khiyār* or the light green *qithī*, the latter often picked and eaten in the field where it grew), which were then in season; and, as fruit: watermelons, sweet melons, figs and grapes, which were also in season. Eating a *mansaf* with his fingers for the first time as the guest of a local bedouin chief, Rustum praised God for the existence of soap (124).

The regular beverage in the Jebel was coffee, prepared for guests after the roasted beans had been pounded with a pestle in their presence to varying rhythms:

> Coffee is much used in these parts, while it is [now] rare and extremely expensive in Damascus; it is held in [high] esteem and offered at frequent intervals. Most often, the [coffee beans] are bought in *qintārs* [quarter-ton units], like wheat and barley, because [of the extent to which] people here are accustomed to [the beverage]. [Coffee] is the drink of this country just as beer is the drink of the Germans, wine the drink of the French and whiskey the drink of the English. When a distinguished guest arrives, they spread out . . . the mattresses, cover them with carpets and rugs [and] then prepare the fire for the coffee, bringing in the chest (*ṣundūq*) and the pestle and beginning pounding... . People [here] accustom their children to coffee from infancy (125). [As for] tobacco, the Druze rarely use it..., [unlike the people of] Hawran and Damascus, and they care little for intoxicating drinks (*wa qallamā yaʿtanūn bi'l-muskir*) (139).

A three-year-old girl chewed a mouthful of ground coffee beans in Rustum's presence, saying how delicious it tasted (*mā atyabuh*). She was Dina, the daughter of Husayn al-Atrash: a beautiful, self-confident and playful little girl with an olive complexion, black eyes and a round face, who spoke with the accent of the Jebel. "She wore a robe (*qamīs*)," says Rustum, "the upper part of which was like a vest (*siḍriyya*) and the lower part pleated like a skirt (*tannūra*); a string of red, yellow, black and blue beads was around her neck; her thick hair was dressed in little braids tied at their ends with green, blue and red ribbon[s]" (125).

The *shaykhs* of the Jebel did not consider it beneath their dignity to play music and sing for their guests. Husayn al-Atrash, Rustum notes, played the *rababa* with much skill (150); so did his kinsman, Mustafa al-Atrash, the brother of Sultan, who also sang *qaṣidas* composed in vernacular Arabic by Shibli al-Atrash (1850-1904), the late bard of the Jebel whose odes, with their folk wisdom, had become "the Bible (*al-Kitāb al-Muqaddas*)" of the Druze there (138).

Rustum saw the Druze of the Jebel perform their special dance, called the *sahja,* at two wedding celebrations which he attended. In one, the men and the women, ranged in separate lines, danced jointly (123); in the other, only the men danced. He comments upon the "strange and evocative steps" and how "the dancers formed a crescent around a leader and keep on dancing for two or three hours, while he egged them on" (144).

Rustum appears to have been fascinated by the wedding customs of the local Druze, elaborating upon them at some length:

> After the betrothal, a young man may not meet his promised bride, nor speak to her; [as for her,] she flees him if she spots him anywhere; and should she enter [his] village, it would be better for her to stay in the house of someone not of [his] kin (146-47)... . People begin celebrating the wedding a few days before [the event]. . .; they assemble in the house of the bridegroom to dance, sing and fire shots and so build up enthusiasm... . [On the appointed day,] the relatives of the bridegroom go to the quarter or village where the bride [is waiting]; her relatives object to [their taking her away], but they allay their objections with some presents, then return [with the bride] (144)... . When the bride leaves [her parental home], the only people who bid her farewell are her mother and sisters (146)... . Before [the bride and the people accompanying her] reach the bridegroom's village, the men, old and young, ride out to perform feats of horsemanship before the bride. [She arrives] on a horse led by one of her relatives; a woman walks on each side of the horse, the men around [them] chanting in triumph (*yuhallilūn*), while the women behind sing songs to the accompaniment of a small drum... . Every time she passes before a house, the owner invites her in, [until] she finally accepts the invitation of some notable of the village to spend the night [in his house]. The next day, the bridegroom is brought [there] to claim his bride (*yuzaff*). Riding a horse, he stops by the village square, where a horse-race begins amidst singing and chanting. A feast follows in the evening, then the *nuqūt* (gifts in money or kind) [are presented]—an old custom probably instituted to help the bridegroom [set up his new home]. An old man (*shaykh*) stands [to acknowledge each gift as it comes, by] shouting out: "[May God] compensate so-and-so! (*Yikhlif ʿalā fulān!*)" (144).

At the Jebel wedding attended by Rustum, he and his friends offered the bridal couple Ottoman gold pounds in the name of Feisal, whose eldest son was called Ghazi; and each time a pound was paid, the old man would shout out: *Yikhlif ʿalā Abu Ghāzī*! (144-45).

Rustum's party was staying with Sultan al-Atrash in his hometown, al-Qrayya, when the latter received a letter from the commander of the Sharifian forces at al-Azraq (today in Jordan) urging him to prepare for military action. Rustum took up the letter to read it. It was written in appalling Arabic and at the top of the page were some printed words that had been effaced. Upon closer examination, the printed words turned out to be the Koranic phrase "Truly, the [Muslim] faithful are brothers (*Innama al-muʿminūna ikhwatun*)." To Rustum, it seemed clear that the author of the letter had purposely effaced this phrase, assuming that it might offend Sultan or that it would not apply to him as a Druze (142).

Passing through the Jebel once more on 28-29 September 1918, as the Sharifian and British forces were making their final push towards Damascus, with each side reportedly trying to get there first (183, 184), Rustum stopped at al-Qrayya, where he was told that Sultan al-Atrash had seized Busra, in Hawran, from the Ottomans: "He put the Arab Ottoman troops who remained [there] in Sharifian uniform; and every time a man entered Busra, he made him kiss the [Sharif's] flag and say: "May God give him life (*Ḥayyāhu-ʾLlāh*)" (182). As Rustum proceeded further north, he arrived on 3 October at the desert border-town of Dayr ʿAli, where he learnt from a fighting band of Druze from the Jebel that Damascus had finally been taken. They were proud that the Arab army had entered the city before the British, but more proud to tell him that it was the Druze who had entered first (186).

On the same day, Rustum Haydar went into Damascus with Feisal. From that moment, the Druze episode of his career was behind him and he apparently never visited the Jebel again.

Michael Provence

Druze Shaykhs, Arab Nationalists and Grain Merchants

In 1925, a local Druze leader led a major revolt against the French mandate in Syria. The revolt began in the rural Druze homeland of Jabal Hawran, but it soon spread to most of the area under French control, including parts of the new state of Greater Lebanon. The uprising was the most significant challenge to French rule during the two and a half decades of the mandate (1920-46). The Syrian participants in the revolt—and many, though not all, historians since then—have argued that the uprising was a forceful expression of Syrian Arab nationalist feeling and aspirations. The participants in the revolt called it *al-thawra al-Sūriyya al-waṭaniyya*. French scholars and colonial civil servants called it the Druze revolt and claimed that it was a reaction of backward Druze feudal lords against the enlightened reforms of French mandatory officials. The 1925 uprising was the largest anti-government revolt to emerge in the Druze region, but it was not the first.[1]

There had been many uprisings against the previous Ottoman government in the Hawran. Earlier revolts mobilized varying segments among the Ḥawran Druze and sometimes other local inhabitants against Istanbul and its representatives. The 1925 uprising, however, was the first general 'Syrian' uprising and the first to utilize nationalist language. Among the many written accounts of the 1925 uprising, only those of the French emphasize the sectarian identity of the rebels. For the French, it was always the 'Druze Revolt.'[2] For the people who took part, Druze, Muslim and even Christian, it was the 'Syrian Nationalist Revolution.' Between 1917 and 1925, Syrian nationalism supplanted Druze particularism as the language of revolt in Jabal Hawran. This paper examines some of the ways in which this change came about.[3]

In 1925, the leader of the insurgency, Sultan al-Atrash, was 35 years old and had already been involved in 15 years of agitation against the Ottomans and the French in turn. His anti-government campaigns against outside rule and colonial occupation were not universally popular in Jabal Hawran and, in 1925, as before, opposition to his efforts came from within his own family. The Atrash were the leading family of the region, but they were not united in their approach to outside authority. In 1918, on the eve of the Ottoman defeat in World War I, Sultan al-Atrash aligned himself and his followers with Emir Faysal ibn Husayn and, through him, with Great Britain. On this occasion, his stance also provoked influential opposition from his own family. I shall argue that, in 1918, both Sultan and his main rival, Salim al-Atrash, were principally preoccupied with the interests and preservation of their Druze community. Their rivalry was based upon differences in definition, not intent.

In unsettled and uncertain times, ideologies, identities and politics are changeable and fluid. People can and do hold widely differing positions simultaneously and with utter conviction. By insisting upon the changeable nature of political tactics, ideology and identity, I am not suggesting that the beliefs of Salim or Sultan al-Atrash—or their followers—were not sincerely held. I do not to wish to argue, for example, that Sultan al-Atrash was not a genuine Syrian nationalist or to claim, as his Druze rivals did at the time, that he was unconcerned with the communal welfare of his coreligionists. What I would like to point out is that factional struggles among the Druze emerged not principally from ambition or personal rivalry, but from competing and rapidly-changing notions of community, identity and communal welfare. It is evident that, in 1918, both Sultan and Salim were concerned with the interests and welfare of their community, despite their bitter disagreements. It is likewise evident that, at some undefined point, Sultan expanded his notion of the community and its welfare to include much of the new Syrian nation beyond Jabal Hawran.

In 1925, mandate apologists argued that rebels fought to preserve Druze feudal privileges. Ottoman and Damascene opponents of an earlier generation of Druze rebels made similar arguments.[4] Conversely, Druze critics and rivals claimed that rebel leaders, both in 1925 and before, were insufficiently concerned with Druze communal welfare. Others claimed that the Druze rebels pursued a strictly sectarian agenda and that those non-Druze who followed them had been tricked. Likewise, rebel leaders questioned the patriotism of their more cautious brethren, both among the Druze and, in 1925, among the larger Syrian population.

In September 1918, Emir Salim al-Atrash, titular head (*shaykh al-mashāykh*) of the Hawran Druze, wrote a letter to his cousin, Sultan al-Atrash. The letter was a sarcastic response to Sultan's agitation in the Jabal on behalf of Emir Faysal ibn Husayn's revolt against the Ottoman state.

25 September 1918
To the leader of the great Druze army, Sultan Pasha:

I was informed of your message to the villagers [of a list of villages] asking them to join you in Busra Eski Sham with the sharif. You must stop your endless revenge against the Ottoman state. Our noble ancestors were divided between the British and the [Ottoman] state. You must not divide the Druze again. The [people] have rejected and turned away from your furious excesses and outrages.

[If you do not reject revolt,] we will expel you from the community.

Do not be fooled by illusions. You have deceived the people by claiming that Nablus has fallen with 30,000 prisoners. We do not know this.

Before anyone understands what is really happening, you are trying to convince the ignorant Druze to join the 'snuffbox army' of the sharif.

You must know that, if you continue, both your village and your huge army will be destroyed.

We are not disloyal and our ancestors were not disloyal. They were firmly behind the throne of the state in the time of Sultan Salim [against the Mamluks] and during the time of Ibrahim Pasha al-Masri. This was the way of our ancestors: to fortify the besieged; not your way: the way of disloyalty for money and of subverting the feelings of the community. Division is not the way of our ancestors.

Salim al-Atrash

Sultan al-Atrash replied the following day.

26 September 1918
To the leader of the Turkish army, Salim Pasha al-Atrash:

Today I was informed of your fraudulent letter, which was dictated to you by the Turks. I wanted to answer every bit, but my time is too valuable to permit it, especially since you commemorate the dying Turkish state and describe it using words that even the [state's servants] do not themselves use, since they admit the state's impotence.

As for your charges, honoured cousin, it is not we who are disloyal. We have not dined at the Damascus Palace Hotel or entered the garden of the municipal *sarāy*. And we have not met any Turk, the murderers of our fathers, and those who disgraced our country.

Read the poems of your grandfather, Shibli, [that] great man of the Druze, who is calling you from his tomb and who told you that you must arm yourself against your enemy, [not against] your friend, and take caution with the treacherous and tyrannical Turks.

We declare a sacred war against the starving remnants of the Turkish army. We advise you to be wise enough to save your remorse. It will not help.

The news that we heard of the fall of Nablus and the victory in Tiberias is [that they came] at the hand of the state of the world, the master of the seas, Great Britain, our old friend.

As far as the destruction of our community (*tā'ifat al-Durūz*) is concerned, this news [from Nablus] is reality; it is not news manufactured in Germany or by Ottoman intelligence. It is accurate information.

If you desire the greatest air force in the world, we can deliver it to you. As for the wireless and the telephone, and all of the most advanced means of communication, they are at our disposal because ours is the faction of God. Praise God, the exalted master of all.

As for your debased Turks, '*Malta yok*,' in other words, everything they [offer] is lacking, even bread. In the name of our noble family, I will not depart from the way [of our ancestors].

As for the 'snuffbox army,' it is your army that is [a snuffbox army]. Now we are aligned with the great state [of Britain], which rules the *mutaṣarrif* of Hawran.

God willing, we will be good heirs to our ancestors and we will protect the honour of the Druze and their future; and we will not allow them to be trampled upon, as you wish to put them under the boot of the most savage state on earth.

Your cousin,
Sultan al-Atrash[5]

The letters are intriguing for many reasons. While both are replete with references to Druze honour, they are illustrative, at a most basic level, of two divergent views for safeguarding the community's well-being. In most of the sources for 1925 and after, these sorts of concerns do not appear. Nationalist language and appeals predominate, at least in written sources. In 1918, however, the language of communal welfare predominated as each writer tried to colour the actions of his rival as inimical to Druze interests. Salim accused his cousin of being motivated by revenge against the state. In this way, he de-legitimized the opposition that Sultan represented. He further claimed that Sultan acted hastily and endangered the community by preparing to join the Faysali rebels without sufficient information. Sultan had thus abandoned, at least as far as Salim was concerned, the customary caution and reticence that characterized responsible leadership. As a sectarian minority perched, sometimes uncomfortably, at the edge of a larger Islamic society, noncommittal discretion was often a crucial Druze leadership trait. Finally, Salim accused Sultan of financially-motivated treason. This accusation is surely based on the extensive wartime contacts between Druze *shaykhs*, Damascene grain merchants and well-funded agents of the British government, about which more will be said shortly.

Sultan's reply vividly indicates that he had glimpsed a post-Ottoman political order not yet visible to his cousin. It also demonstrates that, for Sultan, the Ottoman state was defined ethnically; thus, although the ethnicity of the Syrian nation with which Sultan would soon associate the Druze went unmentioned, the negatively-defined opposition was already clear.[6] Sultan rebutted Salim's charge of financial treachery by accusing Salim of dining in the Damascus Palace Hotel and strolling in the gardens of the government palace. Salim's unmentioned companion was presumably Jamal Pasha, the wartime Ottoman governor of Syria from November 1914 to December 1917, whom Sultan saw as an undifferentiated representative of the entire Turkish nation, "the murderers of our fathers." It is notable and certainly not coincidental that Jamal Pasha was also personally responsible for the execution of a number of alleged Arab nationalist leaders in Beirut and Damascus in 1915 and 1916. None of those executed were Druze, but many who escaped sought refuge in Jabal Hawran with Druze *shaykhs*, particularly Sultan al-Atrash.[7] Those murdered were viewed as non-Druze national martyrs—non-Druze, so not among the "fathers" that Sultan mentions, but possibly 'brothers' in an extended national family.

Like Salim, Sultan evoked history and the example of Druze heroes of the past. Unlike Salim, however, he mentioned a specific individual, Shibli al-Atrash, the grandfather to both Salim and Sultan, as well as his personal traits, among which was caution in dealing with the Turks. Finally, Sultan indicated that he sought to attach communal fortunes to the new power of the age, Britain, and he enumerated the marvels that Britain possessed and emphasized that it had the favour of God. In contrast, the Turkish army lacked everything, including bread. This reminded Salim that the Druze had successfully resisted wartime Ottoman efforts to confiscate the Jabal Hawran wheat crop, while Druze *shaykhs*, including Sultan, had helped to supply the Faysali and British forces with Hawrani wheat. The Ottomans had to confiscate wheat when they could: the British paid in gold.

By 1918, contact between the Hawran Druze and the Ottoman state had long been close and often contentious. While such contact had been continuous, the state had never exercised unquestioned control. Druze migration to the Hawran increased dramatically after the 1860s and the Druze came to be the masters of an increasingly important and profitable grain trade. In 1860, on the eve of massive Druze migration, the Hawran was characterized by rural insecurity and most agricultural settlements were occupied only seasonably, if at all. The potentially rich, rain-fed farmland of the Hawran plain and most of Jabal Hawran were the preserve of the bedouin and were exploited only for pasture. But as Druze migrants settled and pacified Jabal Hawran and the plain, they began to take advantage of the agricultural export market. The migrants knew the importance of exports from their experience in the silk business in Mount Lebanon. Mulberry trees, silk worms and silk cocoon production were impossible to sustain in the relatively arid climate of Jabal Hawran, but the migrants were adaptable and they learned from their neighbours how to grow the hardy and drought-resistant wheat native to the Hawran. Damascus, Beirut and Haifa were ready outlets for their grain and the more enterprising *shaykhs* opened commercial relations on behalf of their villages with merchants from those cities, particularly Damascus.[8] The Druze—and particularly members of the Atrash family—subsequently felt that they had earned the right to dominate Jabal Hawran and the Hawran and they resisted assertions of state control over their newly-prosperous region.

This tension led to major revolts and state incursions in 1879, 1881, 1884, 1889-90, 1895-96 and 1910. Usually the leading *shaykh* of the Atrash family led resistance against the state but, in 1889, a group of secondary chiefs and peasants formed a coalition to challenge the local rule of the Atrash chiefs in an uprising called the *ʿĀmmiyya* or Popular Revolt. The conflict divided the community and the Atrash family itself was split into opposing camps. This conflict had been simmering for several years and, when it finally came into the open, the Ottoman state exploited the opportunity to impose some form of government rule on Jabal Hawran. The power of the great chiefs declined. Peasants earned secure title to their land—or at least their communal shares—and the chiefs gave up half of their shares, bringing the amount of land that they controlled in most villages to no more than an eighth. Involuntary evictions of peasants by chiefs stopped and Jabal Hawran was relatively peaceful for almost twenty years.[9]

The 1889 *ʿĀmmiyya* brought an enduring division within the leading Atrash family of the Jabal. Some members of the family, mostly centred around Suwayda', moved into the Ottoman camp. They became Ottoman civil authorities in Jabal Hawran as the Ottoman state fitfully extended its revenue collecting and conscription authority beyond urban centres through local intermediaries or rural notables, employing a shifting array of enticements and threats. Other members of the family, centred in the southern Jabal, around the original Atrash stronghold in al-Qraya, opposed state control and the state-sponsored domination of the Jabal by their Suwayda' cousins. These two villages, Suwayda' and al-Qraya, were the birthplaces and the hereditary domains of the above correspondents, Salim and Sultan al-Atrash.[10]

In 1910, two years after the Unionist Revolution in Istanbul, Ottoman soldiers were back in the Hawran. This time they came in response to fighting between Druze and local bedouin. With 30 battalions of Ottoman troops, Sami Pasha al-Faruqi met insignificant resistance. While some Hawran Druze leaders were aggressive in defence of what they saw as their rights, none were suicidal. In the wake of the invasion, Sami al-Faruqi disarmed the Hawran Druze and took some of the Jabal's young men as conscripts into the Ottoman army. Among them was a twenty-year-old named Sultan al-Atrash. He spent six months serving in the Balkans where, among other things, he learned to read and write. Whatever goodwill the experience may have fostered was destroyed when the young man returned to find that his father, Dhuqan al-Atrash, *shaykh* of al-Qraya, had been publicly hanged by the Ottoman authorities in Damascus, along with five other recalcitrant Druze *shaykhs*.[11] The executions were not soon forgotten in Jabal Hawran and they would be cited again and again as proof of Ottoman savagery and, anachronistically, as proof of Druze sacrifices for the Syrian Arab nation. For Sultan al-Atrash, the rulers of the Ottoman state had become "the murderers of our fathers."[12]

Execution and exile freed the state from dealing with its most trenchant foes, but a new generation of leaders was emerging. The Ottoman authorities had hanged several leading *shaykhs*, including Sultan's father. The head of the Hawran Druze, the *shaykh al-mashyakha*, Yahya al-Atrash, the last son of the famous founder of the clan, Isma'il al-Atrash, had also been sentenced to death. Sami Pasha al-Faruqi overturned his sentence, however, fining him 3000 gold Ottoman pounds and exiling him to the island of Rhodes. When Rhodes was occupied by Italy in 1912, Yahya went to Egypt before finally returning to Syria, where he died in 1914.[13]

His successor, Emir Salim al-Atrash, was born in 1874 and elected governor of Jabal Hawran in 1914. Succession skipped a generation when the comparatively young Salim became *shaykh al-mashyakha.* As noted above, he came from the branch of the Atrash family based in Suwayda'. Many among the Hawran Druze apparently considered him unfit to be the principal leader, both because of his inexperience and because of his endorsement by the Ottoman authorities. His actions during the war, however, indicate that he was not an unquestioning partisan of the state, but rather a cautious advocate for Druze autonomy. His cousin Sultan, born in 1890 in the original Atrash village of al-Qraya on the southern frontier, opposed his election from the beginning.

The Ottoman state reluctantly entered World War I in October 1914. The Unionist government, in power since 1908, had already fought a series of devastating wars in Libya and the Balkans. By 1914, war and crisis had transformed the Unionist government into a dictatorship headed by a trio made up of two army officers and a civil servant. Secret alliances signed with Germany and Austria-Hungary obligated the Ottoman state to enter the war on the side of the Central Powers against Britain, France and Russia. One of the trio of Ottoman leaders, Ahmad Jamal Pasha, soon became wartime governor of the troublesome geographical Syria and commander of the Ottoman Fourth Army headquartered in Damascus. Shortly after his arrival in Damascus, the government issued a call for global *jihād* in defence of the besieged empire and its caliph.[14]

At the same time, Salim al-Atrash became *shaykh al-mashyakha* of Jabal Hawran. Salim assumed the mantle of Druze leadership on 10 November 1914 with a dramatic gesture; he led a procession of 500 Druze horsemen to Damascus, where they were reviewed by Jamal Pasha in front of the government palace in Marja Square. The spectacle of 500 heavily-armed horsemen must have impressed the newly-appointed governor, for he resolved to involve Druze fighters in the war effort. Amidst government calls for *jihād*, conscription and patriotic sacrifice, Salim demonstrated Druze military prowess and loyalty to the Ottoman state, while simultaneously resisting Ottoman demands for a Druze contribution to the army and the war effort.[15] In keeping with traditional aspirations, the Druze avoided conscription, taxation and seizure of their grain throughout the war.

Jamal Pasha did not give up easily in his efforts to harness the Druze to the Ottoman military. He suggested that Salim and Nasib al-Atrash take up residence in Damascus and offered to arrange lodging for them. Jamal Pasha wished both to gain their support and to keep them under surveillance. He further suggested that an élite Druze military force be formed and visited the Jabal several times to advance this idea. In the Jabal, he distributed stipends and government medals and titles. He gained the conditional support of some leaders and many accepted his gifts, but he failed to attract backing for a Druze military force. Among those who received his gifts but refused to support him was Sultan al-Atrash, who was granted the title of Pasha by the Ottoman state in 1917.[16]

Salim al-Atrash also played a complicated diplomatic game, all the while managing to prevent conscription, taxation, seizure of the Jabal grain crop and any practical extension of central control into Jabal Hawran. He refused a lavish gift of 1000 gold Ottoman pounds, intended to purchase his acquiescence to the formation of a Druze military force. Salim skilfully engaged the Ottoman authorities in endless cordial negotiations, first, with Jamal Pasha and, after December 1917, with his successor, Jamal Pasha "the lesser."[17]

Ahmad Jamal Pasha instituted a reign of terror in Damascus during the war years. He never extended his rule to Jabal Hawran, however, and he treated the Druze, as represented by Salim al-Atrash, with caution and respect. While Salim negotiated with the Ottoman authorities, Sultan, on the mountain's southern flank, negotiated with emissaries from Sharif Husayn. He also extended the customary Druze sanctuary and sustenance to virtually all of the fugitive Arab nationalists able to escape Jamal Pasha's dragnet. Dozens of prominent nationalists found refuge in Jabal Hawran with Sultan and ʿAbd al-Ghaffar al-Atrash. Among them were Dr. ʿAbd al-Rahman al-Shahbandar, Nasib al-Bakri, Ahmad Mudri, Rafiq al-Tamimi, Shaykh Saʿad al-Bani, ʿAbd al-Latif al-ʿAsali, Zaki al-Durubi, ʿIzz al-Din al-Tanukhi, Nazih al-Muʾayyad al-ʿAzm, Tahsin Qadri, Khalil al-Sakakini, Rustum Haydar and Khalil Saydah, as well as many others.[18] One can only imagine the countless conversations that took place in the Atrash *madāfa* (guest house) in Sultan's village between Druze *shaykh*s and nationalist fugitives from the Ottoman government.[19]

Nasib al-Bakri was the first link between Emir Faysal and Sultan al-Atrash. Faysal had stayed in the Bakri family house in the village of al-Qabun early in 1916, before the beginning of the Arab Revolt.[20] The village was just outside of Damascus, not far from the Druze village of Jaramana. The ties of Nasib and his brother, Fawzi al-Bakri, with Faysal dated from before the war and originated with their fathers, ʿAtallah al-Bakri and al-Husayn ibn ʿAli, the sharif of Mecca. Husayn cemented the connection by appointing Fawzi al-Bakri to be his personal bodyguard. During Faysal's stay in 1916, Nasib al-Bakri organized a meeting of Druze *shaykh*s, including Sultan and Husayn al-Atrash, and some Damascene nationalist members of the secret society, *Al-Fatāt*, to try to gain support for a revolt against Ottoman rule.[21] It was natural that Bakri would call upon the Hawran Druze for such a project since their antipathy and periodic armed resistance against the Ottoman state were widely known. Sultan and Husayn al-Atrash met Faysal and were impressed with him, but declined to lend more than their conditional support to the revolt.

The Arab Revolt began in the Hijaz in June 1916. The population of Syria remained quiet and contributed little to the revolt. Simple survival was more important than all else and, as the war progressed, a crushing famine gripped much of geographical Syria. Jabal Hawran, however, was spared the famine and contributed local surplus grain to the rebel forces. Grain merchant families, long and intimately associated with the Hawran Druze, served as emissaries between nationalist fugitives, revolt leaders and the Druze. Many Damascene grain merchants had summer houses in Druze villages and, as war and famine gripped Damascus, they moved their families to the relative safety of the Jabal.[22] In Syrian and Lebanese usage, famine and military conscription are still collapsed in the Turkish word for land mobilization, *seferberlik*, which evokes all aspects of the horrible suffering of the war years. Linda Schilcher has shown that, while grain speculators bore some of the blame for the famine, the most devastating element was the effective British blockade of all Arab Mediterranean ports. At the time it was realized, though apparently not by the Ottoman high command, that the grain shortages in Arabia and starvation among the tribes were the principal reasons why the bedouin joined the revolt. While the British kept any grain from entering the country, the Ottoman command, with insufficient food for the army, cut supplies to the coast due to the suspicion that unscrupulous grain speculators would either hoard grain in Beirut or export it to obtain still higher prices. Meanwhile, with insufficient funds to buy grain on the open market, the Ottoman command resorted to a policy of price fixing for grain producers. When the command was unable to impose a stable grain price, the policy changed to one of more or less forced confiscation, with token payment, of grain stores from both producers and merchants. Only the

Hawran Druze had enough independence from the central government to resist confiscation.[23]

British war policy led indirectly to the deaths by starvation of hundreds of thousands in the cities of geographical Syria and in the Ottoman Army. The Ottoman high command in Istanbul bore responsibility, too, and had evidently decided, by early 1918, that Syria was lost and that re-supply was futile. After the Armistice, the British and French flooded the cities of geographical Syria with embargoed and hoarded grain, reaping the good will of a grateful populace, who blamed the famine on the defeated Ottomans, rather than on their victorious liberators.[24]

Sultan al-Atrash reported that the Jabal sheltered and fed 50,000 refugees from the Ottoman army and the famine. He mentioned this to deflect the periodic charge of Druze war profiteering owing to their refusal to sell Hawrani grain to Ottoman-held Damascus at fixed government prices and their preference for more profitable sales to the British-bankrolled Sharifian army, a trade which the British encouraged with every means available.[25] While the Druze sheltered and fed thousands of refugees on a daily basis, the grain trade continued in cooperation with Maydani merchants and local bedouin. Lines of transport, though, moved south towards the British line, rather than north towards Damascus or east towards Haifa, as they had before the war.[26]

In September of 1918, as the Sharifian army entered the Hawran, it was joined by Sultan al-Atrash and a number of Druze horsemen from Jabal Hawran for the final advance on Damascus. As the above letters demonstrate, Salim opposed the Druze forces' efforts, while his cousin, Sultan, organized and led them. Before the Druze forces joined Faysal, however, they signed agreements with his representatives guaranteeing a high degree of regional autonomy in the state anticipated to emerge from the Ottoman withdrawal.[27] While he certainly flew his own standard, Sultan al-Atrash was the first to raise the Arab flag over the Jabal.[28]

Emir Faysal kept his pledge to the Hawran Druze and stayed out of their affairs for the duration of his short rule, though he hardly had the power to interfere during those turbulent eighteen months.[29] Others did not keep their pledges and, when France insisted upon enforcing the division of geographical Syria secretly planned with the British and later validated by the League of Nations, Britain did not support Faysal's kingdom and stood aside as its European wartime ally brought an end to the government of its Arab wartime ally. French intelligence agents had already been circulating in Jabal Hawran to help smooth the way for French rule. When the agents arrived, they found the Hawran Druze divided toward their mandate along much the same lines as they had been divided toward Ottoman rule. Salim al-Atrash supported the mandate, as he had supported Ottoman rule, while his cousin, Sultan al-Atrash, led the opposition.

Salim and Sultan represented rival factions and rival world-views among the Hawran Druze. Neither was undisputed leader: Salim was elected and received Ottoman and later French sanction as titular head of the Hawran Druze, symbolized by his state-bestowed title of *amīr*; Sultan assumed the position of war leader among the Druze, first by virtue of his descent from a series of legendary fighters and martyrs, including his father, but finally by his own actions in 1918, 1921 and the revolt of 1925.[30] Their differences were significant and they continued until Salim's early death in 1923. Salim identified Druze communal interests with the state, which was the only institution seemingly powerful enough to insure stability in turbulent times. He sought to maintain his traditional role as leader, extending cooperation and nominal submission to the state, while carefully retaining as much autonomy as possible. Sultan, by contrast, had glimpsed a future in which the old Ottoman-dominated world would necessarily crumble. New identities would emerge and the possibility of a new and, perhaps, more just, post-war political order was within reach.

NOTES

[1] See my *The Great Syrian Revolt and the Rise of Arab Nationalism* (Austin, Texas, 2005) Philip Khoury's *Syria and the French Mandate: The Politics of Arab Nationalism, 1920-1945* (Princeton, 1987) has four chapters on the 1925-27 period.

[2] See, for example, General Charles Joseph Andréa. *La révolte druze et l'insurrection de Damas* (Paris, 1937); and Captain Gabriel Carbillet, *Au Djebel Druse: Choses vues et vécues* (Paris, 1929). Recently, a Druze emphasis has come to the fore in secondary sources, notably, in the excellent works of Hasan Amin al-Buʿayni and Kais Firro. These works set out, of course, to tell a history of the Druze in the Arab nation, rather than the story of the Revolt. The two books were written during and just after the war in Lebanon.

[3] For a short discussion of the events and more general views of the Hawran Druze, see Kais Firro's definitive work, *A History of the Druzes* (Leiden, 1992), 249-50. See, also, the contributions of Kamal Salibi and Abdul-Rahim Abu-Husayn in this volume.

[4] Samir Seikaly, "Pacification of the Hawran (1910): The View from Within," unpublished paper presented at the XII Congress of the Comité International des Etudes Ottoman et Pre-Ottoman (CIEPO), n.d. This paper reviews the

Damascene press and shows Damascene hostility to the Druze in 1910. My thanks to the author for providing me with a copy.

5 The letters are reproduced in Hanna Abi Rashid, *Jabal al-Durūz* (Cairo, 1925; reprinted Beirut, 1961). Copies of the 1925 edition are extant, but I refer to the more common 1961 edition; see pages 131-33. Dhuqan Qarqut also reproduces the letters, without attribution, in his *Taṭawwur al-Haraka al-Waṭaniyya fī Sūriyya, 1920-1939* (Damascus, 1989), 264-66. It is important to note that Sultan himself referred to and documented the authenticity of the "famous letters" in his dictated memoirs; see Sultan al-Atrash, "Mudhakkirāt Sultān," serialized in *Bayrūt al-masāʾ* (1975-76), 97-120. His memoirs show that, rhetorically at least, he apparently mellowed with age and came to regard his rivals more charitably with the passage of time.

6 Ranajit Guha shows that the idea of "negation" is a crucial element in subaltern insurgent consciousness; see Ranajit Guha, *Elementary Aspects of Peasant Insurgency in Colonial India* (Delhi, 1983), 18-77. See, also, Partha Chatterjee, *The Nation and Its Fragments: Colonial and Post-Colonial Histories* (Princeton, 1993), 161-62.

7 See Sultan's dictated memoirs in "Mudhakkirāt Sultān," part 98, 36. For Jamal Pasha's wartime policies, see Hasan Kayali, *Arabs and Young Turks: Ottomanism, Arabism, and Islamism in the Ottoman Empire, 1908-1914* (Berkeley, 1997).

8 I have drawn on the work of Linda Schilcher for the importance of the grain trade. See Linda Schilcher, "The Grain Economy of Late Ottoman Syria and the Issue of Large-Scale Commercialization," in *Landholding and Commercial Agriculture in the Middle East,* edited by Çaglar Keyder and Faruk Tabak (New York, 1991), 173-95; Linda Schilcher, "The Hauran Conflicts of the 1860s: A Chapter in the Rural History of Modern Syria," *International Journal of Middle East Studies* 13 (1981): 159-79; and Linda Schilcher, "The Great Depression (1873-1896) and the Rise of Syrian Arab Nationalism," *New Perspectives on Turkey*, nos. 5-6 [Suraiya Faroqhi, guest editor] (1991): 167-89.

9 See ʿAbdallah Hanna, *Al-ʿĀmmiyya wa al-intifādat (1850-1918) fī Jabal Hawran* (Damascus, 1990), for the best treatment of this period.

10 Firro dates the split within the Atrash family from the death of Ibrahim al-Atrash in 1869; see Firro, *A History of the Druzes*, 249.

11 The events of 1910 have been recounted elsewhere. See for example, al-Atrash, "Mudhakkirāt Sultān," part 97, 36; and Firro, *A History of the Druzes*, 243-44. See, also, the article by Engin Akarli, "Some Ottoman Documents on Jordan: Ottoman Criteria for the Choice of an Administrative Center in the Light of Documents on Hauran, 1909-1910," Publications of the University of Jordan (Amman, 1989). I thank Professor Akarli for kindly giving me a copy of this arti-

cle. Fandi Abu Fakhr owns a copy of the death warrant for Dhuqan al-Atrash and some other *shaykhs*, signed by the grand vizier, which is reproduced in his *Tārīkh liwā' Ḥawrān al-ijtimā'ī: Al-Suwaydā'- Dar'ā- al-Qunaytra- 'Ajlūn, 1840-1918,* document 13, 344.

[12] Abi Rashid, *Jabal al-Durūz*, 125, 133.

[13] Niqulaws al-Qadi, *Arb'ūn 'āman fī Ḥawrān wa Jabal al-Durūz* (Beirut, 1927), 46-47. Qadi, then Greek Catholic archbishop of the Hawran, claimed partial responsibility for convincing Sami Basha to spare Yahya's life. I thank Professor Abdul-Rahim Abu-Husayn for sharing this source. See, also, Hasan Amin al-Bu'ayni, *Jabal al-'Arab safahāt min tārikh al-Muwaḥḥidīn al-Durūz (1685-1927)* (Beirut, 1985), 245.

[14] Kayali, *Arabs and Young Turks*, 187.

[15] Bu'ayni, *Jabal al-'Arab*, 250-51.

[16] Ibid., 251. See Jurj al-Faris, *Man huwa fī Sūriyya, 1949* (Damascus, 1950), 32. According to this biographical dictionary, Sultan received the second- and third-degree Majidi medals and the title of *bāshā* in 1917. In the following year, Sharif al-Husayn ibn 'Ali offered him the title of *amīr*, which he refused. He never accepted employment or payment from any government in later years and he never used the title *bāshā*, though others referred to him by it.

[17] Bu'ayni, *Jabal al-'Arab*, 251.

[18] Al-Atrash, "Mudhakkirāt Sultān," part 98, 36.

[19] See Kamal Salibi's contribution to this volume for a rare contemporary record of such a visit and of the conversations between Rustum Haydar and Sultan al-Atrash.

[20] Abi Rashid, *Jabal al-Durūz*, 126-27. Biographical information on Fawzi and Nasib al-Bakri appears in al-Faris, *Man huwa fī Sūriyya*, 67-68. See, also, Linda Schilcher, *Families in Politics: Damascene Factions and Estates of the Eighteenth and Nineteenth Centuries* (Stuttgart, 1985), 156.

[21] George Antonius, *The Arab Awakening* (reprinted Beirut, 1969), 149-53; and James Gelvin, *Divided Loyalties: Nationalism and Mass Politics at the Close of Empire* (Berkeley, 1998), 57-58.

[22] Muhammad Sa'id al-Qasimi, *Qāmus al-ṣinā'āt al-Shāmiyya* (reprinted Damascus, 1988), 55. Grain dealers were called *ba'ika*, plural *buwayki*, in Damascus. On grain merchants in Jabal Hawran, see al-Atrash, "Mudhakkirat Sultan," part 98, 25. The importance of these relationships did not end with the Great War or even the Revolt of 1925. Sultan al-Atrash's son, Mansur al-Atrash, married the daughter of his father's Christian Maydani grain merchant. The merchant, Yusuf Shuwayri, had a house in their village. Yusuf 'Aflaq, grain merchant and father of Ba'th party co-founder, Michel 'Aflaq, also had a house in the village of al-Qraya. Salah al-Din al-Bitar, the other founder of the party, was

also the son of a Maydani grain merchant who dealt with Jabal Hawran. See Hanna Batatu, *Syria's Peasantry, the Descendants of Its Lesser Rural Notables, and Their Politics* (Princeton, 1999), 134 and 142. Mansur al-Atrash joined the Baʿth while a student at the American University of Beirut and followed the party's leaders to pursue advanced studies in Paris. He was minister of education in the first Baʿthist government in 1963.

[23] On the *seferberlik,* see Linda Schilcher, "The Famine of 1915-1918 in Greater Syria," in *Problems of the Middle East in Historical Perspective, Essays in Honour of Albert Hourani,* edited by J. P. Spagnola (Oxford, 1992), 229-58. See also, Najwa al-Qattan, "Safarbarlik: Ottoman Syria and the Great War," in *From the Syrian Lands to the States of Syria and Lebanon,* edited by Thomas Philipp and Christoph Schumann (Beirut, 2004), 163-73.

[24] In what might be considered a typical complaint of a front-line officer, Liman von Sanders, commander-in-chief of Turkish forces on the Arab front, wrote in his memoirs that Istanbul seemed not only uninterested in reinforcing his troops, but actively sought to divert men and equipment to other fronts. The unmistakable implication is that Enver, at least, sought to strengthen the more 'Turkish' regions. See Liman von Sanders, *Five Years in Turkey* (Baltimore, 1928), 254 (for officer re-postings), 257-59 (for re-supply problems) and 265 (for British propaganda). See Kayali's *Arabs and Young Turks,* for a more nuanced view of Ottoman wartime policy.

[25] Schilcher, "The Famine of 1915-1918 in Greater Syria," 246.

[26] See al-Atrash, "Mudhakkirāt Sultān," part 98, 35; and von Sanders, *Five Years in Turkey,* 262. The latter reproduces an intelligence report dated 19 August 1918, from a Dr. Brode: "For about two months an organized caravan traffic has existed from Akaba across the Huarun, [*sic*] the Druse mountains. Sugar, coffee, and cotton goods are imported, and apricot paste is exported, together with great quantities of grain from the Hauran." Elsewhere (236), von Sanders writes, "Had the money been available, all requirements of the Army Group, and large additional supplies, could have been purchased from the Arabs. As the money was not forthcoming, a large part of the harvest of the Arabian grain lands and thousands of camel loads from Hauran, inhabited by Druses, went to the British, who paid in gold."

[27] The autonomy agreement is controversial. Abi Rashid reproduced it in his *Jabal al-Durūz,* 128-29, but Sultan al-Atrash disavowed it in his memoirs. See, also, Firro, *A History of the Druzes,* 250-51.

[28] Al-Atrash, "Mudhakkirāt Sultān," part 98, 36.

[29] Gelvin's *Divided Loyalties* covers this period in detail.

[30] Abi Rashid, *Jabal al-Durūz,* 122-25.

LESLIE MCLOUGHLIN

Fuad Hamza as an Observer of the Kingdom of Saudi Arabia

THE AIM OF THIS PAPER is to recall attention to Fuad Hamza, a man who has been curiously neglected despite the importance of his work. For a quarter of a century, he was a prominent figure in the service of King ʿAbdul ʿAziz ('Ibn Saud') of Saudi Arabia and, for most of this time, he was active in international affairs.

Fuad Hamza has, at any rate, the distinction of having left his name on maps of the Middle East. Anyone studying the history of Saudi Arabia must take note of the process to define the country's frontiers. Ibn Saud negotiated for many years with the British over the thorny question of the country's eastern border—negotiations that had, of course, much to do with the likely presence of oil. It was Fuad Hamza who was entrusted by Ibn Saud with working out the details during this long drawn-out process. As a result, one of the lines on the map indicating the Saudi position in negotiations is called, to this day, the Fuad Line, much as a line in the Polish-German frontier settlement of 1919 was known as the Curzon Line.

In order to understand the significance of Fuad Hamza's work and the positions that he took, it is important to note the chronology.

Hamza was born in the predominantly Druze village of ʿAbey in Lebanon in 1899. He was 15 years old when World War I broke out and 17 years old when the Ottomans hanged certain Lebanese and Syrian patriots in Beirut and Damascus—the 'martyrs' who, in Beirut, gave their name to the very busy traffic junction of the old city, the Place des Canons, also known as Martyr's Square. At the time, Hamza was a student at the American University of Beirut and this exercise of Ottoman power proved to be a turning point in his development as an Arab nationalist. When the mandatory system was imposed after World War I, he spent 10 years as its active opponent and as an energetic advocate of the independence and freedom of the Arab world. During this time, he worked in Lebanon, Syria and Palestine, in the educational field mostly, while acquiring some legal knowledge as well. His energy and diligence in pursuing his profession gained him favourable notice from the authorities, as did his knowledge of English which, while not perfect, was well above the average.

The authorities in Syria were less enamoured, however, of his activities on behalf of the Independence (*Istiqlāl*) Party, which is why he judged it wise to leave for Palestine. Even there, however, he was not safe and, in 1926, he fled just as the British were about to implement an arrest warrant issued by the French authorities in Syria. At the time, the French were in the process of suppressing the Druze revolt of Sultan Atrash Pasha, which had begun in 1925.

Fuad Hamza joined the service of Ibn Saud in 1926, that is, at the age of 27. From that time onward, he was unwavering in his support for Arab causes. Like many young Arabs from Egypt, the Levant and Mesopotamia who worked for Ibn Saud in the 1920s and 1930s, he regarded the future founder of the Kingdom of Saudi Arabia as a symbol of resistance to foreign imperialism. He accepted the official Saudi view that the territories which would later make up the kingdom had never been subject to foreign rule. For him, as for them, Ibn Saud was to be cherished as a symbol of what the Arabs might achieve if only they had freedom and independence. For the next 25 years, Hamza's Arab nationalist motivation was the constant in the various roles that he played. Regrettably, this was not understood by the many foreign representatives with whom he dealt for a quarter of a century, especially the British. One of the themes noticeable in the British documents that mention him throughout this long period is the tendency to underestimate him and, at times, to make fun of him.

Fuad Hamza was initially employed by Ibn Saud as a translator and interpreter. By 1932, he was accompanying Prince Feisal bin ʿAbdul ʿAziz, the nominal foreign minister, to London and the Soviet Union. By 1940, he was ambassador to France until, fleeing the German occupation, he was transferred to Turkey, where he served as ambassador until shortly after the end of World War II.

In post-war Saudi Arabia, Hamza was the minister responsible for development at the moment when oil revenues were poised to change the country in a fundamental way. He was also a close adviser to Ibn Saud concerning the growing difficulties with Britain over the eastern frontier, particularly in relation to Buraimi. At the height of the first phase of the Buraimi crisis, he fell victim to the bad health from which he had suffered since about 1930 and returned to Lebanon to recover. There he succumbed to a heart attack and died.

The remainder of this paper will look at his work decade by decade.

The 1920s: The Kingdom of the Hejaz

Fuad Hamza arrived in Jeddah shortly after the expulsion of the Hashemites and the proclamation, on 8 January 1926, of the new Kingdom of the Hejaz. Even at this early stage in his relations with the British, the tendency to underrate him is clearly apparent. A potted biography by Robin Bidwell in his *Dictionary of Modern Arab History* (London, 1998) says that he came to the Hejaz to give English lessons to the sons of Indian merchants (174), while one of the earliest official documents in which he is mentioned describes him as "an out-of-work schoolmaster, who arrived. . . two years ago. . . to devil for his countryman, Yusuf Yassin." In actual fact, he had been recruited from Cairo specifically to serve as an interpreter for Ibn Saud. Moreover, the reference to "his countryman" indicates yet another failing of the official record. At various points, he is described as a Syrian or Palestinian and it is only much later, when he takes a wife from Lebanon, that the record becomes more accurate.

At this point in time, what was later to become the Kingdom of Saudi Arabia was a kind of dual monarchy. Ibn Saud was king of the Hejaz and, at the same time, sultan of Nejd (and its appendages), but he was a ruler with very limited resources, which would soon be further reduced by the world economic slump, and very serious internal problems. Before the end of the decade, he would be involved in a rebellion by elements of the tribes which had furnished his assault troops. These 'Ikhwan' had won new territories for Ibn Saud and bitterly resented the fact that they had not been given key posts in return, such as the governorship of Medina or Mecca. Fuad Hamza was a privileged and responsible observer of all of this.

From an early date, Hamza's qualities had been recognized by Ibn Saud, who utilized the skills that the younger man had acquired in Lebanon, Syria and Palestine, his superior education and his knowledge of English and made him into something between acting foreign minister and head of the primitive administration which then existed in the Hejaz. Hamza was so energetic in the latter role that the Jeddah legation was reporting to London by mid-1929 that he "appears to have collected in his own hands the reins of government." Such was his zeal in attending to the minutiae of his task, even when it came to issuing bicycle licences, that the British commented that his supervision of the project "satisfies Fuad Hamza's lust for administration." However, it is his activities in foreign affairs that are of greater concern to us here.

Although the Saudi ministry of foreign affairs (MFA) was nominally in the hands of Prince Feisal, who had visited Britain and France at the age of 14 and knew something about Europe, in practice, all was left to Fuad Hamza, since the greater part of foreign relations involved dealings with the British. As the Jeddah legation reported: "As Faisal now takes no step without consulting Fuad the latter is virtual ruler of the Hejaz in the absence of the King... . [Fuad] now has a well-appointed Foreign Office in Jedda, where he is able to receive foreign representatives rather than himself visit them."

A review of the official British record for 1929 reveals that Fuad Hamza was a key figure in various matters with MFA content.

At the end of 1928, he and Yusuf Yassin manoeuvred to have the young Iraqi, ʿAbdullah Damlugi, tender his resignation as minister of foreign affairs once he had served as Ibn Saud's principal instrument in negotiations that led to British recognition of the kingdom in the treaties of 1925 and 1927.

In early 1929, Hamza was a close adviser to Ibn Saud on the delicate matter of frontier disputes between Iraq and Nejd, which naturally involved Britain in the role of Iraq's protector. Hamza also negotiated with the British to ensure that a Royal Navy ship did not visit Jeddah while Saudi troops were deploying in the eastern regions; he made this request so that no one would get the impression that the British were making a show of force to deter Ibn Saud from invading Iraq. Similarly, he worked with Britain to obtain sea transport for 1000 fighting men being sent to al-Hasa province. Hamza was also the key figure in negotiations with Transjordan aimed at ending cross-border incursions in both directions.

Most important of all, through the British legation, he kept Britain as closely informed as possible about the complexities of the military situation between Ibn Saud and the Ikhwan rebels, recognizing that the success of the rebellion might lead to the collapse of Ibn Saud's regime. By the end of 1929, he was instructed to ask the British to attack the main rebel leader, Feisal bin Duwish, in Kuwait, where he had taken refuge.

We may also take note of one aspect of Fuad Hamza's activities which further demonstrates the trust placed in him by Ibn Saud. As is well known, Ibn Saud had a keen appreciation, from an early date, of the power of modern technology as an instrument of government. By 1929, it was clear to him that he needed air power to control his vast domains and he assigned the task of developing an air force to Hamza. Hamza began this undertaking by founding, to the vast amusement of the British in Jeddah, the Arab Aeronautical Society in 1930.

The 1930s: The emerging Kingdom of Saudi Arabia

The first half of the decade

The story of the lands ruled by Ibn Saud in the 1930s is one of very serious threats to the survival of the regime. Indeed, as early as 1925, D. G. Hogarth had observed that "nothing would surprise him less than to find, within five years or so, the Wahhabis deposed from the Hejaz and the Sharifian family again in authority there."

Relations with the Sharifians, that is, the sons of the former king of the Hejaz, Hussein bin ʿAli, represented only one of the kingdom's existential problems, but an important one. As a result of the suppressed hostility between the two groups, there were seemingly interminable clashes across the borders with Transjordan and Iraq. In 1932, an armed uprising that occurred in the area north of Jeddah was alleged to have been fomented by Emir ʿAbdullah of Transjordan.

The decade began, however, with the resolution of what was probably the most serious internal conflict in the regime's history, the one between Ibn Saud and dissident elements of some of the Ikhwan tribes. Put very briefly, dissident elements of the Mutair, Ajman and Otaiba tribes were suppressed through Ibn Saud's application of superior technology, namely, armoured vehicles and machine guns, and modern communications for command and control. Ibn Saud also made use of his relationships with the British and Kuwaitis to force the Mutair leader, Feisal bin Duwish, into an impasse, from which the only escape was surrender on the Kuwaiti border.

The British next arranged what was supposed to be a reconciliatory meeting between Ibn Saud and the king of Iraq, Feisal bin Hussein, aboard the HMS Lupin, which was off of Kuwait. In view of the long hostility between the Saudis and the Hashemites (on which Kim Philby, the son of St. John Philby, was to wax eloquent as *Observer* correspondent as late as 1963), this did no more than paper over the cracks. It was a start, however, to the gradual ending of clashes on the border with Iraq. This eventually led, in turn, to the signing of a treaty between Saudi Arabia and Iraq.

When the related problems of tribesmen and borders had ceased to threaten his regime, Ibn Saud was faced with the monumental challenge presented by the collapse of his few sources of revenue. By 1931, the world economic recession, which began with the Wall Street collapse of October 1929, had ruined the pilgrim trade to Mecca and Medina. According to St. John Philby, Ibn Saud said to him on one occasion that same year, "If anyone would offer me a million pounds now he would be welcome to all the concessions in my country."

The impact of the loss of revenue was so severe that Ibn Saud's finance manager—it would be an exaggeration to call him minister of finance—was forced to take refuge in increasingly ignominious expedients. On one occasion in 1931, ʿAbdullah Suleiman gave instructions for raids on the vehicle storage depots for all companies in Jeddah and the removal of petrol stocks to fuel the royal cars. The following year, the desperate need for funds led Ibn Saud to dispatch his son and foreign minister, Feisal, on a mission to Europe and the Soviet Union to raise loans, with Fuad Hamza as his counsellor.

The trip abroad must have seemed an enormous relief to Hamza since the British record shows that he was in despair, by October 1931, over the future of the country. His anguish can only have been increased by the failure of his attempts (in conjunction with Philby) to persuade Ibn Saud to undertake the reform of administrative institutions.

Feuding with the Hashemites, internal dissension and lack of funds were not the only problems facing Ibn Saud at the beginning of the 1930s. Since the end of World War I, there had been areas of conflict on the southern borders with the territories of the *imām* of Yemen. Asir had been assimilated in a brief campaign led by Prince Feisal in 1923, but conflict continued over the southern coastal areas, Najran and the highlands. Matters were resolved for the short term by a brief war in April-May 1934, which ended with a treaty in which both parties swore "perpetual peace and firm and everlasting Muslim Arab brotherhood." Almost exactly one year later, Ibn Saud survived an assassination attempt by three former Yemeni soldiers while he was performing the Hajj ritual of circumambulating the Kaaba at Mecca.

Let us pause here, half-way through the decade, in order to evaluate the role of Fuad Hamza in all that had occurred up to this point.

British records make clear that it was Hamza who was the main link with Britain (the effective protecting Power) over cross-border clashes with Transjordan and Iraq before some kind of resolution was achieved. In the former case, incessant negotiations with the British representative in Jeddah, Andrew Ryan, led to a treaty between Transjordan and Saudi Arabia that was signed on 27 July 1933. When Hamza left for Cairo for the final meeting concerning the treaty's terms, he was seen off, in a very fulsome gesture, by Ryan.

However, their relationship was not always a smooth one. A year earlier, Hamza had been a principal actor in a drama which had almost led to Ryan's expulsion from Jeddah. The near *casus belli* involved a slave seeking manumission from the British legation, a question which directly involved the king as the slave in question was said to be one of his. Ryan hardly helped his position by arranging for the slave to be smuggled onto a ship calling at Jeddah, the same ship upon which he himself was planning to depart. Fuad Hamza eventually arranged a settlement whereby an apology was made by Ryan.

The treaty of Bon Voisinage, arranged following the meeting on the HMS Lupin between King Feisal of Iraq and Ibn Saud, was an important milestone in ensuring the stability of the latter's territories. It was co-signed by Fuad Hamza and another expatriate in the service of Ibn Saud, the Egyptian, Hafez Wahba.

Hamza also played an important role in resolving the conflict with dissident elements of the Ikhwan. Throughout 1929 and until the final denouement in 1930, it was he who kept the British legation informed of the moves being made to deal with the problem, from meetings with the Ikhwan, to personal negotiations with Ibn Saud and, finally, to armed conflict.

In relation to the financial crisis, Hamza carried out three important tasks: he stayed in close contact with the British legation to keep Britain informed; he emphasized to Ibn Saud the need for proper administrative and financial management; and, most importantly, he accompanied Prince Feisal to Europe and the Soviet Union in search of relief for the kingdom's pressing financial problems.

Hamza and Feisal's 1932 visit to Italy, France, Britain and the Soviet Union is the clearest indication of the trust placed in Hamza by Ibn Saud and the king's appreciation for his contributions. This contrasts strangely with the British judgement, made in a 1932 report from Jeddah, that he was "more subtle than intelligent."

By this time, Hamza was coping with considerable responsibility while troubled by severe illness. As early as 1930, he had been unable to continue his work because of heart and liver problems and eventually, in January 1931, he had to be sent to Egypt for treatment and convalescence. For the first time, Yusuf Yassin took over from him at the MFA, in an arrangement that would be repeated many times later in the decade.

When returning from his overseas trip with Prince Feisal, Hamza travelled overland from Kuwait. During this journey, he was able to view the military preparations for the final skirmish to put an end to the Bin Rifada revolt in the Hejaz in July 1932.

Henceforth, Hamza would be heavily preoccupied with the next major crisis—relations with Yemen. Commencing in early 1933, he was in constant contact with the British legation and informed them of new developments, for instance, the flight of the Idrisi to Yemen following an uprising against Ibn Saud. This sort of information was important since the (British) Protectorates, Eastern and Western, bordered the *imām*'s domains just as much as Ibn Saud's kingdom did. (At one stage, the Jeddah legation reported to London that "relations between His Majesty's Minister [ambassador] and the Saudi Government, i.e. Fuad Bey Hamza, were sweeter than sugar throughout the month.")

Tension was clearly growing between Ibn Saud and the *imām* to the extent that an official Saudi delegation was finally taken hostage. This was no trifling matter since one of the hostages was Khalid Gargani, the Libyan nationalist, who had joined Ibn Saud's service. (He was to be a key figure in negotiations with Nazi Germany in 1939.)

Fuad Hamza was so closely concerned with the Yemen crisis that, taking a break from his liaison work in Jeddah (he was now routinely at the MFA each Saturday to receive visitors), he personally visited the Abha region in January 1934. In mid-April of the same year, he returned to Jeddah, where he at once assumed control over the MFA, which had been left in the hands of Yusuf Yassin. Military operations under Princes Feisal and Saud were soon over and the peace treaty with Yemen was signed on 25 May 1934.

Hamza, Philby and books

Philby arrived in the Hejaz in 1926 as H. St. John Badger Philby, but came to be called ʿAbdullah after his conversion to Islam in 1930. His arrival in the kingdom coincided almost exactly with Fuad Hamza's, although he stayed past the time of the latter's death. The two men also had a similar gap in their residence in the kingdom during World War II: Philby was in jail in Britain (obtaining his release in 1943), while Hamza was *en poste* in Paris and Ankara from late 1939 to 1946.

The two men often came into contact, since Philby attended the *majlis* of Ibn Saud in Riyadh. Moreover, owing to the close *ex-officio* contact that Hamza had with the British legation, he could not help but be aware of the many irons that Philby had in the fire—if not bees in his bonnet. Philby's major preoccupation, according to one British ambassador, Bullard, was ensuring that Britain was always found on the side of the forces of darkness. Such comments could only interest Hamza since Philby was continually involved in a number of endeavours that affected the future of Saudi Arabia. Since the focus here is upon Fuad Hamza and not Philby, I will list them only briefly, even though the story of Philby's relationship with Ibn Saud and other Saudis is quite engrossing.

1 Philby was the first non-Arab to make the east/west crossing of the Empty Quarter (at the turn of 1931-32), a feat noted in the first of Fuad Hamza's books (see below).
2 Philby was a paid adviser to the Standard Oil Company of California (CASOC) and helped it to obtain, in 1933, an oil concession that began producing oil in commercial quantities in 1938.
3 Philby served Ibn Saud well by surveying large areas of his country, especially in Asir and Najran, between 1936 and 1937.
4 Philby produced a major crisis between Ibn Saud and the British by his disingenuousness in making his way to Mukalla in July 1937 with an armed Saudi escort. This led the British to adopt a more forward policy and to move their border with Yemen further to the north.
5 Philby created a major embarrassment for Ibn Saud in 1939 by appointing himself as an intermediary between Zionists and Arabs over the Palestine question. As a consequence, Ibn Saud was obliged to put out a disclaimer through the official Saudi gazette to the effect that Philby was not authorized to speak on behalf of the Saudi government.

All of these matters and much else besides in Philby's conduct and history were of official concern to Hamza. It is worth noting, however, that for Hamza, as for many other people, the real truth about Philby and his motivation remained a mystery. He said to him on one occasion that the only possible explanation most Saudis could find for his presence in the country was that he worked for the British Secret Service.

Philby, of course, was the most prolific chronicler of and commentator on Ibn Saud's reign in English; because he did not have regular employment, he had considerable leisure time to explore, study and write. Hamza expressed admiration for Philby's feat in crossing the Empty Quarter, but had no time for similar endeavours or for all of the reading and writing that he might have wished to do. But the fact that he managed to produce three books in Arabic on Ibn Saud's domains is of significance in evaluating his role as an observer of the monarch's life and times.

In chronological order, Hamza's three books are: *In the Heart of the Arabian Peninsula* (1933; index; no maps or illus.); *Saudi Arabia* (1936; no index, but detailed chapter and section headings; no maps or illus.); *In Asir Country* (1951; no index, but subject headings; maps drawn by the author). Although written in the last year of his life, the Asir book is centred on the time he spent in Abha just before the Saudi-Yemen war of 1934.

These books are of considerable value for the researcher since they are, by and large, contemporary records by a participant observer in the development of Saudi Arabia. Moreover, all of them contain essential topographical and physical information about areas rarely covered in scholarly Arabic works of the 1930s. Finally, Fuad Hamza had the curiosity about people that one might expect of a very intelligent Lebanese accustomed to the anthropological variety of Lebanon, Syria and Palestine. Hence, some of his most charming prose is on Saudi Arabians of African origin, the Ismaʿilis of Najran, the Shiʿa and so on. Being a practiced linguist, he also displays a passionate interest in the dialectal curiosities of Saudi speech, as well as Arabic poetry, both classical and popular.

There is another literary curiosity from the 1930s relevant to the relationship between Hamza and Ibn Saud, namely, the latter's English-language biography by H. C. Armstrong. Armstrong visited Saudi Arabia in 1933 and had numerous interviews with Ibn Saud, with Hamza acting as interpreter. Hamza also worked with Armstrong on the text and the book eventually saw the light in 1934 as *Ibn Saud, Lord of Arabia.*

The second half of the decade

The latter half of the 1930s saw a continuation of earlier themes in the relationship between Fuad Hamza and Ibn Saud, with two significant differences. The first is that the kingdom had finally emerged from a delicate period during which its very survival had been in question—a period marked by Hamza's intimate involvement in the country's fate. Possibly the best indication of the fact that Ibn Saud felt more secure was his decision to move, in 1935, from the fortress in Riyadh which he had occupied since 1902, into a new palace that he largely designed himself, the Murabba, located in what were then the city's suburbs.

The second significant difference is that Hamza became much more active on the international scene. This occurred partly because of the change in the kingdom's circumstances after CASOC had begun to develop Saudi oilfields and partly because Saudi Arabia's strategic location naturally involved the country in international power politics.

In the previous section, I noted some of Fuad Hamza's activities in the field of foreign affairs, many of which may be loosely described as 'fire-fighting,' such as the border conflicts with Yemen, Iraq and Transjordan. However, he also played significant roles in other aspects of Saudi foreign relations, some of which were to continue to preoccupy him up to 1940. For instance, during the years 1933-35, he was involved in the following: working with Britain, Italy and Egypt in order to acquire aircraft and train Saudi personnel to build a Saudi air force; multilateral discussions on the future of the Hejaz Railway; cultivating relations with Italy, especially after the treaty to end the Yemen war was signed; and furthering relations with the Arab sheikhdoms in the Gulf (in 1935, he indicated clearly to Ryan that Arab independence must include these territories as well). In the latter half of the decade, two new subjects would take up increasing amounts of his time, namely, oil and the Palestine question.

Hamza took the keenest interest in the negotiations that led to the granting of the oil concession to the Americans in 1933 and was bitter about Philby's role in persuading the king to accept their offer. Once the deal was done, however, he turned his attention to handling its ramifications. He worked with Lebanese entrepreneurs seeking other oil concessions and, more importantly, closely monitored the development of the eastern oil regions. He was to pay many visits to al-Hasa, on one famous occasion accompanying the British ambassador from Riyadh when their vehicle broke down far from civilization.

Curiously, Fuad Hamza was not in Saudi Arabia in March 1938, when Well Dammam No. 7 became operational, a turning point in the country's history. He had left just before for a very extended leave and convalescence, hoping to find relief from his chronic health problems. As a result, he was out of the country until December of 1938.

It was the Palestine issue that brought him back to active diplomacy. In March 1939, he attended the Round Table Conference on the Palestine question in London, where he acted as counsellor to Prince Feisal. The conference was potentially of crucial importance, hence, it received much press coverage; indeed, Hamza's photograph may be found in the London *Times* of that period. One short-term result of the conference was the British government's realization that attempts to limit Jewish immigration to Palestine would have a positive effect on its relations with Arab countries.

At this point, Philby returns to the story, for he had convinced himself that behind-the-scenes negotiations between Saudi and Zionist representatives, managed by himself, could produce a satisfactory solution. He therefore arranged with Namier and Chaim Weizmann to hold a meeting at his London home in 1939, with Fuad Hamza present. No second meeting was held, however, and the rejection of Philby's ideas may have been Fuad Hamza's greatest act in the service of Ibn Saud. The subject continued to be raised during the war years, when neither Philby nor Hamza was in Saudi Arabia, but Ibn Saud expressed the greatest indignation when the Americans proposed, in formal talks, a deal similar to the one discussed by Philby and the Zionists in London, whereby Ibn Saud would receive a large payment for welcoming Palestinians displaced by Jewish immigrants.

Following the London conference, Fuad Hamza returned to Saudi

Arabia by way of Cairo, Beirut and Damascus, where he discussed many matters relevant to Arab nationalists.

The British had long been suspicious that Ibn Saud was giving secret support to the Palestinians by arranging for weapons to be smuggled to them during the Intifada of 1936-39. Fuad Hamza was aware of the famous occasion in 1938 when the British ambassador, Bullard, had travelled to see Ibn Saud in Riyadh in order to hear the first transmission of the BBC's Arabic Service. It was a memorable occasion for the first news item concerned the hanging of a Palestinian by the British: Ibn Saud wept as he recalled the incident.

Egypt was suspected as a source of smuggled arms, for the country was not, as yet, independent, with British troops still in Cairo itself. One consequence of the close relations between Egypt and Saudi Arabia was that they would work together during the final years of the war to establish the Arab League.

During Hamza's visits to Lebanon and Syria there was much agitation against France, the mandatory power. This period saw the arrest of many nationalist leaders who would later become famous, such as the future Lebanese ambassador and distinguished novelist, Tawfiq Yusuf ʿAwwad. The French were greatly resented at the time for their willingness to cede the province of Alexandretta to Turkey, which they did in June of 1939.

As a senior Saudi representative, Fuad Hamza had access to people in high places and, during his stay in Syria, he had discussions with the French high commissioner. It is indicative of the way in which those involved in international politics at that time indulged in lateral thinking that the high commissioner asked Hamza for his views on an idea then current—that a son of Ibn Saud might become king of Syria.

It was June 1939 when Fuad Hamza returned to Riyadh, just three months before the outbreak of World War II. During the two increasingly tense years before the war, Saudi Arabia had studied all options, which explains the meeting of Khalid Gargani, representing Ibn Saud, with Hitler in June 1939. This meeting was the climax of a period of intense contacts with Nazi Germany, during which arms exports to Saudi Arabia were discussed. Since a final German condition was a guarantee that Saudi Arabia would remain neutral, the deal in question, involving the construction of a German arms factory in Riyadh, was not consummated. Fuad Hamza had brought Bullard, the British ambassador, the text of the draft agreement.

By September 1939, it had been decided to open a Saudi legation in Paris and it was Fuad Hamza who was appointed to be the first ambassador. Bullard reported, somewhat unkindly, that he was in two minds about his new appointment: "divided between joy at his escape from Saudi Arabia... and terror at the prospect of being bombed in Paris."

However, the final British comment on Hamza in the 1930s was to note that, on his way to Paris, he made a notably pro-Allied speech in Istanbul.

Fuad Hamza presented his credentials to the French government on 4 November 1939 and remained in Paris during the phoney war, leaving only after the breakthrough in early May 1940 and the entry of German forces into the capital in June 1940.

The 1940s

After leaving Paris, Fuad Hamza remained in Vichy until 1943, when he was instructed to take up the post of Saudi ambassador to Turkey. He spent the remaining war years *en poste* in Ankara. Because the period 1940-45 fall outside of the strict terms of reference of this paper, namely, Fuad Hamza as an observer of developments in Saudi Arabia, they will be left out of this chronological account. It is known, however, that he paid a visit to Jeddah in 1944.

There may well be relevant material about Hamza in the archives of the Turkish, French, British and Saudi governments for the war years and the period up to the time of his return to Saudi Arabia. These may shed light on his diplomatic work in Turkey, a country that saw much intrigue: the arrival of the Ankara train in Aleppo was always eagerly awaited, not least by intelligence agents from France and various other foreign powers, not to mention Syria, which was striving to actualize its nominal and newly-obtained independence.

It is in connection with Syria that Fuad Hamza again emerges in British documents during the last days of the war. In its report for May 1945, the British legation in Jeddah made note of what it saw as nefarious activities by "Sheikh Fuad Hamza" in Damascus. According to the legation, he was having a wholly harmful influence on the Syrian president, Shukri Quwatli (the same man who had introduced him to Ibn Saud in 1926), raising with him the possibility that he might be removed from power and replaced by Emir ʿAbdullah of Transjordan. Curiously, the report says that the ambassador at Jeddah had been able "to obtain the return of Fuad Hamza from Syria, where he had been staying far too long, to his post as Saudi Minister [ambassador] at Angora [Ankara]."

When Fuad Hamza returned to Saudi Arabia in 1946, he found Ibn Saud at the very heart of international manoeuvrings over Palestine. Following Ibn Saud's meeting with American President Franklin D.

Roosevelt in early 1945, it had been assumed that the United States was committed to FDR's written pledge that he would consult with Arabs and Jews before taking a stand on the matter of Jewish immigration to Palestine. The president's death in April 1945 led the new president, Harry Truman, to abandon that position and, indeed, to call for unrestricted Jewish immigration, beginning with immediate approval for the migration of 100,000 European Jews to Palestine.

Until the time of the proclamation of the state of Israel on 15 May 1948, Fuad Hamza was heavily involved in Ibn Saud's attempts to moderate the United States' new total commitment to monumental demographic change in Palestine.

One major consequence of events in Palestine was a rapprochement of sorts between Ibn Saud and the Hashemites, which was intended to take account of all possible future developments. In 1948, when Ibn Saud received the Transjordanian king, ʿAbdullah, in Riyadh, the British legation in Jeddah gave Fuad Hamza credit for arranging the meeting and noted that it excluded Yusuf Yassin. However, the reconciliation was brief since Ibn Saud disapproved strongly of ʿAbdullah's move, in 1949, to annex part of Jerusalem and the West Bank in order to form a new entity, the Hashemite Kingdom of Jordan.

Thereafter, Hamza's major preoccupation was the sequel to pre-war talks with the British over the eastern borders of Saudi Arabia. From 1949 to 1951, he was the principal figure in the complex process of negotiations over matters connected to the borders with Qatar, Abu Dhabi and Oman. He did not, however, accompany the delegation that Prince Feisal bin ʿAbdul ʿAziz took to London for talks on border questions between 7-25 August 1951.

Eventually, disagreement between Saudi Arabia and Britain threatened to lead to armed conflict over the Buraimi oasis but, before this point was reached, Fuad Hamza was gone. In November 1951, he left Saudi Arabia for Lebanon, where he died of a heart attack on 21 November, ironically, the eve of that country's Independence Day.

Conclusion

Fuad Hamza has suffered undeserved neglect. He is mentioned only once, for instance, in a major Saudi study (in 862 pages) of the life of Ibn Saud by Sheikh ʿAbdul ʿAziz al-Tuwaijiri of the Saudi National Guard. Similarly, he has not been done justice by those British officials, such as Bullard and Ryan, who published their diplomatic memoirs: these contain only glancing references to the person who was almost their sole link to Ibn Saud over a long period of time and who was of pivotal importance for the conduct of Saudi-British relations. Contemporaneous official British reports on him take an equally disparaging view.

The writer of the Annual Report on Arabia for 1951 describes Fuad Hamza as one of the old guard of foreign advisers, "older, richer and even less liable to give the King any valuable advice than previously."

It is hoped that this brief paper will stimulate further research (in the archives of a number of countries) into the quarter of a century which Fuad Hamza spent in the service of Ibn Saud.

Eyad Abu Chakra

The Druze and Arabism

Arabism is an all-encompassing and vague term not easily delineated or defined. However, the notion of an Arab 'identity' has existed since that time in distant history when Arabia and its inhabitants, the 'Arabs,' were first recognized and described.

In this paper, 'identification' is my term of reference regarding 'Arabism' and the relationship(s) of the Druze to it. 'Arabism' is here considered as an aggregation of traits, facets and phenomena, not as a model for exclusivity or activism—particularly in relation to the relatively recent socio-political movement known as 'Arab nationalism.' No attempt is made here to endorse or refute any aspect of 'Arabism' wholesale. This paper is meant to be informative and investigative, rather than defensive, apologetic, or justificatory.

Ethnography provides one important approach to 'Arabism,' especially when it comes to self-identification and what may follow in terms of limited or qualified interaction on behalf of both claimants and subscribers. When we consider the criteria recognized by many anthropologists, such as John Gulick,[1] it is clear that 'Arabism' is central to the Druze ethnographic character. These criteria are geography, language, claimed ancestry or self-identity and common history.

The Levant: Abode of the Druze

Geography undoubtedly ties the Druze to Arabism. Both Druzism (*madhhab al-tawḥīd*) as a movement and the Druze as a community were born and have remained concentrated in the heart of what we today call the Arab world. The antecedents of the Fatimid *daʿwa* (or 'call') were in Arab North Africa—in Tunisia, to be precise; the Fatimid Caliphate was based in Egypt; and, even at present, the vast majority of Druze live in the Arab Levant, namely, Syria, Lebanon, Palestine/Israel and Jordan.[2] According to some, a few Druze also live in southern Turkey, across the present Syrian/Turkish border.[3]

In fact, historical sources suggest that the Druze inhabited the Levant since the beginning of the *dāʿwa* in the late tenth and early eleventh century AD. The *dāʿwa* found its warmest reception in the valleys and mountains of present-day Syria, Lebanon and Palestine, most of which were inhabited by Arab tribes well before the advent of Islam. The Tayyʾ, Kalb ibn Wabra, Tameem, Kilaab, Judham and Qidhaʿa tribes, as well as the Lakhm and Ghassan, all settled in geographical Syria and Iraq at an early date. The latter two, the Lakhm and Ghassan, both of which were of Yemeni origin, created pre-Islamic vassal states in southern Iraq and southern Syria respectively. Other sedentary tribal federations, most significantly, the Tanukh (whose name actually means settled or sedentary tribes or tribal groupings), spread out from Iraq into various parts of northern and western Syria.

Some of those whom Druze and non-Druze historians and chroniclers describe as 'Tanukh' were linked to the Lakhm, Qidhaʿa, or Bahraʾ tribes. It was the Tanukhs of Lakhm, however, who may have had the most significant association with the Druze. The two houses of Buhtur and Arslan were said to be descended from the Tanukhs of Lakhm; along with the house of Maʿn of Rabiʿa, these houses were the ones that provided the community with notables or commanders (*umarāʾ*) at various periods in early Druze history.[4]

The earliest Druze settlement centred upon Wadi al-Taym, which comprises the Rashayya and Hasbayya districts in today's Lebanon. Hence, together with Jabal al-Aʿla, the Acre plain and Damascus (with its environs), Wadi al-Taym is regarded as the Druze community's oldest centre,[5] the heartland from which al-Shuf, al-Gharb and al-Metn, as well as Iqlim al-Ballan (the Golan Heights), were later settled. Ultimately, the Shuf, Gharb and Metn (collectively making up the major part of Mount Lebanon) became the most important regional power base in the community's history.[6]

From Mount Lebanon, the Druze subsequently extended their presence southward to the regions of Iqlim al-Tuffah, Iqlim Jazzin and Iqlim al-Rihan.[7] South of Damascus and al-Ghuta (the fertile region surrounding the city that includes the town of Jaramana), the Druze settled the region of Wadi al-ʿAjam and established the villages of Sehnaya, al-Ashrafiyya and Deir ʿAli.[8]

Today, Druze villages are found as far north as Jabal al-Aʿla (Jabal al-Summaq), in the extreme north-western part of Syria, and in the plain lying south-east of this mountain, in the districts of Harem and Idlib in Idlib province,[9] and they exist as far south as al-Azraq oasis in Jordan.[10] The villages of Daliyat al-Carmel and Isfiya on Mount Carmel mark the westernmost limit of Druze habitation in the Middle East, while the villages in the eastern foothills of Jabal al-ʿArab (Jabal al-Druze), namely, al-Rushaydah, al-Sʿana and al-Shbekeh, represent the easternmost limit.[11]

The largest concentration of Druze, however, is found in the Syrian province of Suwayda (Jabal al-ʿArab or Jabal al-Druze), which was populated, since the late seventeenth and early eighteenth centuries, by waves of Druze immigrants[12] from northern Syria (making up the 'Halabiyya,' that is, the Aleppine clans), Mount Lebanon (the 'Shawafneh,' namely, those who hailed from the Shuf), Wadi al-Taym (the 'Rashaniyya,' related to Rashayya) and northern Palestine (the 'Safadiyya,' denoting the link with the district of Safad there). In addition, tens of thousands of Druze today live in the capital cities of Beirut, Damascus and Amman; many of them were born there, while the rest are migrants or seasonal residents.

The language

The Arabic language is a fundamental part of the Arab Druze identity. Arabic is not only the mother tongue of the Druze and the national language in the Middle Eastern political entities that they currently inhabit; it is also the language of the Druze epistles and of major religious chronicles and poems.[13]

Emir Shakib Arslan, famous in Arab literary circles as *amīr al-bayān* (the prince of speech), made particular mention of the pure Arabic spoken by the Druze and their uncorrupted pronunciation.[14] Many Druze cherish an unusual attestation to their Arabism in this respect: the Lebanese Christian man of letters, Maroun ʿAbboud, who lived for years among the Druze in the town of ʿAley. In a long poem about the Druze, 'Abboud says:

> What runs through their veins is pure Arab blood,
> the proof of this is their impeccable speech.

> يجري الدم العربي في أعراقهم
> صرفا صراحا والدليل المنطقُ [15]

Numerous Druze authors, poets and journalists, all writing in Arabic, have left an indelible mark on Arab cultural and literary life, whether in the Arab East or in Europe and the Americas. Many families, such as the Nasser Eddins of Kfar Matta, the Taqi Eddins of Baʿaqlin, the Arslans of

Shouweifat, the ʿUbayds of Suwayda and al-Qassems of al-Rameh in Galilee, have produced famous literary figures: Amin Nasser Eddin, Saʿid and Amin Taqi Eddin, Shakib Arslan,[16] ʿAli and Salameh ʿUbayd[17] and Samih al-Qasim.[18]

In the field of Arabic calligraphy, several Druze have attained renown in the Arab world, particularly, Nassib Makarem and Fahd and Bahij al-ʿAndary.[19] In the Americas, such Druze figures as Farid Abu-Muslih (Fred Massey) of the United States[20] and Najib al-ʿAsrawi of Brazil[21] were known both as men of letters and as brilliant translators of works from the Arab/Islamic heritage into English and Portuguese.

Claim of ancestry and self-identity

The vast majority of Druze clans claim descent from Arab tribes and entertain no other origin, although it would be difficult to confirm most of these genealogical assertions. Historical sources disagree greatly on the question of Druze descent. Richard Pococke, Henry Maundrell, G. W. Chassaud, Canon Joseph T. Parfitt, as well as the Lebanese American historian, Philip Hitti, all dismissed Druze claims to Arab descent.[22] Others, like Carsten Niebuhr and the anthropologists cited by Nejla Abu-Izzeddin, as well as most Druze historians and chroniclers, have maintained that their Arab descent is beyond doubt.

Abu-Izzeddin makes the argument that Arabs inhabited geographical Syria long before the Muslim conquest in the seventh century AD and that this Arab presence had, in fact, facilitated the conquest.[23] She also advances another argument, namely, that the Druze claim to Arab origin was not motivated by considerations of self-interest, for the Arabs were no longer in the ascendant when the Druze community was constituted during the first half of the eleventh century AD. Non-Arab dynasties, like the Ayyubids, Saljuks, Mamluks and, eventually, the Ottomans, were the dominant powers at that time and for centuries afterward.[24]

In an editorial that appeared in *Al-Shūra* newspaper, Emir Shakib Arslan contended, like almost all Druze historians, that the Druze are pure Arabs, going so far as to say: "No Arab outside of the Arabian peninsula is as close to Arab purity as the Druze." However, he did admit that a few families of notables are of Turkish and Kurdish origin, a fact known to every Druze. He also noted that historical records possessed by the Lebanese Druze and their neighbours suggest that the Druze of Mount Lebanon are descended from twelve Arab tribes that used to inhabit the Aleppo/Maʿrrat al-Nuʿman region in northern Syria before many of them migrated south during the ʿAbbasid period.[25]

A more recent researcher, Nadim Hamzeh, confirms that the Tanukh federation, from which the Tanukhs of Mount Lebanon are descended, was made up of Azd, Qidhaʿa and Lakhm sub-tribes, although he disputes the full account found in *Al-Sijill al-Arslānī* (the Arslan emirs' genealogical tree).[26] A related point deserving attention is the fact that, with the possible exception of the inhabitants of Palestine, where the Qaysi-Yemeni rivalry and its related alliances survived well into the twentieth century, it has been the Druze of Mount Lebanon who have been the most loyal to—or, rather, afflicted with—this traditional, pre-Islamic enmity.[27]

Traditionally, Druze and other Lebanese historians and chroniclers have made this Qaysi-Yemeni rivalry into a hallmark of Druze-dominated Mount Lebanon. The often-mentioned Battle of ʿAin Dara (AD 1710/1711), where it is said that a Qaysi grouping defeated a Yemeni leadership, has been portrayed as "the beginning of the end" for unchallenged Druze supremacy and the event that allowed the non-Druze Shehabis to become the powerbrokers and, eventually, the actual governors of Mount Lebanon.[28]

As for the more detailed Druze sources on the earliest settlements, the Druze religious epistles, as well as such works as al-Ashrafani's *ʿUmdat al-ʿārifīn*, mention several Arab clans or sub-clans, including al-ʿAbdullah in the Gharb and Shuf, al-Turab in northern Palestine and al-Sulayman in Wadi al-Taym, as being the first to accept the *dāʿwa*. Al-Ashrafani also mentions the "*mashāyikh* [pl. of *shaykh*] of al-Bustan" in greater Damascus and the "*mashāyikh* of Jabal al-Anwar [Jabal al-Aʿla, near Aleppo]" in relation to the beginnings of their respective communities.[29]

A brief political history

'Arab Nationalism' as we know it today was born in the second half of the nineteenth century. In explaining how the "Arab awakening" took place, George Antonius writes: "Patriotism in the national sense was unknown. All creeds and sects, had, it is true, much in common: language, customs, racial kinship; and, above all, hatred of the Turkish rule of which they all desired to be rid. But in their aspiration towards freedom they were moved by different impulses."[30]

According to Antonius, foreign missionaries, especially American Protestants and French Jesuits, played a crucial role in the drive toward Westernization and emancipation from Turkish rule. Arab Christian intellectuals like Nassif al-Yaziji and Butrus al-Bustani also assisted in this effort, which eventually gained momentum from younger nationalists educated at institutions of higher learning founded by missionaries, such as the Syrian Protestant College, which later became the American University of Beirut. No Druze joined the first two societies established to promote Western culture, namely the American-inspired Society of Arts and Science (1847) and the Jesuit-supported Oriental Society (1850). However, the situation began to change after the founding of the Syrian Scientific Society (*al-Jamʿiyya al-ʿilmiyya al-Sūriyya*) in 1857. In fact, Emir Muhammad Arslan, a prominent Druze intellectual, headed this society, which was independent of missionary influence, for several years.[31]

Emirs Amin and ʿAdel Arslan were later involved in the creation of the Qahtaniyya Society (Qahtan is eponymous forefather of the Yemeni Arabs, or al-Arab al-ʿAriba, meaning the original Arabs)[32] against the background of the growing Turkification of the Ottoman Empire.

Other Druze 'Arabists,' like Emir Shakib Arslan,[33] ʿAdel's brother, believed that the dividing line between upholding Arabism and maintaining support for the Islamic Caliphate, as embodied by the Ottoman sultan, was too thin to support. The dynamics of this issue were evidently being decided by overall regional and international political developments. After the end of World War I, to their grave disappointment, the nationalist or secular Arabists had to contend with the new and disappointing realities of the French and British mandates and, of course, the Balfour Declaration.

Druze Syrian Arab Unionists, like ʿAdel and Amin Arslan and Rashid and Saʿid Taliʿ (as opposed to Lebanese 'Kayanists,' from *kayān*, meaning 'entity,' who supported a Lebanon fully independent of Syria), were now in open confrontation with the French Mandatory authorities in Beirut, which finally passed death sentences on ʿAdel Arslan and Rashid Taliʿ.[34] The Great Syrian Revolt, started by Sultan al-Atrash, the Druze leader in Jabal al-ʿArab, ensured deeper Druze involvement in Arab causes.

In Syria and Lebanon, more Druze became involved in Arab and anti-Mandatory groupings, such as the Nadi al-Ahli (National Club) of 1929, whose leadership included Saʿid Taqi Eddin and Mohammad ʿAli Hamadeh; the *Hizb al-Istiqlal al-Jumhuri* (Republican Independence Party) of 1931, which counted among its leaders Emir Sami Arslan and Muhammad ʿAli Hamadeh; and the *Usbat al-ʿAmal al-Qawmi* (League of National Action), founded after the Qurnayel Congress in 1933 in the Druze Metn village of Qurnayel and led by ʿAli Nasser Eddin.[35] This last party expanded into Syria and became the largest political organization in Jabal al-ʿArab, one joined by thousands of young Druze men.[36]

The Druze Arabists were not, however, limited to Druze living in the Levant. In North America, under its secretary-general, ʿAbbas Abu Shakra, the Hizb Suriyya al-Jadida (New Syria Party) played a pivotal role in supporting the Great Syrian Revolt of the 1920s. Sultan al-Atrash corresponded with Abu Shakra regarding the party's continued assistance to the rebels.[37] The party, which was based in New York City, had around 50 branches in North America, primarily in the United States, and provided the revolt with almost half of its funds.[38]

In addition to his involvement with *Hizb Suriyya al-Jadida*, Abu Shakra was also active in the two oldest Arab nationalist newspapers in the United States: *Al-Bayān* (The manifesto) and *Nahdat al-ʿArab* (The Arab renaissance). *Al-Bayān* was founded in Detroit, Michigan, in 1910 by Sulayman Baddur, a Druze from the town of Baʿaqlin, who was helped by ʿAbbas Abu Shakra with the editing and publishing. *Nahdat al-ʿArab* was founded by the two Druze brothers, Amin and Saʿid Dawoud Fayyadh, in 1947.[39]

Still other Druze were active in Arab causes in various capacities throughout the Americas, including Salman Yusuf ʿAzzam and his son, Mahmud, in the United States; Emir Amin Arslan, the editor of *Al-Istiqlāl* (The independence) newspaper in Argentina; Muhammad Saʿid Massʿoud in Canada; and Najib al-ʿAsrawi in Brazil.[40]

The Baʿth Arab Socialist Party

After World War II and the establishment of the state of Israel, many Druze continued to identify with the two main causes of Arabism: Arab unity and the liberation of Palestine. In particular, two pan-Arab political parties attracted the Druze of Syria and Lebanon and provided them with powerful vehicles in the political arena; indeed, Druze played prominent roles in these parties and reached the highest positions in both of them: the Baʿth Arab Socialist Party in Syria and the Progressive Socialist Party in Lebanon.

After the Sixth National Congress of the Baʿth Arab Socialist Party, held in Damascus from 5-23 October 1963, a Syrian Druze, Hammoud al-Shufi, joined the enlarged 13-member National Command. The following year, after the Seventh Congress (12-18 February), two new Druze members, Mansur al-Atrash and Shibli al-ʿAysami, also joined the National Command reversing the then leftist trend—led by al-Shufi.

Al-Atrash and al-ʿAysami maintained their positions after the Eighth Congress of May 1965, less than one year before the major split between the Syrian Regional faction, which took political control of Syria, and the National Command, which did the same in Iraq.

Al-Shufi was also a member of the Provisional Regional Command (RC) in Syria after his appointment by the National Command in June 1962. In fact, al-Shufi became secretary of the First Regional Congress between 10 and 16 September 1963, when two more Druze, Mahmud Nawfal and

Hamad ʿUbayd, also joined the leadership. However, in an extraordinary session held 1-5 February 1964, the new Regional Command included three Druze members: al-ʿAysami (secretary of the RC), ʿUbayd and Jamil Shayya. ʿUbayd and Shayya maintained their position in the Second RC in 1965 before the RC was dissolved by the National Command. The provisional RC appointed later included al-Atrash and al-ʿAysami. Salim Hatum, another Druze Baʿthi officer, had joined the RC earlier that year (see Devlin). Both ʿUbayd and Hatum were members of the Military Committee, which brought the Baʿth party to power in 1963,[41] while Fahd al-Shaʿir, then one of the highest ranking officers—and also a Druze—was the leader of what was known as the Military Bureau.[42]

Kamal Junblat and the PSP

Kamal Junblat, a scion of one of the richest and most influential Druze families in Lebanon, was the founder of the Progressive Socialist Party.[43] Junblat had always felt that the Lebanese political system, which was based upon confessionalism, could not provide social justice, equal rights and secularism. But what began as a tentative liberal approach to politics in the late 1940s[44] metamorphosed into an idealist ideological quest during the 1950s.[45]

The 1958 Lebanese uprising, which was supported by a popular Arab Unionist/Nasserist groundswell against President Camille Chamoun and his pro-Western policies, guaranteed that Junblat would not only become the paramount Druze leader but would also attain a central position in the Lebanese political system as a 'kingmaker.'[46]

The 1950s saw a clearer pan-Arab flavour added to the PSP's principles and stances owing to the position of the Arab Near East as an arena for the rivalry between two superpowers, the United States and the Soviet Union, which manifested itself through the Eisenhower Doctrine and the Suez Crisis. Junblat became an admirer of the Egyptian president, Jamal ʿAbdel Nasser, whom he met for the first time near Cairo in 1955.[47] He also established political links with the Baʿth Party in Syria in 1954.[48] This development was not at all unlikely owing to the broadening cooperation between socialist, communist and Arab nationalist forces throughout the area and their alliance with Nasserist Egypt.

Indeed, this phenomenon was perhaps best exemplified in the creation of the Baʿth Arab Socialist Party itself by the merger of the former Arab Baʿth Party, very much a nationalist intellectual group, led by Michel ʿAflaq and Salah al-Bitar, and the Arab Socialist Party, a class-conscious and activist socialist grouping led by ʿAkram al-Hawrani.[49]

Judging by the results of general elections in the early 2000s, the PSP is still the strongest political entity in Lebanon's Druze areas to date. Most of the party's senior leadership and its deputies in the Lebanese parliament continue to be Druze.[50]

NOTES

[1] John Gulick, *The Middle East: An Anthropological Perspective* (Pacific Palisades: Goodyear Publishing Company, Inc., 1976), 36-37.

[2] Nejla Abu-Izzeddin, *The Druzes: A New Study of Their History, Faith, and Society* (Leiden: E. J. Brill, 1984), 1-4; ʿAbbas Abu-Salih and Sami Makarem, *Tārīkh al-Muwaḥḥidīn al-Durūz al-siyāsī fī al-Mashriq al-ʿArabī* (Beirut: Al-Majlis al-Durzi lil-buhuth wal-inmaʾ, 1980), 39-50; and Nadim Hamzeh, *Al-Tanūkhiyyūn* (Beirut: Dar al-nahar lil-nashr, 1984), 15.

[3] Kamal Junblat and Philippe Lapousterie, *I Speak for Lebanon*, trans. by Michael Pallis (London: Zed Press, 1982), 27; here Junblat claims that about 60,000 Druze lived in southern Turkey at the time of writing.

[4] Shakib Arslan, *Banū Maʿrūf, ahl al-ʿUrūba wal-Islām,* edited by Suʾud al-Mawla (Beirut: Dar al-awda/Al-Majlis al-Durzi lil-buhuth wal-inmaʾ, 1990), 34-35 and 71-73; see, also, Hamzeh, *Al-Tanūkhiyyūn,* 15-18; Abu-Salih and Makarem, *Tārīkh al-Muwaḥḥidīn al-Durūz*, 19-23; and Abu-Izzeddin, *The Druzes,* 6-10.

[5] Muhammad al-Ashrafani, *ʿUmdat al-ʿarifīn fī qisas al-nabiyyīn wal-umam al-sālifīn* (manuscript).

[6] Abu-Salih and Makarem, *Tārīkh al-Muwaḥḥidīn al-Durūz*, 133-138.

[7] Yusuf Abu-Shaqra, *Al-Harakāt fī Lubnān ilā ʿahd al-Mutaṣarrifiyya* (Beirut: Matbaʿat al-ittihad, 1952), 151-59.

[8] Hafiz Abu-Muslih, *Waqiʿ al-Durūz,* 2d ed. (Beirut: Al-Maktaba al-haditha lil-tibaʿa wal-nashr, n.d.), 244.

[9] The villages of Jabal al-Aʿla and the neighbouring plain are: Bnabel, Qalb Lozeh, Tal Titha, Kfar Kila, Bshindalaya, Kukku, Hilleh, Ibraita, Illatha, Jedʿin, Kfar Mares, Tall al-Doweir, Arshin, Kfar Binneh, Keftin, Biret Keftin and Martahwan (also known as Maʿarrit al-Ikhwān). See, also, Kamil ibn Hussein al-Bali al-Halabi al-Ghazzi, *Nahr al-dhahab fī tārīkh Ḥalab* (Aleppo: Matbaʿat al-Maruniyya, 1962), 214-16; Ahmad Wasfi Zakariyya, *Jawla athariyya fil-Bilād al-Shāmiyya* (Damascus: n.p., n.d.); Yusuf Saleem al-Dubaysi, *Ahl al-Tawḥīd al-Durūz wa-khasaʾis madhhabuhum al-dīniyya wal-ijtimāʿiyya* (Beirut: By the author, 1992), 3:114; and Norman N. Lewis, *Nomads and Settlers in Syria and Jordan, 1800-1980* (Cambridge: Cambridge University Press, 1987), 90.

[10] Abu-Muslih, *Waqiʿ al-Duruz*, 243.

[11] Kais Firro, *A History of the Druzes* (Leiden: E. J. Brill, 1992), 31-42 and 47-53; see also Lewis, *Nomads and Settlers,* 77-95 and the maps in both volumes.

[12] Estimates of the Druze population in the Levant are taken from Gabriel Ben-Dor, *The Druzes in Israel, a Political Study* (Jerusalem: Magnes Press, 1979), 255; and Intisar J. ʿAzzam, *Change for Continuity: The Druze in America* (Beirut: MAJD Entreprise Universitaire d'Etude et de Publication [SARL], 1997), 29. The figures are: Syria (mostly Suwayda province), 170,000; Lebanon, between 130,000 and 135,000; Palestine/Israel, 35,000; and Jordan, between 6,000 and 10,000. Note that the numbers for Syria, Lebanon and Palestine/Israel were first published in 1981.

[13] The epistles and all other religious Druze texts are written in Arabic, as is the case with religious poetry and chronicles by such authors as Sheikh al-Fadil Mohammad Abu Hilal, Sheikh Zein al-Din Abdul Ghaffar Taqi Eddin, Sheikh Yusuf al-Kfarquqi and others. See also the poetry of the Buhturid emirs in Salih bin Yahya, *Tārīkh Beirut* (Beirut: Dar al-fikr al-hadith lil-tibaʿa wal-nashr), 58 and 65-74.

[14] Arslan, *Banū Maʿrūf,* 71; Abu-Izzeddin, *The Druzes,* 14.

[15] Al-Dubaysi, *Ahl al-Tawḥīd al-Durūz,* 4:208-09.

[16] Najib al-Buʿayni, *Rijāl min bilādī* (Beirut: Dar al-Rihani, 1984), 40-50, 98-112, 136-42 and 154-60.

[17] Al-Dubaysi, *Ahl al-Tawḥīd al-Durūz,* 5:135-36 and 5:225-36.

[18] Wafiq Ghuraizi, *Muʾānāt al-Muwaḥḥidīn al-Durūz fil-arāḍī al-muḥtalla* (Beirut: Dar al-kateb, 1984), 106-08.

[19] Muhammad Khalil al-Basha, *Muʿjam aʿlām al-Durūz* (Mukhtara: Dar al-taqaddumiyya, 1990), 2:245 and 2:417-19.

[20] Ibid., 1:103-04.

[21] Ibid., 2:178-80.

[22] Sadik Assad, *The Reign of al-Hakim bi Amr Allah, 966-1021* (Beirut: Arab Institute for Research and Publishing, 1974), 156-57; see, also, Abu-Salih and Makarem, *Tārīkh al-Muwaḥḥidīn al-Durūz,* 15-19.

[23] Abu-Izzeddin, *The Druzes,* 4-9.

[24] Ibid., 11.

[25] Written in Geneva on 12 September 1925; see Arslan, *Banū Maʿrūf,* 71-72. For a summary of the clans' descent, see al-Basha's *Muʿjam aʿlām al-Durūz.*

[26] Hamzeh, *Al-Tanūkhiyyūn,* 10 and 22-26.

[27] Moshe Ma'oz, ed., *Studies on Palestine during the Ottoman Period* (Jerusalem: Magnes Press, 1975), 284-91 and 358-68.

[28] Kamal Salibi, *A House of Many Mansions: The History of Lebanon Reconsidered* (London: I. B. Tauris, 1988), 109-112 and 149-150; see, also, Abu-Izzeddin, *The Druzes,* 198-203; and Abu-Salih and Makarem, *Tārīkh al-Muwaḥḥidīn al-Durūz,* 151-56.

[29] Al-Ashrafani, *ʿUmdat al-aʿārifīn*, see ref. 5.

[30] George Antonius, *The Arab Awakening* (New York: Capricorn Books, 1965), 33.

[31] Ibid., 51-53; see, also, al-Basha, *Muʿjam aʿlām al-Durūz* 1:164-66.

[32] Antonius, *The Arab Awakening,* 110; see, also, N. al-Buʿayni, *Rijal min biladi,*149-151.

[33] Ibid., 35-38; see, also, al-Basha, *Muʿjam aʿlām al-Durūz,* 1:146-49.

[34] Raghid Solh, "Attitude of the Arab Nationalists towards Greater Lebanon during the 1930s," in *Lebanon: A History of Conflict and Consensus,* edited by Nadim Shehadi and Dana Haffar Mills (London: Centre for Lebanese Studies/I. B. Tauris, 1988), 151-52. Note that ʿAdel Arslan became a prominent Syrian statesman, serving as a deputy and cabinet minister, and Rashid Taliʿ became Transjordan's first premier.

[35] Ibid., 154-55; N. al-Buʿayni, *Rijāl min bilādī,* 199-213.

[36] Hasan Amin Buʿayni, *Durūz Sūriyya wa Lubnān fī ʿahd al-intidāb al-Faransī, 1920-1943* (Beirut: Markaz al-ʿArabi lil-abhath wal-tawthiq, 1993), 368-69.

[37] Hanna Abi-Rashed, *Hawran al-damiya,* 2d ed. (Beirut: Maktabat al-fikr al-ʿArabi wa matbaʿatuha, 1961), 533-40. See, also, H. al-Buʿayni, *Duruz Suriyya wa Lubnan,* 223; and Amer Ibrahim al-Qandilchi, *Al-ʿArab fil-mahjar al-Amrīkī: Wujūduhum, sahāfatuhum, jamiʿyyātuhum* (Baghdad: Dar al-hurriyya lil-tibaʿa, 1977), 113. Note that George Antonius declared that what had started with Sultan al-Atrash as a Druze revolt had became a national insurgence; see Antonius, *The Arab Awakening*, 377.

[38] See Abi-Rashed, *Hawrān al-dāmiya;* and Saʿid al-Zughayyar, *Banū Maʿrūf fil-tarīkh* (Qurayya: Matabeʿ Zein Eddin, 1984), 642.

[39] Al-Qandilchi, *Al-ʿArab fil-mahjar al-Amrīkī,* 58 and 61-64; and H. al-Buʿayni, *Durūz Sūriyya wa Lubnān,* 219.

[40] Al-Dubaysi, *Ahl al-Tawḥīd al-Durūz,* 5:42.

[41] Hanna Batatu, *Syria's Peasantry, the Descendants of Its Lesser Notables and Their Politics* (Princeton: Princeton University Press, 1999), 146-49, 164-66 and the Appendix. See, also, John F. Devlin, *The Baʿth Party: A History from Its Origins to 1966* (Stanford: Hoover Institution Press, Stanford University, 1975), 39-40, 67, 141, 301 and appendices A, B and C.

[42] Nikolaos Van Dam, *The Struggle for Power in Syria: Sectarianism, Regionalism, and Tribalism in Politics, 1961-1978* (London: Croom Helm Ltd., 1979), 67-75.

[43] Junblat and Lapousterie, *I Speak for Lebanon*, 26-33.

[44] Igor Timovief, *Kamāl Junblāṭ: Al-Rajul wal-ustūra,* translated by Khairi al-Damin (Beirut: Dar al-nahar, 2001), 154-60.

[45] Ibid., 172-76.

[46] Ibid., 227.

[47] Ibid., 247-79.

[48] Patrick Seale, *The Struggle for Syria* (London: I. B. Tauris, 1986), 178.

[49] Seale, *The Struggle for Syria*, 154-59; and Devlin, *The Baʿth Party*, 64-68.

[50] See the official results of the Lebanese general election in 2000, particularly in the Shuf and ʿAley-Baʿabda constituencies (available online at <http://www.lp.gov.lb>). A PSP candidate, Ghazi al-ʿAridi, won the only Druze seat in the Lebanese capital, Beirut, while Anwar al-Khalil, a former ally of Walid Junblat, won the only Druze seat in South Lebanon.

Amir Taheri

Remarks on Some Communities with Druze-Like Affinities

The idea for this paper arose from discussions that I had with Druze friends, especially Shaykh Salim Kheireddine and Walid Abi-Merchid, who had taken an interest in a book that I published in 1989 about Muslims in the now defunct Soviet Union. They were intrigued by the affinities that I had detected between aspects of their own faith and those of some of the communities mentioned in that book.

I was no stranger to the Soviet Union when I started research for the book in 1985. Covering the USSR as a journalist for much of the 1970s, I had travelled to that giant empire several times and established a few contacts, especially in regions where peoples of an Islamic background formed the majority of the population. My initial focus in researching the book was to test the strength of a theory then in fashion in Western academic and decision-making circles, especially in France, where I happened to live at the time, namely, that the USSR was heading for implosion and that the *denouement* signalling its end would come from Muslim revolts in Central Asia and the Caucasus. Ultimately, my research showed that, while the USSR was doomed, its end would not come from any Muslim revolt. But that is another story.

In an illustration of the law of unintended results, my travels and the many interviews that I conducted revealed a religious diversity in the region that I had not expected to find.

The Western maps that painted the vast expanses of Central Asia and Kazakhstan, plus a part of Siberia and virtually the whole of the Caucasus, green, the classical colour of Islam, were too simplistic. Looking closer, one could find many different shades within that green and, often, even spots of other colours.

To be sure, my approach to the subject was political and cultural—not religious and certainly not theological. This is why I did not conduct specific research into matters of doctrine and rite. But, in most cases, religion, politics, ethnic identity and culture were so closely interwoven that formal compartmentalization was difficult.

My own country, Iran, has always been a land richly varied in religion and culture. By the latest count, no fewer than 69 languages are spoken in various parts of the country, some of them being among the oldest in the world. Iranian history is a narrative of religious diversity.

This paper is intended to attract attention to some of the affinities that exist between the Druze and a number of communities in several countries, including some that once formed part of the USSR.

But let me start with a caveat.

This is not an academic research paper. Nor is it intended as a study in comparative theology. What I am offering is a series of observations recorded in a reporter's notebook during the course of journalistic investigations. In some cases, I may have seen more than I should have; in others, perhaps not enough. In some cases, the mosaic of affinities that I perceived may well be deemed by experts to be nothing more than a colourful mural sealing a cul-de-sac; in others, I may have missed broader horizons altogether.

A word, too, on the method.

My aim here is to detect existential affinities among communities that I believe resemble the Druze in one or more ways.

Using an algebraic shorthand, one may organize the principal qualities of an entity into three elements, symbolized by three successive letters of the alphabet. Each new trio begins with the last letter of the previous one. Thus, one gets ABC, followed by CDE, then EFG, followed by GHI and so on. The further we move from the original ABC trio, the fewer the affinities. Yet, even then, the trio furthest removed from the first one still retains a measure of affinity with it, what the French call *un air de famille*.

The first element that these communities have in common is the way in which they are regarded by others, principally, the Muslim majorities among which they live.

The attraction/repulsion that alterity exerts almost invariably shapes the image of these communities in the broader context of the Islamic culturescape.

At the very least, the majority Sunni Muslims regard them as schismatic and describe them as *rafiḍi*s, *baṭini*s and, in one or two specific instances, even *mulḥid*s. Duodecimain Shiʿi Muslims often use the generic term *ghulāt* or 'extremist' to characterize these communities. Until recently, they were all regarded with a mixture of suspicion and awe. Some have been subject to slanderous allegations concerning their practices, which include accusations of incest and worshipping a golden calf—or even Qitmir, the dog of the People of the Cave (*Ashāb al-Kahf*)—and worse. Many also have reputations as warriors and/or the ruthless assassins of their opponents.

Muslims are not alone in having projected their greatest fears and fantasies onto these communities. From the nineteenth century onward, a number of Western travellers and writers have also indulged in such flights of fancy. Rudyard Kipling claimed that Freemasonry originated in Kaffiristan, present-day Nuristan in Afghanistan. (Incidentally, others have identified the Druze, on the supposition that they have either French or English ancestry, as the founders of Freemasonry!) James Hilton located his Shangri-La in the high mountains of Tajikistan, the home of the *ghulāt*. G. I. Gurdjieff, the charismatic charlatan who attracted numerous adherents in France and the United States in the 1940s and 1950s, claimed that a secret global government was located among those communities.

The fact that these communities have developed a tradition of secrecy concerning their beliefs, often as a defence mechanism, which has been interpreted as dissimulation (*kitmān*) or obfuscation (*taqiyya*) by others, has facilitated the projection of all manner of fantasies upon them.

The second element that these communities have in common is a history of suffering from persecution, repression and, in some cases, who we would now call 'ethnic cleansing.' Some of them, such as the Khurramites or the Sarbedaran, which once ruled parts of south-western Khorassan, have been wiped out completely, while others, like the Qarmatis, who once shook a good part of Muslim space, have coalesced into broader and/or newer communities. Still others, like the Mushaashaiyah in south-eastern Iran, disappeared underground for long periods only to make a surprising reappearance elsewhere at a later date.

The third element that needs to be mentioned is that virtually all of the communities in question began as political movements that quickly redefined themselves in terms of theological schism. This was almost inevitable in societies in which the main organizing principle was religion. A peasant revolt against landowning barons, a craftsmen's rebellion against exploiting masters and even an intra-dynastic feud could all quickly translate into conflicts over rite and doctrine.

The fourth element is the common attempt by all of these communities to open some windows onto the broader universe in what experts call *religio perennis*, the perpetual religious quest of mankind that, like a subterranean river, emerges and re-emerges in different places, at different times and in different forms.

Islam itself, in its early stages, had tried to remain receptive to some of the religious experiences and traditions that had preceded it. The followers of all prophets before Muhammad, from Adam to Jesus, were described as muslims with a lower case 'm.' In fact, the concept of islam, with a lower case 'i,' is quite clear in the Qur'an itself. Schismatic communities often emerged when the dominant politico-military power tried to impose a uniformity of belief with the help of official theologians.

These communities began by opening windows, or at least *wasitas*, leading not only to other religions, such as Zoroastrianism, Christianity and even Manicheanism, but also to very different ways of perceiving the cosmos, as in Hinduism and Buddhism, and to Greek philosophy, with special attention to Plato and Plotinus and, in some cases, metaphilosophy: hence, the importance of such figures as Hermes Tresmegistus and the Amshasepandan in the doctrines of some of the communities. Almost all, however, ended up by becoming closed spaces themselves, buildings within the larger Islamic fortress that had already closed its windows and pulled down the shutters. In almost every instance, a period of daring—the orthodox might say reckless—theological innovation was followed by an ice age in which speculation was ruled out, dissent frowned upon and mere suppositions frozen into intellectual givens.

In general, the theologians of these communities have become mere custodians of orthopraxy, perceiving their role as one of perpetuating a tradition shielded by secrecy. The effective separation of the sacred and the profane within these communities—with political leadership in the hands of an élite distinct from the theologians—has also contributed to the fetishization of theology.

The closing of the debate, the freezing of theology, has led to an overemphasis on ethnic identity. Most of these communities began with militant proselytization (*daʿwa*), drawing adherents from many different tribal and ethnic backgrounds. Over time, however, they abandoned the *daʿwa* and, partly because of endogamous marriage practices, developed a new ethnic identity that encompassed all of the initial elements to create a single entity. At times, that ethnic identity has been stronger than the community's religious core, leading to curious cases in which one might, for example, be an Izadi in ethnic terms, but convert to Christianity or even profess atheism in religious ones. The ethnic aspect is further accentuated by the shared belief that the community consists of a single whole divided in three segments: the living, the dead and the yet-to-be-born. Thus, the community can neither grow nor dwindle, but remains locked in an eternal cycle of birth, life and death.

The conflict between ethnic and creedal membership in a community has been one of the motors of Islamic history and has occurred throughout the Islamic world.

The fifth element is the disproportionate role that many of these communities have played in secular political movements in their own regions. The Druze, for example, have been in the vanguard of pan-Arabism, along with many Arab Christians. In Iran, the Caucasus and Central Asia, the many *ghulāt* communities have espoused causes such as pan-Iranism, pan-Turanism and even communism. In every case, the aim has been to promote political unity in the hope of safeguarding religious diversity. In other words, opening oneself to a broader political identity was a means of ensuring one's right to a closed religious identity. Because almost all of these communities abandoned their initial proselytizing zeal long ago, their principal aim in politics was the protection of their separate rights to be religiously different.

In Central Asia, the Caucasus and Iran, many leaders of political reform—from Ismail Agha to Ibrahimov, Akhundzadeh, Ayni, Fitrat, Danesh, Ruhi, Kasravi and others—belonged to communities that were often described by their opponents as minority 'sects' within broader Muslim societies. Virtually all of those from Central Asia and the Caucasus who became active in the various left-wing movements in the Tsarist Empire from the middle of the nineteenth century onward belonged to one or another of the 32 'heretical sects' of Islam identified by an Okhrana survey in 1886.

The 'pan' movements, as well as the various proto-communist ones, aimed at projecting enemies against whom all native inhabitants of the land could unite regardless of their differences. The message was: the enemy is without, not within our frontiers. Paradoxically, however, the politics of nationalism and/or class solidarity incited further animosity toward the *ghulāt* communities, mainly from the traditional circles of Islam (with an upper case 'I'). Members of these circles claimed that the communities, by promoting a secular political ideology as society's organizing principle, were actually trying to undermine the dominant position of Sunni Islam.

The sixth element that these communities have in common is their nexal, as opposed to serial, structure. Changes of political regime or even the cataclysmic experience of communism over seven decades seldom undermined the deep sense of solidarity that ensured their unity. Even geographical dislocation, such as the wholesale transportation of the Chechen nation from the Caucasus to Siberia in 1944, did not destroy a nexus based upon deep-rooted religio-ethnic self-definition. A serial identity melts away as soon as one is removed from its context. A nexal identity, by contrast, is interiorized as a second nature and is not dependent upon proximity. The difference between these two types of organization is best reflected in the German words *Gesellschaft* (association) and *Gemeinschaft* (community).

The seventh element concerns life-style issues. Most members of the community, whether in the countryside or in cities, live simple, if not frugal, lives. Monogamy is often the rule. Respect for elders, sometimes (as in Central Asia) exaggerated into a cult of the *ishān*, is routinely practiced and may be complemented by ritual visits to the tombs of ancestors and holy men. Formal places of worship either do not exist or are visited only on special days, often Thursdays or Wednesdays. These places are called different names, the most common being *khalwāt, khalwatkadeh, zāwiya, chelleh-neshin, jamaat-khaneh, diwan*.

Another common feature is a general disregard for ritualistic practices, such as regular prayers and fasting, although individuals might wish to keep up appearances and "be of the same colour as the majority," as the Persian proverb puts it. A more equitable treatment of women, compared to the broader Muslim community, a greater emphasis on the value of education and a keen sense of social hierarchy and family links are also among the distinguishing features of these communities. Moreover, many of them have survived thanks to the remoteness of their abodes in mountainous regions of the West Asian plateau. If one drew a line connecting these often inaccessible safe-havens together, the image would be that of an archipelago of religious defiance stretching from North Africa to the Indo-Pakistani subcontinent and into the heart of China.

Often these so-called *ghulāt* practices overlap with those of the Sufi fraternities. Indeed, there are many examples of the élite (*khawāṣ*) being organized into Sufi fraternities, while the masses (*ʿawām*) are left solely with their communal identity. (The Bektashi movement, spreading from Xinjiang to Turkey via Iran and Transcaucasia, comes to mind).

Using the tools of linguistic archaeology, one might draw another fascinating map, this time of the Muslim world, from the heart of Asia (Kazakhstan) to the western Mediterranean (Spain). Traces of these so-called heretical movements remain to this day in place names taken from words like *jazīra, rabāt, zāwiya, qalāt* (*qalāt al-daʿwa*) and *astaneh*. (In the case of Algeria, this is true of the entire country: *al-Jazāʾir*.)

Many of these *ghulāt* communities have strong roots in the guilds, trade fraternities and professional associations that once were the backbone of civil society in predominantly Muslim countries. In Iran, for example, the Heydaris virtually monopolized the textile business, which included silk weaving, until the twentieth century. Guilds specialized in masonry, metalwork (both ferrous and precious), and the manufacture of other goods for export were often dominated by these communities. In more recent times, many of their members have been attracted to the professions, such as medicine, law and engineering, which are often organized into syndicates.

When it comes to theology proper, however, it is not easy to offer a full account of the systems developed by these communities, often over centuries, owing to cultic secrecy, suspicion of outsiders and, in some cases, the genuine absence of an easily accessible body of organized written material. Almost all of these communities claim to have their own master-texts, often referred to as 'the book,' 'the secret book,' 'the book of shadow,' 'the holiest book,' or something of the sort. In every case, outsiders are denied access to what is clearly more of an icon, if not a relic, than a living text subject to normal examination and exegesis.

On a few occasions, reporters have been able to draw at least the silhouette of some of these doctrines, for example, during several sessions spent with Isma'ili theologians in Najran, Saudi Arabia, or during a number of lengthy interviews with the Izadi Emir Muawiyyah ibn Isma'il in 1982, which resulted in what was probably the first, if not the only, direct account of Izadi doctrine to be published in English.

Almost all of the communities acknowledge at least some affiliation with islam (with a lower case 'i'), if only because they share its first and foremost principle: the oneness of God. Many of the communities reject the names given them by their adversaries—appellations with hostile or pejorative connotations or designed to reduce the alterity of the community to a matter of purely ethnic, clannic, or sectarian identity. Thus, most of these communities prefer to be called the Monotheists (*Muwaḥḥidūn*), or Khodaparastan (God-Worshippers), or Allahverdis (those who chant God's name).

Because most of the communities in question do not expressly reject their classification as Islamic 'ways' or *madhab*s, or *tarīqāt,* a cloak of uniformity hides the fact of diversity. In a sense, what looks from the outside to be an almost monolithic whole is no more than an external pose, if not a statistical abstraction. The reality that it shrouds is one of a large number of nexal communities facing the outside world in a serial manifestation.

Having temporarily merged with the latest of the Abrahamic revelations before re-emerging from it, the undercurrent of *religio perennis* to which all of these communities belong rejects such concepts as heaven and hell except as metaphors for absolute knowledge and absolute ignorance. The belief that God cannot commit his own creatures to perpetual punishment in hell is an important article of faith. Using Islamic terminology, they insist upon *ta'wīl* as the key to *tawḥīd* and juxtapose the concept of *ẓahir* ('appearance') or ritual religion to *baṭin,* which is true faith or *īmān*. To all of this is added the neo-Platonic doctrine of *al-ʿaql al-kullī* (the universal intelligence) that emanates from the Creator. *Al-'Aql al-kulli* originally manifested itself in the person of Adam, the first human being, and then in the *ulū-ʿazm* prophets, followed by the *imāms* of the various communities; some communities believe that this emanation extended still further to encompass specific political and military leaders. A few names recur across most of the communities as personifications of the universal intelligence, including Jethro (Shuʿayb), Salman Farsi and ʿAli ibn Abi-Taleb.

The Persian poet, Hafez, posits that all of creation is a reflection (*tajallī*) of the universal intelligence, which is the principal attribute of the Creator. God the Creator withdrew from man's sight after Adam's fall, starting a period of divine concealment (*sitr*) that serves as a test for mankind. This eventually ends with a new period of revelation (*kashf*) in which all religions become irrelevant. In some cases, of course, the idea of *tajallī, taqammus* and *hulūl* are taken to their extreme metempsychosic expression to assert that the Creator is Himself revealed through reincarnation in the person of a particular leader.

Most of these communities turn Dostoevsky's celebrated dictum, "If there is no God, all is permitted!" upside-down to read "When there is *only* God, all is permitted." The ultimate aim is to become one with the Creator which, paradoxically, also means annihilating His identity. In the meantime, the common folk (*am*) are invited to observe the rituals of formal religion, while the élite (*khawās* or *khasan*) are exempted.

An examination of the many different sources of these doctrines will reveal borrowings from Hinduism, Buddhism and Zoroastrianism, as well as the Abrahamic faiths. Here, I will only make brief mention of the impact of ancient Greek philosophy in transforming gnostic myths about the origin of the world and about redemption into a system of neo-Platonic concepts.

From the end of the eighth century, partly owing to the efforts of the 'Abbasid caliph, Mamoun, who briefly patronized the Muʿtazila, a number of texts on philosophy and the natural sciences were translated from Greek, first into Syriac and Aramaic, and then into Arabic. The adoption of the works of Plato and Aristotle, as well as the neo-Platonist, Plotinus (d. 270), helped to foster an independent Islamic school of philosophy that eagerly absorbed ancient learning and tried to harmonize it with revelation and the *sharīʿa*. Long before Thomas Aquinas 'baptized' Aristotle, al-Kindi (d. 870) and his two prominent successors, al-Farabi (d. 950) and Ibn Sina (d. 1037), tackled the task of reconciling philosophy, the realm of doubt, with religion, the realm of certainty. A counter-attack by al-Ghazzali to 'cleanse' religion of philosophy posed a temporary setback to such efforts and forced their proponents to seek the space that they needed on the margins of mainstream Islam. The real founder of the neo-Platonic movement known as the Persian School was the *dāʿi*, Muhammad al-Nasafi, of Neishapour (executed in 943). From a position of critical support, Razi continued on the path indicated by al-Nasafi, while al-Sistani's prolific writings influenced the subsequent doctrinal developments of virtually all of the so-called *ghulāt* communities. Al-Kermani and Nasser Khosrow, both of whom, unlike their illustrious precursors, probably had direct access to key Greek texts, later expanded upon their work. The central justification for their speculations was that, if the universe is a book authored by the Creator, as the Qurʾan suggests, it should support an infinite number of readings. Translated into the politics of coexistence, this means that unity need not mean uniformity. Nasser Khosrow's assertion that knowledge (*ʿilm*) is superior to theology (*fiqh*) is a philosophical rendition of the tradition attributed to the Prophet according to which thinking is the first stage of faith (*īmān*) and an hour's thinking (*taffakur*) is better than a year's prayers. The emphasis on faith (*īmān*) as opposed to islam (with a lower case 'i') echoes the sentiment expressed in the Qur'an, which includes 573 references to "*iman*" and fewer than 80 to "*islām*."

The broadest label used by outsiders, both friend and foe, to describe these communities is Shiʿi and it is clearly off the mark in some cases, for example, in relation to the Ibadis of Algeria and Oman. Within Shiʿism itself, these communities are considered to be extremist and, depending on time, place and the persons involved, are treated either with the amused condescendence shown toward a child's *polissonnerie* or the outright hostility reserved for schismatic enemies.

Another generic name often used to describe extremists and distinguishing them from the duodecimains is Sabees or Seveners, which is both too much and not enough. It is too much because it implies a degree of theological uniformity that is simply not there. While many communities—and the Druze are a good example—did start and develop within the original Sabee tradition for a time, most ended up by finding their own ways and evolving distinct identities. The term is not enough because it ignores these specificities.

Sometimes, in an attempt to make the definition more precise, the generic term used is Isma'ilism. But even this may be regarded as insufficient, if not actually misleading. The Isma'ilis are themselves divided into different groups, the largest of which is the Nizaris, who are further subdivided into the Imami Khojas, led by the Agha Khan, and several smaller communities—especially in Iran, Saudi Arabia, Tatarstan, the Ferghanah valley and the Caucasus—which shun specific labels. The Agha Khan has been able to re-absorb, not to say annex, some of these latter communities, for example the Isma'ilis of Gorno Badakhshan in Tajikistan, owing to a mixture of missionary work and humanitarian aid. A similar case is that of the Isma'ilis of the Afghan portion of the Badakhshan highland. When I first visited them in the 1970s, they had virtually no links with the Agha Khan. Since the fall of the communist regime, however, much of the community has been re-absorbed into the movement that he leads. The only other group presently undertaking missionary work is the Mustali Tayyebis, who are present in both Yemen and the Indian state of Gujarat. They are also trying to absorb isolated communities in Central Asia, Kazakhstan, Tatarstan, Bashkortstan and the Caucasus.

Similar communities also exist in the Kulyab region of Tajikistan and around the city of Osh in Uzbekistan.

The Khojas, whose stronghold is the north-west of the Indo-Pakistani subcontinent, largely developed from the conversion to Islam of the Lohanas, a Hindu trading caste. Even today, the Khojas are largely traders. Their centres are in the Punjab (Ush, Moltan, Rawalpindi), in Sind on the lower Indus (Karachi and Larkhanah) and in Gujarat (Kutch, Khatiwar, especially the towns of Nawanagarm Jungarah, Patan and Ahmadabad).

The uplands of Kashmir, divided among India, Pakistan and China, are home to a wide variety of '*ghulāt*' communities, which often have little formal contact with the outside world or even one another. There are also similar communities in the Northwest Frontier province of Pakistan (Chitral) and on the upper Indus in the region of Karakaoum (Hunza and Gilgit), as well as in the western Tarim basin in East Turkestan (Xinjiang), especially in Kashgahr and Yarkand. In Afghanistan, communities exist, as already mentioned, in Badakhshan, but also in Wakkhan and Nuristan (former Kaffiristan).

Communities with close affinities are also present in various parts of Iran, especially in Quhestan (Qa'en and Brijand), as well as Yazd, Kirman and Khorassan (Zuzan). There are also remnants of the original Nizaris in the Zahra-Blok, near Qazvin, not far from the legendary Alamut. The oasis city of Mahallat and particularly the village of Anjudan, 100 kilometres southwest of Qom, remain strongholds. Still more similar communities, which survive under different appellations, also exist in Talesh, along the Caspian coast (divided between Iran and the Republic of Azerbaijan)

The Heydaris, who follow Heydar, son of Junaid, as their eponymous *imām*, are present in the provinces of Zanjan, East Azerbaijan and Hamadan. In many Iranian towns, one still finds the remnants of the Heydar-Khaneh or whole districts named Heydarieh, reminders of a community that was once strongly present throughout the country, but was gradually wiped out by the Safavids. Sabee communities may be found in Khuzestan, especially Ahvaz and the Shadegan plain. The Sitri community is present in the Pishin district of Baluchistan, while the Mustali Tayyebis have a presence in Saravan and Chah-Bahar.

A number of other communities also merit mention. One is known to outsiders as the ʿAli-Allahis, 'those who deify 'Ali', but to insiders as Ahl-e-Haq or 'people of the truth'. This community is strongly present in the Iranian provinces of Luristan, Kurdistan, Kermanshahan and West Azerbaijan, but also has adepts in Tehran, as well as Tajikistan, Uzbekistan, Kyrgyzstan and Daghestan. The term ʿAli-Allahi is off the mark because ʿAli ibn Abi-Taleb, though revered by the community, occupies a subordinate place in its religious ideas.

Smaller communities, such as the Akhbaris, the Shaykhis, the Ahl-e-Tariq and the ʿAlawis are also present in many parts of Iran, especially in the western and north-western provinces. More controversially, one may even include the Babis, the Sobhis, the Azalis and, finally, the Bahaʾis, although I am sure that some of their adepts would not agree.

Another such community is known as Yazidis to outsiders and Izadis to insiders. It is present in north-western Iraq and south-eastern Syria and also has adepts in the Iranian provinces of Kurdistan and Ilam and in south-eastern Turkey. In recent years, some of the leaders of the community have described it as merely an offshoot of Zoroastrianism. But while the Izadi cosmogony does indeed possess many Mazdaic themes, it also shares many theological notions and philosophical motifs with the broad category of *ghulāt* movements.

The Nusayris, especially populous in Syria, but also present in Turkey and Iraq, also deserve mention. Less known is the fact that small Nusayri communities also exist in Mazandaran, along the Caspian, where the movement had its first stronghold under the Buyid dynasty in the tenth century.

As already noted, similar communities live in southern Saudi Arabia, especially Najran, with roots in neighbouring Yemen and offshoots in the Hadramawt valley, along the Gulf of Aden.

The Caucasus, known as the 'mountain of languages,' is also the land of numerous religious communities broadly classifiable as Christian or Muslim, plus small Jewish groups. The communities that interest us here are almost routinely described as either Imamis or Isma'ilis. Under their broadest appellation, Imami, they account for some 90 percent of the population of the Republic of Azerbaijan, where the overwhelming majority consists of duodecimains. But *ghulāt*-type groups also exist in the plain of Qarabagh, in several villages around Ganjeh (formerly Lenin-Abad) and north of Baku. The Ahl-e-Haq have a presence in the Lachin uplands and the enclave of Nakhchevan. In some cases, for example, among some communities in Abkhazia and Adjaria in Georgia, and the Darband and Makhach-Qalah areas in Daghestan, specific religious identities have blurred into those of the Sufi fraternities. In Chechnya, Ingushetia and Southern Ossetia, virtually all of society is organized into Sufi fraternities that often contain within them religious communities, in the manner of Russian *matreshka* dolls, with key elements of *ghulāt* doctrines serving as the theo-philosophical backbone of belief systems.

This brief reportage does not even scratch the surface of what is an immense and, as yet, largely untouched subject. Most scholars have approached the issue as if the communities in question are little more than fading historical curiosities. But many communities that are presented by scholars as having completely disappeared continue to exist, either under new names or as branches of broader movements. The fact that the presumed (Sunni) majority consists of numerous minorities is ignored in favour of myths about a uniform and increasingly militant Islam that is supposedly preparing for a clash of civilizations with the West.

The disintegration of the USSR in 1991 and the collapse of the Taleban regime in Afghanistan in 2002 have allowed some of the communities to re-assume their identities and they may, in time, open themselves to *bona fide* scholarly studies.

But, for the most part, the authorities do not yet provide the degree of safety and security—even in India, a secular republic—for the communities to consider a genuine effort to reveal and, thus, expose themselves. Fear of religious persecution is so deeply entrenched in many of these communities that they have not entertained candid dialogue, even among themselves, for decades, if not centuries.

Even in the democratic societies of Western Europe and North America, which now have substantial minorities that originated in the Muslim world, these various communities, which have so much in common, have not succeeded in developing meaningful contacts and fostering dialogue. In some cases, this is due to old historic feuds and pseudo-theological disputes that provoked the initial schismatic ruptures. But, more often, the real cause is the belief of these communities that safety lies in keeping as low a profile as possible.

The Cartesian dictum, "*vivons cachés, vivons heureux,*" remains the rule. In the meantime, large chunks of the map continue to be presented in a uniform green, hiding the rainbow reality of life in a turbulent part of the world. The Muslim world—the whole world, for that matter—is the poorer for it.

JUDITH PALMER HARIK

Coping with Crisis: Druze Civic Organization during the Lebanese Civil War

THE DRUZE HAVE LONG BEEN perceived as feisty mountaineers with superior military skills and strong communal solidarity. It is commonly held that these characteristics allowed them to maximize the effects of their relatively small numbers when they faced challenges from out-groups and those wielding central authority.

The recent Lebanese civil war provided observers with an opportunity to measure these perceptions of Druze prowess against the reality of their behaviour on the battlefield and in defence of their home territory. The latter became a particularly daunting task as a result of the destruction and dislocations of the 1983 War of the Mountain. This ferocious, week-long battle, in which the military wing of Walid Junblat's Progressive Socialist Party (PSP) attempted to eject militiamen of the Christian Lebanese Forces (LF) from Druze areas in Mount Lebanon, dealt a heavy blow to government agencies that were still operating in the battle zone and left the PSP with the task of re-establishing civic organization in the areas under its control.[1]

This paper looks at the efforts taken by Druze leader Walid Junblat and PSP officials and members to cope with the 1983 emergency from a resource mobilization perspective. It seeks answers to the following questions: What were some of the community features and political factors that facilitated the establishment of civic organization and how were they exploited? How were party, community and state manpower and material resources developed and marshalled to manage urgent emergencies swiftly and re-establish social and public services that the Lebanese government was in no condition to provide?

To help guide this research, theories of conflict and minority behaviour were sought that identified and explained some of the important factors involved in successful efforts by groups to ward off outside pressures or threats. These propositions are presented below, along with a brief discussion of their relevance to the Druze condition and experience in general.

Coping with threats and pressures

Mordechai Nisan, an expert on Middle Eastern minorities, mentions several factors that have contributed to the persistence of these groups. Among them is shared historical experience. Nisan suggests that the serious existential threats faced by many minorities at one time or another explain important developments in their communal life, from the intensification of existing social bonds to the evolution of political institutions. In his opinion, the persecution of the Druze for their schismatic doctrine in the early days of the faith was one of the major factors in their early social and political development.[2] Their survival depended upon centralized leadership, planning and tight organization, as well as members' solidarity and cohesiveness.

These traits also served the Druze well later, as they began to assert themselves politically. For instance, historian Kamal Salibi points out that the Druze were continuously at war with the Crusaders and their local proxies, the Maronite Christians, during the two centuries that followed the first crusades.[3] In Salibi's view, this experience caused the Druze to develop as a "community of mountain peasants organized for war." Because of their martial skills, Druze chieftains continued to be given regional commands by the central authorities and their successes on the battlefield were rewarded with subsidies and titles. Hourani claims that this situation greatly influenced the community's social structure, since it encouraged the concentration of power in the hands of a few aristocratic families whose ascendancy was legitimized by the clergy.[4]

The capacity of the Druze to put aside power rivalries within the community and close ranks behind the dominant leadership in times of trouble is well known and cannot be emphasized too much. As sociologist Leo Coser explains, "Any schemes devised to maximize the influence of small numbers in times of group stress are most efficiently promoted by centralized leadership… . [I]n times of crisis a group must centralize power in order to meet the challenges faced."[5]

That being said, there is still no substitute for astute leaders who are capable of formulating effective strategies and tactics, and adequately exploiting available human and physical assets. When numbers are few and resources are scarce, planning and efficient management are decisive factors. Few would dispute the fact that the Druze of Mount Lebanon were singularly fortunate in the quality of their ascriptive leaders over the centuries or that the modern descendants of traditional ruling families are capable of meeting their community responsibilities.

Besides the importance of a tight hierarchical chain of command that can mobilize and direct offensive or defensive operations efficiently, the capacity of leaders to elicit sentiments of loyalty and solidarity from their partisans and to sustain them during hard times is also vital when small groups face grave threats.[6] In this respect, the recorded military exploits of the Druze certainly suggest the strong presence of a certain *esprit de corps* among the fighters. Westerners visiting Druze areas in the nineteenth century, such as C. H. Churchill and Lady Hester Stanhope, recorded vivid impressions of Druze solidarity.[7] Writing in 1833, Stanhope, for example, notes that "although the Druze army did not exceed 2,500 men, due to their resolute action each man is worth twenty."[8] During the recent civil war, it was widely known that, although the Druze militia counted only some 4,000 fighters, thousands more could be mobilized in the blink of an eye if called upon to defend their area and way of life. That remains the case. Such impulses and convictions provide a bedrock of support that can be counted on and exploited whenever the community's interests appear to be in jeopardy.

In addition to capitalizing on the leadership and manpower available in the community, minorities use other means to protect their interests and expand their influence. For instance, some minorities lessen their isolation by adapting mainstream political ideals and positions. Gubser and Firro refer to the ideologies adopted by Druze communities in different countries as indicative of their pragmatic response to environmental conditions.[9] The adoption of Arab nationalist ideology by the Lebanese Druze is a case in point. Members of the two ruling Lebanese Druze families—the Arslans and the Junblats—were well known for their Arab nationalist sympathies and actions. Kamal Junblat's pan-Arab beliefs facilitated his leadership of Lebanon's National Movement—a loose coalition of leftist Muslim groups, including Palestinian factions—in 1975. This alliance gained him access to the training and logistical support required to rapidly transform his motley group of volunteers into a small army with professional capabilities. Yet, it must not be forgotten that the sense of relative political and social deprivation—the gap between expectations and material achievements[10]—was the principal impetus for the Druze break with passivity; and that the ready availability of foreign assistance, so often a catalyst when frustrated minorities turn to violence, also came into play in this case. The later point refers, of course, to the international and regional rivalries which developed as a result of the Arab-Israeli conflict and which resulted in the 'fishing' of foreign powers—especially Syria and Israel—in Lebanon's troubled sectarian waters.[11]

Certain constants, such as geographical location and demographic characteristics, also help or hinder groups' capacities to cope with persecution or other threatening situations. It is no accident that many Middle Eastern minorities chose residence in the rugged hinterlands of the region.[12] In the Druze case, access to their mountainous and forested areas was, and still is, restricted to a few main roads, which are not difficult to patrol, while the strategic location of areas of Druze concentration presented many advantages in the struggle against government troops and Maronite militias that began in 1975.

A minority's compactness, as opposed to its dispersal over a large area or several areas, is another asset for the maintenance of political cohesion and group security. During the recent civil war, this feature was accentuated as increasing numbers of Christians left Druze areas to take refuge with their brethren in other locales. The Shuf, ʿAley and parts of the Matn districts became more Druze than ever and were thus more easily defended.

In summary, then, minorities must efficiently exploit all possible community resources and assets, and fill any gaps quickly, if they are to prevail against opponents greater in number and potential. The Druze of Mount Lebanon possess many advantages that help them in this regard: legitimate and capable leaders with the ability to centralize their authority and assert organizational skills; historical experience and military traditions that heighten group solidarity, volunteerism and performance when community threats are perceived[13]; and a compact and defensible home territory. Furthermore, at the time of the civil war, the emerging power on the ground—the Junblati faction of the community—espoused an Arab nationalist ideology and a view of Lebanon's problems that were shared by other local opposition groups and regional powers. This permitted the formation of helpful alliances that greatly expanded the power of the community, which counts for only about 6.5% of Lebanon's total population.

The task now is to explore how and to what extent these assets and resources were exploited as Walid Junblat, Kamal's son, and his partisans rapidly tried to respond to the 1983 emergency and its aftermath.

Leadership and institutional assets: Kamal Junblat and his Progressive Socialist Party

As we have seen, a major factor in a small group's capacity to cope effectively with threats involves its ability to centralize leadership and, thus, acquire the organization and hierarchical chain of command essential to dealing with crises of all kinds. In this respect, it is impossible to understand the PSP's capacity to cope with the emergencies of 1983 without being familiar with the institutional groundwork previously laid by the party's founder, ascriptive Druze chieftain Kamal Junblat.

It is difficult to overstate the importance of Kamal Junblat's action in establishing a modern political party capable of mobilizing a mass following and assisting with the incentives necessary to retain and enlarge the clientele networks so important in Lebanese politics, particularly when it comes to the party's impact on his own political influence. Since the focus of this paper is on the organized delivery of social and public services in Druze areas, a few words are in order on the general topic and on Junblat and the PSP's background in this field of endeavour.

Like all Lebanese *zuʿama*, Druze leaders are expected to use their influence and even, at times, their own financial resources to assist partisans and potential partisans in need. Early in the PSP's development, party officials and close Junblat associates began facilitating this process through the institution of specialized party offices. In 1977, the PSP charter specifically committed the party to "public usefulness" through its social affairs and health bureaus. It should be said, however, that these bureaus were not always a substitute for the well-known Lebanese institution, the weekly *majlis*. This is a sort of public audience or open house during which the *zuʿama* receive visits from constituents seeking assistance, expressing gratitude for past favours, or merely seeking an opportunity to rub shoulders with members of the élite. For a visitor who has been promised help with a hospital bill, a scholarship for his or her child, or a water well for the village, the next step often was—and still is—a visit to the party official charged with taking down the specifics, filing the papers and seeing that the job gets done. The specialized offices of the PSP were, therefore, conceived as standing service providers that implemented the directives of the party's president by developing procedures and finding ways to ensure that clients saw results. The importance of this work in attracting partisans is evident when it is understood that most rural Lebanese fall right through the social safety net extended by the government and thus incur an obligation to whomever helps them.

In addition to providing social support facilities in return for political allegiance, Junblat and, therefore, the PSP also attracted partisans for ideological reasons. Because it transcended the narrow issues of Druze politics through the espousal of Junblat's versions of universal (socialism), regional (Arabism) and local ('Lebanonism') ideologies, the party was open to anyone, Druze or non-Druze, whose views and values meshed with its mission of working toward reform and social justice.[14] Although some claim that the socialist doctrine espoused by this hereditary leader was merely a political ploy to gain a more broadly-based following, there are indications that Junblat took the tenets of socialism quite seriously. Most importantly, however, whether for ideological or other reasons, he succeeded quite well in mobilizing partisans from different sectarian affiliations to his positions.

In addition, the many interviews which I conducted over the years with Druze of various political persuasions convinced me that perceptions of Junblat's charisma, popular pride in his intellectual depth and his very 'Druzeness' (owing to his interest in Sufism, an austere and contemplative lifestyle influenced by Hinduism, and deep understanding and concern for mountain society) were also significant factors, at least in his capacity to gain adherents among members of his own faith and thus carve out a preponderant role in his community's politics. For many he was the *muʿallim* or 'teacher', a man whose personal qualities and convictions were believed to set him apart from the ordinary Lebanese politician. Junblat's allure might also be explained by his ability to reinforce Druze inner convictions about the community's unique identity and contribution to Lebanese political life.

Kamal Junblat's speeches and writings, which contain analyses of Lebanon's problems at the time and suggestions on how to redress them, not only enhanced his stature in the Druze political arena, but made him the natural spokesman, in the early 1970s, of the opposition forming against the Lebanese government.[15] However, it was his capacity to mobilize a considerable body of individuals ready to fight fiercely for the causes that he articulated within the framework provided by the PSP, as well as the locale of the confrontation between government loyalists and their opponents, which were primarily responsible for the prominent role that he played in the National Movement, a loose coalition of leftist Muslim and Palestinian forces that had joined forces to combat the mainly Christian Lebanese Front. This alliance permitted the fighting wing of the PSP, the *jaysh al-shaʿbī* (people's army), access to Palestinian trainers and shipments of war *matériel* from the Soviet Union—supplies sent from Eastern Europe and forwarded to Lebanon by the Syrian government.

From interviews with a range of Druze intellectuals in the 1990s, I gathered that many believed that Junblat's political positions during this critical period were simply more practical and more consistent with Druze historical interests than those adopted by his major Druze rivals, the Arslans. At the time, the Arslans nurtured close attachments to some of the leaders of the mainstream Maronite Christian community, whose militias were being armed by Israel.

Thus, at the outbreak of civil strife, Kamal Junblat was reaping some of the advantages of his birthright and his prior performance as a Druze and national leader, and making good use of the multi-purpose political instrument he had founded in 1949. Core PSP members and other volunteers were quickly mobilized into structured fighting units, while party officials tried to come to grips with the social effects unleashed by the military mobilization and the hostilities.

The 1976 Popular Administration

The arming of thousands of fighters and the PSP's alliance with other militias was thought by some to be a bit of a mixed blessing in 1976, when the combined Palestinian and Lebanese militias of the National Movement flooded into ʿAley and other Druze areas and began military operations. In addition to the retaliatory bombardments that their actions drew, residents experienced security problems that emanated from the presence of the free-wheeling militiamen themselves. In an effort to protect the civilian population and bring some order to the prevailing chaos, Kamal Junblat established the Popular Administration, an institution that provided the conceptual and organizational model for the much broader experiment in Druze civic organization, the Civil Administration of the Mountain (CAOM), which followed in 1983.[16]

As ʿAref al-Aʿwar, the vice-president of the Popular Administration, told me, Junblat's first act was to establish a tribunal to handle citizens' complaints against the hordes of heavily armed and sometimes unruly young militiamen.[17] With that problem under control, committees were formed to deal with logistics in the areas that had been placed on a wartime footing. Party loyalists were appointed to important posts: for instance, Hisham Nasreddine, who later directed the CAOM, was Junblat's personal representative in the Popular Administration and was responsible for the ʿAley district. According to its by-laws, the Popular Administration was intended to 'activate' what remained of government services since contacts with administrative headquarters had been lost. Nasreddine reports that he did his best to keep daily garbage collection on track, manage water and electricity problems, and keep health centres supplied and open, aided by the considerable staff which he acquired to help him.[18] PSP militiamen manning checkpoints collected tolls on major roads to finance these operations and efforts were also made to collect taxes and the normal fees for government services from citizens.

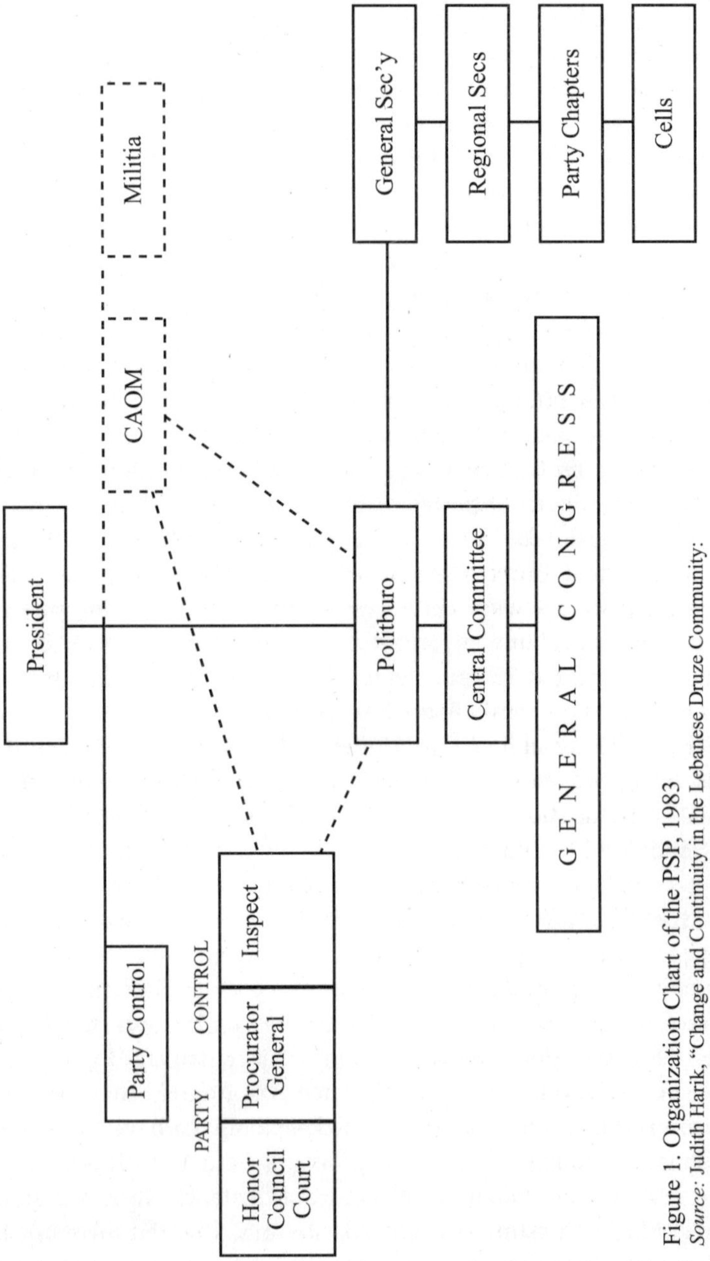

Figure 1. Organization Chart of the PSP, 1983
Source: Judith Harik, "Change and Continuity in the Lebanese Druze Community: The Civil Administration of the Mountain, 1983-1990," *Middle Eastern Studies* 29, no. 3 (July 1993): 383.

The by-laws also reveal that the *ad hoc* administration was meant to be "a model for the organization of public services through popular, democratic participation in public affairs." Some interpreted this statement as an effort to cover a risky parochial undertaking with a mantle of national respectability. Kamal Junblat was known to favour administrative decentralization as a means of rectifying government neglect and promoting local development. Moreover, such a system was consistent with the Druze's age-old goal of acquiring as much autonomy as possible from the central authorities. Seven years later, on 2 October 1983, when the CAOM was announced, it was also rationalized as a model for the state to emulate and described as activating, rather than replacing, flagging government services.

The Popular Administration was closed down by the Syrians later that year, but the tension and uncertainty that continued after 1976 sustained some of the party work that had begun at that time. The PSP's specialized social committees took on larger roles as state agencies further declined into virtual paralysis. Matters were complicated by the fact that local elections had not been held since the 1960s so that many village mayors and councilmen who had died or moved had not been replaced. As fighting spread, government employees in hard-hit areas left their posts. Roads, water, electricity and sewage networks not only suffered from the lack of routine maintenance, but were also damaged or destroyed by shelling.[19]

During this time, the PSP and other Druze institutions and individuals did their best to handle local disruptions and needs on an *ad hoc* basis. When Kamal Junblat was assassinated in 1977, he left the PSP in the hands of his son, Walid, who was faced, before long, with the 1982 Israeli invasion, the arrival of the multinational force and the fierce hostilities that followed.

The War of the Mountain broke out in 1983 as members of the Lebanese Forces tried to take up positions that had been held by the evacuating Israelis in the Shuf and ʿAley. From these positions, the Christian militiamen hoped to 'liberate' Christian villagers and assert full control over the Mountain. The magnitude of the Druze response and the rapidity with which the Lebanese Forces were overcome during that horrendous week in September clearly demonstrated that the Druze were as ready as ever to defend their heartland and autonomy. The battle brought to life all of the historic commentary and folkloric anecdotes about Druze solidarity, cohesion and martial skills.

However, once the military battle had been won, another even graver struggle loomed. An estimated 50,000 Druze and 150,000 Christians had been displaced from the areas of confrontation and extensive material damage had been sustained to homes, businesses and infrastructure.

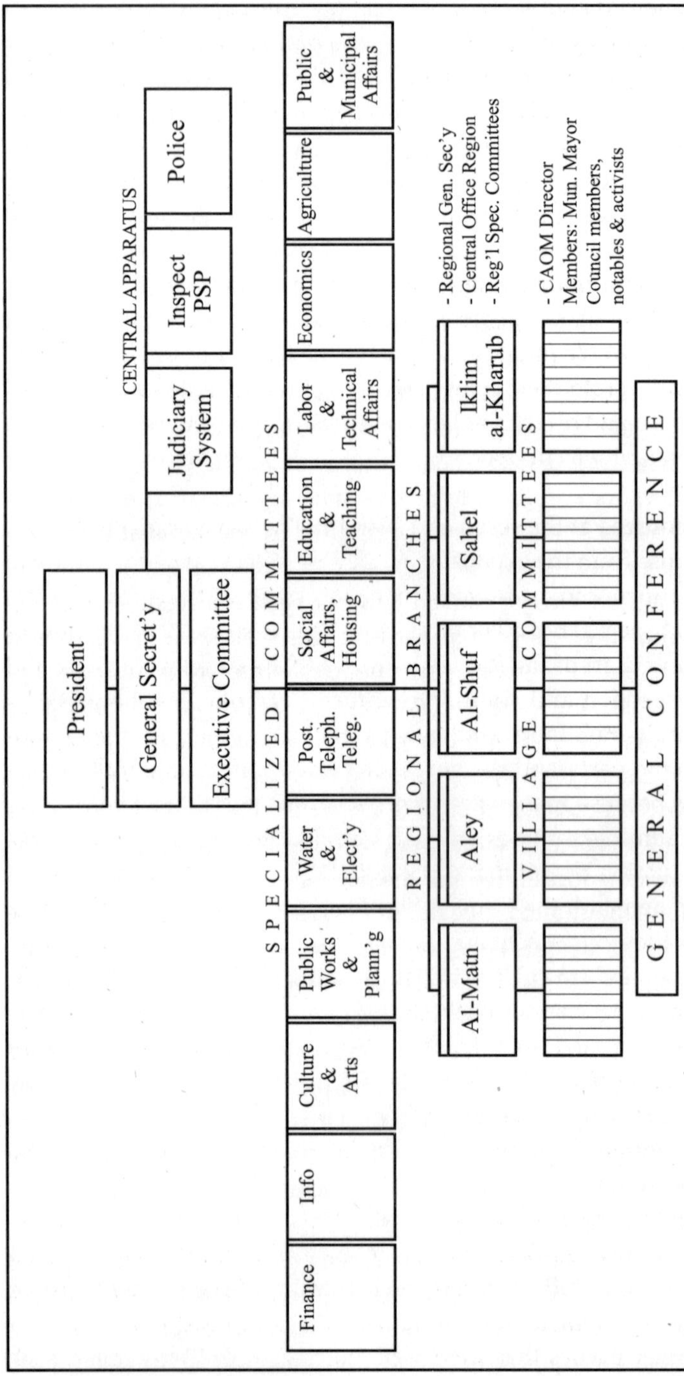

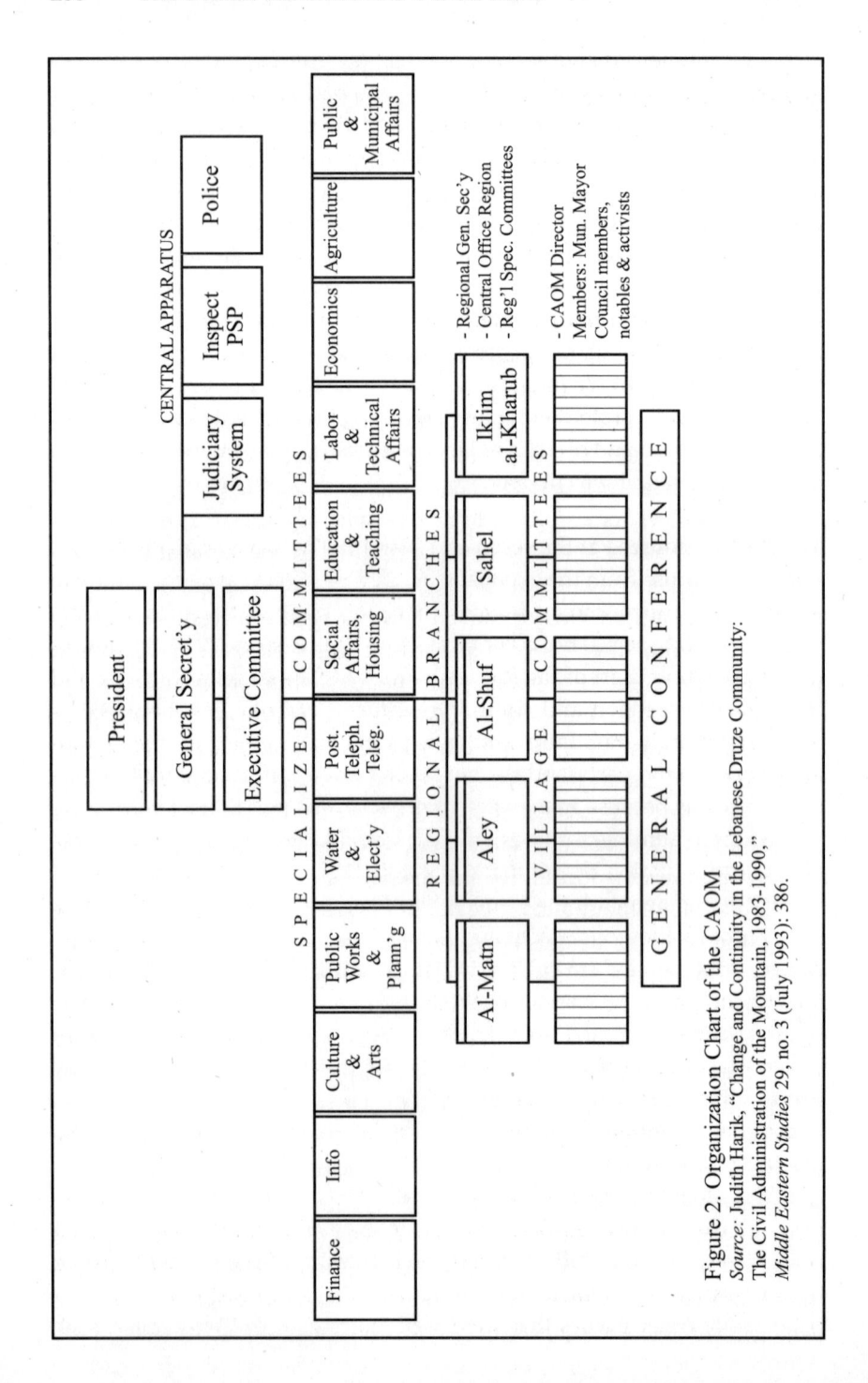

Figure 2. Organization Chart of the CAOM
Source: Judith Harik, "Change and Continuity in the Lebanese Druze Community: The Civil Administration of the Mountain, 1983-1990," *Middle Eastern Studies* 29, no. 3 (July 1993): 386.

Moreover, numerous civil servants—teachers, health workers, bureaucrats and blue-collar employees of all sorts—who had stayed at their posts up until the War of the Mountain abandoned them as hostilities appeared inevitable. As the power on the ground, the PSP faced social emergencies of various dimensions requiring immediate attention. Rule by executive decree became the order of the day and was backed up by the military wing of Walid Junblat's party in all Druze areas. This tight control ensured that decrees were followed to the letter and that civic organization pertained in a uniform manner right across the mountain. With the short-lived Popular Administration before him as a model of how the PSP might be harnessed to provide public and social services, Walid Junblat followed his father's lead, wrote the by-laws of the CAOM, issued personal directives to start it up and established its priorities. By mid-October the surrogate administration was in operation.

The PSP's resources at the service of its administrative branch

The CAOM arose from the expansion of the PSP's General Services Bureau to become a functioning administrative unit endowed with a separate directorate and specialized committees (see Figures 1 and 2). According to the organization chart of the PSP, only the CAOM's secretary-general and its head of inspection and control were formally linked to the party by membership in its Politburo. However, as might be expected, the boundaries between the party and the bureaucracy were, in fact, highly permeable. This was because many party regulars with specialized talents were plugged into administrative positions as rapidly as possible to cope with the chaotic situation that initially prevailed. For instance, as a result of greater public demand, the General Services Bureau, originally in charge of both social and educational affairs, was split into two specialized committees, each headed by a PSP partisan: Walid Fatayri, a young and popular teacher, became director of the Education and Teaching Committee; Khalid Muhtar, who had run the General Services Bureau for years, stayed in place as head of the CAOM's Social Affairs and Housing Committee; Nadim Nammur, an engineer, took over the CAOM's Public Works Committee; contractor Rafiq Hamadi became head of Water and Electricity; and so on.

It is evident that the CAOM drew extensively on a pool of party members and close Junblat associates since, of the 39 CAOM officials heading committees, 21 were PSP members, 14 claimed an 'independent' status, but nevertheless revealed admiration for the Junblats, and only four belonged to other parties that were well established in Druze areas, such as the Lebanese Communist Party and the Syrian Social Nationalist Party.[20] As Figure 2 shows, the CAOM also had regional branches that directed aid from the centre to needy villages within its jurisdiction. Within the villages, CAOM committees operated to fill municipal council gaps, marshal local resources for repair and reconstruction projects, and communicate needs to regional branches.

The Civil Administration was headed by individuals who might be characterized as Junblat's right-hand men. They included Adil Sayyur, Hisham Nasreddine and Daher Ghandour, who were the CAOM'S first, second and third secretaries-general respectively. Nasreddine was still head of General Administration and Services in the party Politburo when he became the director of CAOM on Sayyur's death. The importance of this pool of competent PSP loyalists cannot be overestimated in terms of the party's capacity to deal with social issues of crisis dimensions. All had possessed administrative experience of one kind or another while Kamal Junblat was alive and all could move swiftly into executive positions in 1983. Manpower availability and flexibility were the keywords, as evinced by the fact that, after the CAOM closed down in 1991 and Walid Junblat became minister of the displaced in the following year, Nasreddine was right there with him, this time directing the *government's* Office of the Displaced in Damur. His job was to process the thousands of requests for assistance and indemnities upon which the returns rested.[21] Nadim Nammur, who had headed the CAOM's Public Works Committee, still followed related issues for the PSP at the time of writing and was additionally appointed a member of the Social Fund for the Displaced when that agency was created in the mid-1990s. Junblat remained as minister of the displaced until 1998, when Selim al-Hoss became prime minister and replaced him with Anwar al-Khalil, a Druze leader from Hasbayya, in the southern part of Lebanon. When Rafiq al-Hariri returned to the premiership in 2000, Marwan Hamadeh, who represents himself as an advisor to Walid Junblat, rather than a party member, became minister of the displaced, while another political advisor, Ghazi al-ʿAridi, was named minister of information. Khalid Muhtar reverted to his original role as head of the PSP Social Affairs Committee in 1991 and holds the same position today.

After his stint with the Ministry of the Displaced, Hisham Nasreddine became the director of a PSP bureau that encourages the development of social and public programs in the Mountain by liaising with foreign ambassadors and representatives of the European Union, USAID (United States Agency for International Development) and non-governmental organizations (NGOs). There was, of course, every reason to continue the liaison work started under the CAOM (discussed below) since a great deal remained to be done to restore the quality of mountain life and to address residents' needs. A recent interview with Nasreddine revealed that, as before, he works closely with Walid Junblat; indeed, when interviewed about his role in the CAOM, he emphasized a point that he had originally made to me in 1992, namely, that he acts specifically according to Junblat's instructions.[22]

The Judiciary Committee, headed by Tewfiq Barakat during the CAOM days, provides a good example of Junblat's absolute authority in Mount Lebanon between 1983 and 1991. This committee substituted for the legal state authorities in Druze areas and all of the judges were appointed by the PSP leader. Many of them were not accredited by the state as they had not graduated from the official juridical institute. Moreover, Junblat himself issued various decrees concerning the penalties to be meted out to criminals in some cases. These were explained as extraordinary measures for extraordinary circumstances. Some community members with whom I spoke concerning the legitimacy of these measures indicted that, with armed militiamen all over the place, a functioning police force and justice system answerable to *someone* had been absolutely essential. Junblat, they said, was the only individual with the necessary muscle and authority to make this happen.

Mobilizing community resources

The individuals who manned the CAOM offices sought to deal with the emergencies that confronted them in 1983 in any way that they could. For instance, the Public Works Committee's head, Nadim Nammur, marshalled all available human resources, both volunteers and professionals, to open roads that had been closed as a result of bombing and to remove and repair downed electrical wires. Contractors with heavy equipment were brought in to handle emergencies whose scope surmounted the capacities of local inhabitants. Some of those who participated in these operations became staff members of the CAOM offices or remained on call in case of future problems. In many instances, Druze who had worked in government departments in other regions and who were now unable to go to their jobs were recruited—sometimes under pressure—to handle the same tasks at home. Some worked out of the CAOM headquarters, which had been established in the complex of buildings next to Beiteddine castle; others, such as school teachers, nurses, and public works and electricity company employees, worked wherever they were needed. The tools of their trades and their transportation were provided by the CAOM.

Interestingly, when the situation in the Mountain had become somewhat stable, plans were made and implemented to undertake the regular maintenance of roads, water sources and electrical equipment which had been neglected by the government for years. Some committees also began developmental projects. The Agriculture Committee worked on a beekeeping project and a model dairy farm, while the Education Committee produced history books that were felt to be 'more honest' and civics texts that taught the basics of good citizenship; these volumes were used as textbooks in all schools in Druze areas. Several officials acknowledged that, as time passed, CAOM cadres aimed at making the Druze areas into a model for post-war Lebanon—orderly, clean and green.

Securing external resources

As briefly noted above, efforts were also made to garner as much assistance as possible from non-community sources. One of the oddities of the Lebanese civil war was that, despite their total hostility toward the government, opposition leaders like Walid Junblat jealously guarded the prerogatives of their official positions. Their capacity to wring material and financial assistance from the all but moribund state agencies thus remained intact. It came as no surprise, therefore, when the Ministry of Public Works, under Junblat's direction, found funds for road and electricity repairs in the mountains. However, because they fell short of what was actually needed for such a mammoth project, the CAOM filled the gap in 1988 with the purchase of 30,000 tons of asphalt, which was laid by local contractors.[23]

Junblat's administrators also liaised with their counterparts in public agencies on a constant basis and lobbied the NGOs operating in Lebanon at the time for assistance. For example, CAOM executives and point men worked closely with Save the Children, which repaired war-damaged schools. According to a UNICEF official, Rafiq Hamadi's committee worked closely with his staff on well-digging and maintenance work for water networks.[24] Interviews with the directors of these NGOs indicated that their work was made easier by CAOM's accessibility and its officials' capacity to identify project priorities, supply relevant information about them and provide some of the local labour necessary for their completion. My visits and interviews with CAOM officials gave me the impression that, by the late 1980s, they had worked out an effective system to handle the problems caused by continuous fighting and that they had also made some strides in replacing infrastructure that had simply suffered neglect, rather than actual war damage, during this period.

Financing civic organization

The compactness of the Druze community greatly enhanced the effectiveness of the surrogate administration. For instance, it enhanced the functioning of the vaunted 'Druze telephone,' an informal system of communications based upon word of mouth which could mobilize both fighters and volunteers with lightning speed when emergencies arose. This was particularly vital in those chaotic times when shelling began suddenly and instantaneous backup, whether military or medical, involving damage control or the evacuation of families, was needed. The community's compactness also made it easier to collect the nominal taxes levied on all families and others imposed on businesses. Real estate was taxed at 6% of the assessed value of the land and fees were collected for any legal transactions that took place. The tax collectors with whom I spoke reported that, because contributions were voluntary, sometimes more and sometimes less than the assessed amount was actually paid. Wealthy residents received 'special appeals' for donations. The rents of houses, apartments and agricultural land left by or seized from fleeing Christians also reportedly went into the treasury, as did returns from the Jiyyah and Khaldeh ports, which were operated by the PSP. Figures on income and disbursements were published annually by the CAOM.

In addition to giving the *jaysh al-shaʿbī* and its military helpmates enormous strategic advantages, Druze concentration in one general mountain area also served the local administration well by facilitating the collection of the road tolls that furnished the bulk of CAOM revenue. After 1983, some of the military checkpoints earlier established by PSP soldiers became toll booths for the collection of nominal daily and monthly fees for road use. The relatively limited number of major arteries serving Druze areas made this task far easier for the Druze administration than it was for the one set up by the Lebanese Forces in urban Christian areas.

The socio-political meaning of the CAOM and its implications

The CAOM provides a good example of how the Druze have been able to overcome the handicaps of small numbers and limited resources to protect a cherished identity and way of life. Faced with an emergency of huge and multiple dimensions, a traditional community leader, possessing authority and a pre-existing institutional structure, stepped into the breech and organized a rescue operation that assumed the characteristics and functions of a full-fledged public administration. Loyal secondary cadres took up duties as bureaucrats and called upon community members to lend a hand. Soon, administrative units were operating in most Druze villages and towns—many of which had long lacked such structures. In retrospect, by relying on the *jaysh al-shaʿbī* and the police force created to maintain order and to back up its regulations, the CAOM brought a measure of civic organization to an area that had been all but totally abandoned by the Lebanese government. It might even be argued that, by making life more bearable, as random shelling and concentrated attacks continued over the eight-year period of its existence, the surrogate administration probably limited Druze emigration.

Nevertheless, not everyone welcomed the substitution of the PSP for the legal authorities and the political mileage that the party gained from that situation. Some made known their wish that state agencies might soon take up their duties again and relieve them of the onus of political obligation for whatever assistance they received from the CAOM. There were also some complaints that villages whose inhabitants supported other parties or the Arslans did not rate as high as others on the CAOM's services list. The implication was that PSP partisans came first. These complaints, of course, were firmly denied by CAOM officials, who insisted that fair governance had been the rule. On the other hand, when critics were asked what would have happened had the PSP not taken charge in 1983, the general response was a grudging acknowledgement that there had indeed been no substitute at that time. Furthermore, most of those who complained had to admit that Druze areas had often been the fiefdom of one or another leader during the course of history and that, during the recent war, circumstances had simply favoured the Junblati 'door' of the 'two-door' Druze leadership option. One individual called situations like this "Druze destiny."

There is no doubt that the CAOM greatly enhanced Walid Junblat's capacity to construct and service a clientele network that was larger than ever before. That fact, the strong performance of the *jaysh al-shaʿbī* and the alliance that Junblat had made with Syria saw him effectively crowned the 'king of the Mountain' as the civil war ended and the new political order unfolded. Walid Junblat's post-war authority, with political and security implications for Christians and Druze alike, meant that he would be given the vital post of minister of the displaced and oversee the slow return of refugees that began in 1992. The job was his for six years and, after a brief interval, his close advisor, Marwan Hamadeh, was next placed in charge. Facilitating the return of the displaced meshes quite nicely with recent measures taken by Walid Junblat to forge better relations with Lebanon's Christian community. While it is difficult to say what part the CAOM actually played in these outcomes, it can be argued that its role in maintaining the solidarity of Junblati partisans and attracting still others over the years was not negligible. In short, the organization provided the Junblatis with the capacity to resolve problems afflicting whole villages at a stroke. This capacity was unmatched by any of the PSP's political rivals.

A further implication of Druze civic organization during the Lebanese civil war is the fact that party cadres learned the ropes of resource mobilization and development during the 1980s and are putting this knowledge to good use today. With the state's post-war priorities focused upon rehabilitating the capital and the economy's poor performance, politicians whose fiefs lie in peripheral areas face more demands than ever to provide the assistance required by their constituents. It goes without saying that the very few leaders in possession of well-organized and flexible party instruments are more capable than others of showing the *sustained* interest and performance being demanded at the grass roots and appear to receive their just rewards in terms of votes when it counts. Post-war elections, for instance, record impressive victories by Junblat's ticket in Druze areas and Hizbullah's in two of the three areas where Shiʿi are concentrated. The latter party's constant efforts to provide public and social services to constituents is considered to be a very important part of its appeal. On the other hand, social commitment has its own rewards. A visit to Druze areas today reveals what all of Lebanon might look like if the tree-planting and clean-up campaigns initiated by the Civil Administration had been as faithfully carried out on an annual basis elsewhere.

NOTES

[1] For information on the deterioration of the Lebanese state because of civil strife, see N. Kliot, *The Territorial Disintegration of a State: The Case of Lebanon,* Occasional Papers Series (Durham: Centre for Middle Eastern and Islamic Studies, 1986).

[2] Mordechai Nisan, *Minorities in the Middle East: A History of Struggle and Self-Expression* (Jefferson, NC: McFarland, 1991), 11.

[3] Kamal Salibi, *The Modern History of Lebanon* (London: Weidenfeld and Nicholson, 1965), xix.

[4] Albert Hourani, *Minorities in the Arab World* (Oxford: Oxford University Press, 1947), 67-68.

[5] Leo Coser, *The Functions of Social Conflict* (Glencoe, IL: Free Press, 1956). See also M. Sherif, *In Common Predicament: Social Psychology of Intergroup Conflict and Cooperation* (Boston: Houghton Mifflin, 1966).

[6] See George Simmel, *Conflict and the Web of Group Affiliations* (New York: Free Press, 1955).

[7] See Col. C. H. Churchill, *Mount Lebanon: A Ten Year's Residence from 1842-1852, Vol. 1* (London: Saunders and Otleys, 1853); and C. I. Meryon, *Memoirs of the Lady Hester Stanhope, as Related by Herself in Conversations with Her Physician. . .*, 3 vols. (London: Henry Colburn, 1845).

[8] Ibid., 310.

[9] See Peter Gubser, "Minorities in Isolation: The Druzes of Lebanon and Syria," in *Political Role of Minority Groups in the Middle East,* edited by R. D. McLaurin (New York: Praeger, 1979); Kais Firro, "The Druze in and between Syria, Lebanon and Israel," in *Ethnicity, Pluralism and the State in the Middle East,* edited by J. E. Milton and Itamar Rabinovitch (Ithaca, NY: Cornell University Press, 1988); and Kais Firro, "Political Behavior of the Druze as a Minority in the Middle East—a Historical Perspective," *Orient* 27, no. 3 (1986).

[10] Tedd Robert Gurr, *Why Men Rebel* (Princeton, NJ: Princeton University Press, 1971); Joseph Chamie, "The Lebanese Civil War: An Investigation into the Causes," *World Affairs,* no. 139 (Winter 1976): 171-88; and Ghassan Salameh, *Lebanon's Injured Identities: Who Represents Whom during a Civil War?,* Papers on Lebanon Series, no. 2 (Oxford: Centre for Lebanese Studies, 1986).

[11] See, for instance, Zeev Schiff and Ehud Ya'ari, eds., *Israel's Lebanon War* (New York: Simon and Schuster, 1984); Marius Deeb, "The External Dimension of the Conflict in Lebanon: The Role of Syria," *Journal of South Asian and Middle Eastern Studies* 12, no. 3 (Spring 1989): 37-51; Adeed Dawisha, *Syria and the Lebanese Crisis* (London: Macmillan, 1980); and Moshe Ma'oz and Avner Yaniv, *War and Intervention in Lebanon: Israeli-Syrian Deterrence Dialogue* (London: Croom Helm, 1987).

[12] Nisan, *Minorities in the Middle East,* 11.

[13] See Judith Harik, "The Effects of the Military Tradition on Lebanon's Assertive Druzes," *International Sociology* 10, no. 1 (March 1995): 51-70.

[14] For information about the PSP, see Faris Ishtai, *Al-Ḥizb al-Taqadumī al-Ishtirāki wa-dawruhu fi al-siyāsa al-Lubnāniyya, 1949-1975: Vol. 1* (Mukhtara: Dar al-Taqadumiya, 1989); and Hasan Rashid, *Al-Ḥizb al-Taqadumi al-Ishtirākī fi dawʾ mithāqih* (n.p.: PSP, n.d.).

[15] Kamal Junblat, *Fī majra al-siyāsa al-Lubnāniyya* (Beirut: Lajnat al-Turath, 1978); Kamal Junblat, *Al-Birnāmaj al-marḥalī lil-aḥzāb wal-qiwā al-wataniyya wal-taqadumiyya,* al-Anba, 28 August 1975, 38; and Kamal Junblat and Philippe Lapousterie, *I Speak for Lebanon,* trans. by Michael Pallis (London: Zed Press, 1982).

[16] See Judith Harik, "Change and Continuity among the Lebanese Druze Community," *Middle Eastern Studies* 29, no. 3 (July 1993): 379-80.

[17] Interview with ʿAref al-ʿAwar, Beirut, 13 August 1988.

[18] Interview with Hisham Nasreddine, Beirut, 1 June 2002.

[19] For more information on the chaotic situation, see Walid Khalidi, *Conflict and Violence in Lebanon* (Cambridge: Center for International Affairs, Harvard University, 1979); and Randa Antoun, *War and Administration in Lebanon* (Beirut: Fikr Publications, 1990).

[20] Ibid., 382-83.

[21] The slow return of Christian displaced persons to Druze areas was found to be the result of economic rather than security factors according to a survey carried out by Judith Harik in 1993. See "The Return of the Displaced and Christian-Muslim Integration in Postwar Lebanon," *Islam and Christian-Muslim Relations* 10, no. 2 (1999): 164-171.

[22] Interview with Hisham Nasreddine, Beirut, 1 July 2002.

[23] Interview with Nadim Nammur, CAOM Public Works Committee, Beiteddin, 26 July 1988.

[24] See Harik, "Change and Continuity," 389.

Index

ʿAbbasid(s): 38, 174, 190
Abbeville: 14
ʿAbd al-Nasser, Jamal: 178
ʿAbd al-Qadir, (Emir): 105, 106
ʿAbdel-Nour, Antoine: 111
ʿAbdullah (Emir of Transjordan): 159, 167, 168
ʿAbey: 44, 53, 54, 155
Abha: 162, 163
Abi-Mershid, Walid: 183
Abkhazia: 194
Abu Dhabi: 168
Abu Shakra, Abbas: 176, 177
Abu Shaqra, Muhammad: 86, 87
Abu'l Faraj: 19
Abu'l Fida: 19
Abu-Husayn, Abdul-Rahim: 109
Abu-Izzeddin: Nejla: 174
Abul-Lasan: 129
Adam: 186, 190
ʿAdawiyya, Rabiʿa al-: 66
Adjaria: 194
Afghan: 192
Afghanistan: 185, 192, 194
ʿAfifah: 119
ʿAflaq, Michel: 178
Africa: 171, 188; African: 164
Agha Khan: 82, 192
Agha, Ismail (Ibrahimov): 187
ʿAhira: 119, 120
Ahl al-Haqq: 82 .- *see also:* Ahl-e-Haqq: 193
Ahmadabad: 192
Ahvaz: 193
ʿAin Dara: 175
ʿAjman: 159
Akarli, Engin: 108
Akhbaris (sect): 193
Āl Saud: see Ibn Saud
Alamut: 192
ʿAlawis (sect): 82, 193
ʿAlayili, ʿAbdullah al-: 63
Albania: 118; Albanian: 120, 121
Aleppo: 9, 13, 62, 167, 173, 174, 175
Alexandretta: 166
ʿAley: 173, 200, 203, 205
Algeria: 106, 188, 191; Algerian: 105
Alamuddin, Najib: 82
Ali-Allahis (sect): 193
Allahverdis (sect): 189
Allenby, Edmund: 129
America: 173, 177; American: 134
American University of Beirut: 155, 176
ʿAmir, Yahya: 119, 146
Amman: 173

Amshasepandan: 186
Amsterdam: 14
Anatolia: 119, 120
Anaz: 125
ʿAndary, Bahij al-: 174
ʿAndary, Fahd al-: 174
Anderson, J.N.D.: 99
Anjudan: 192
Ankara: 120, 162, 167
Anti-Lebanon: 1
Antonius, George: 175
Aquinas, Thomas: 191
Arab Aeronautical Society: 158
Arab League: 166
Arab Socialist Party: 178
Arab(s): 20, 65, 69, 74, 83, 84, 85, 87, 88, 89, 96, 108, 115, 116, 117, 129, 139, 148, 149, 163, 171, 172, 173, 174, 175, 176, 177, 178, 199, 200
Arabia: 1, 116
Arabic: 11, 190
Aramaic: 190
ʿAraman: 120
Argentina: 177
ʿAridi, Ghazi al-: 208
Aristotle: 65, 190, 191
Armenian: 130
Arsinoé: 21
Arslan, Adel: 176
Arslan, Amin: 176
Arslan, Sami: 176
Arslan, Shakib: 173, 174, 176
Arslan(s): 70, 172, 173, 199, 212
Asʿad, Asʿad: 86
ʿAsali ʿAbd al-Latif al-: 147
ʿAsali, Shukri al-: 124
Ashrafani, al-: 175
Ashrafieh, al-: 172
Asia: 183, 187, 188, 192
Asir: 163
ʿAsrawi, Najib al-: 174, 177
Assaad: 32, 34
Astaneh: see Istanbul
Atashe, Z.: 61
Atrash, ʿAbd al-Ghaffar al-: 147
Atrash, al- (family): 140, 144, 178
Atrash, Dhuqan al-: 145
Atrash, Hilal al-: 117
Atrash, Husayn Bey al-: 133, 135, 136, 148
Atrash, Ismaʿil al-: 146
Atrash, Mansour al-: 177
Atrash, Mustafa al-: 136
Atrash, Nasib al-: 147
Atrash, Salim al-: 140, 141, 143, 144, 145, 146, 147, 149, 150
Atrash, Shibli al-: 136, 142, 143, 144
Atrash, Sultan al-: 130, 134, 135, 136, 137, 138, 139, 140, 141, 142, 143, 144, 145, 146, 147, 148, 149, 150, 176, 177
Atrash, Yahya al-: 119, 146
Austria: 11, 146
Aʿwar, ʿAref: 203
Aʿwar, Sajiʿ al-: 101
ʿAwwad, Tawfiq Yusuf: 166
ʿAyn Nimrah: 135
ʿAyni: 187
ʿAysami, Shibli al-: 177, 178
Ayyubid(s): 174
Azalis: 193
Azd: 175
Azerbaijan: 193, 194
ʿAzm, Nazih al-Muʾayyad al-: 147
Azraq, al-: 62, 137, 173
ʿAzzam, Fayez: 81
ʿAzzam, Salman Yusuf: 177

Bʿaqlin: 36, 173, 177
Baʿth Arab Socialist Party: 91, 177

Baalbek: 129
Bab Tuma (Damascus): 106
Babis: 193
Badakhshan: 192
Baddur, Sulayman: 177
Badr al-Din al-Husain (Tanukhid emir): 53
Baha' al-Din: 29, 30, 31, 32, 33, 34, 35, 67
Baha'is: 193
Bakri, ʿAtallah al-: 148
Bakri, al- (family): 147
Bakri, Fawzy al-: 148
Bakri, Nasib al-: 147, 148
Balfour Declaration: 176
Balkan(s): 146
Bani, Saʿad al-: 147
Baqʿata: 120
Baradhaʿi, al-: 17
Barakat, Tawfiq: 209
Bashkortstan: 192
Basra: 13
Batatu, Hanna: 61
Bayān, al-: 177
Bayyada, al-: 80,
Beeston A. F. L.: 37, 38
Behistun: 21
Beirut: 14, 85, 105, 106, 107, 109, 111, 116, 129, 143, 144, 148, 155, 166, 173, 176
Beiteddine: 209
Bektashi: 188
Ben Dor, Gabriel: 61
Berlin: 14, 36
Berthereau, Dom: 14
Bible: 16, 29
Bibliothèque Nationale: 18
Bidwell, Robin: 157
Bin Duwish: 159
Bitar, Salah al-: 178
Bodleian Library: 14, 36, 37, 39
Bolu: 120
Bonaparte, Napoleon: 13, 19
Brazil: 174, 177
Brijand: 192
British: 157, 158, 159, 160, 162, 166, 167, 168, 169; army: 129; mandate: 176
British Library: 36
British Museum: 39, 40
Buddhism: 186, 190
Buhtur: 172
Bulwer, Henry Lytton (Sir): 105
Buraimi: 168
Buraykah: 119
Bursa: 138
Busra al-Harir: 119
Busra Eski Sham: 117, 138, 141
Bustan, al-: 175
Bustani, Butrus al-: 175

Cairo: 1, 13, 34, 116, 157, 160, 166, 178; Cairene: 33
Calcutta: 14
California: 163
Calvinism: 16
Cambrai: 14
Cambridge: 36
Canada: 177
Caspari: 19
Caspian: 193
Catholic: 16, 106
Caucasus: 183, 187, 192
Chah-Bahar: 193
Chamoun, Camille: 178
Champollion: 12, 22
Chassaud, G.W: 174
Chechnya: 194
Chelleh-neshin: 188
Chevallier, Dominique: 111

Chézy: 14
China: 12, 188, 192
Christ: 2, 69
Christianity: 15, 20, 23, 186
Christian Lebanese Forces: 197, 211
Christian(s): 20, 22, 31, 36, 44, 55, 62, 63, 69, 106, 107, 108, 109, 110, 111, 131, 175, 187, 198, 202, 203, 205, 211, 212
Churchill, Colonel Charles Henry: 61, 199
Civil Administration of the Mountain (CAOM): 203, 205, 207, 208, 209, 210, 211
Collége de France: 12
Committee of Union and Progress (CUP): 116
Constantinople: 13, 14 .- see *also:* Istanbul
Copenhagen: 14
Coptic: 22
Corfu: 14
Coser, Leo: 198

Daghestan: 193, 194
Daliyat al-Carmel: 173
Damascus: 1, 36, 43, 53, 54, 62, 72, 106, 116, 119, 120, 123, 124, 127, 129, 130, 131, 134, 135, 136, 138, 143, 146, 147, 148, 149, 155, 166, 167, 172, 173, 175, 177 .- Damascene: 126, 135, 148
Damascus Palace Hotel: 142, 143
Damlugi, ʿAbdullah: 158
Damur: 208
Danesh: 187
Dara: 125
Darʿa: 118
Darazi, Muhammad ibn Ismaʿil al-: 1, 17
Darband: 194
Deir ʿAli: 172
Denmark: 11, 13
Dersim: 82
Detroit: 177
Dinbayh: 120
Diwan: 188
Dostoevsky: 190
Dubar Naʿla: 125
Dublin: 39
Dufferin, Lord: 105, 106, 107
Dupont: 14
Durubi, Zaki al-: 147

East Persian: 38
Egypt: 13, 31, 33, 36, 79, 110, 146, 156, 161, 164, 166 .- Egyptian: 21, 24, 110, 161
Eichhorn: 23
Eisenhower Doctrine: 178
English: 13, 136
Enoch: 16
Erpenius: 19
Eshkol, Levi: 91
Europe: 10, 11, 12, 14, 16, 18, 21, 36, 90, 106, 158, 160, 161, 173, 194, 202; European: 36, 39, 107, 110, 111, 149, 168
European commission: 106
European Union: 208
Ewald: 23

Farabi: 39, 40
Farisi, Salman al-: 65, 66, 190
Faruqi, Sami Pasha: 118, 119, 125, 126, 145, 146,
Fatāt, al-: 129, 148
Fatayri, Walid: 207
Fatimid(s): 25, 30, 67, 97, 171
Fayyadh, Amin: 177
Fayyadh, Saʿid: 177

Fehim Bey: 126
Feisal ibn Hussein (Emir, King): 140, 147, 148, 149, 159, 161
Ferghanah: 192
Firro: 199
Fitrat: 187
France: 9, 10, 13, 14, 110, 146, 149, 156, 158, 161, 166, 167, 183, 185; French: 22, 67, 105, 106, 108, 109, 111, 136, 139, 149, 156, 166, 167; mandate: 176
Frankfurt: 14
Fuad Pasha: 106, 107, 109, 110

Galilee: 174
Ganjeh: 194
Gargani, Khalid: 162, 166
Georgia: 194
Germany: 11, 12, 142, 146 .- German: 23, 136, 156, 167, 188
Gesenius: 23
Ghandour, Daher: 208
Gharb, al-: 43, 53, 172, 175
Ghassan: 172
Ghazzali, al-: 191
Ghifari, Abu Dharr al-: 65, 66
Ghulāt: 187, 192
Ghurba: 120
Ghuta, al-: 62, 172
Gilgit: 192
Golan: 62, 73, 172
Gorno Badakhshan: 192
Göttingen: 14, 22
Great Britain: 140, 142, 144, 146, 158, 160, 161, 162, 164
Great Syrian Revolt: 115
Greek: 25, 65, 186, 190
Gubser: 199
Gujarat: 192
Gulf of Aden: 193
Gulf: 69, 165
Gulick, John: 171

Hadramawt: 193
Haifa: 118, 144, 149
Hajj: 160
Hakim bi-Amr Allah al- : 1, 9, 20, 31, 32, 33, 69, 72
Halabi, Salim al-: 132
Halabiyya: 173
Hamadan: 193
Hamadeh, Marwan: 208, 212
Hamadeh, Mohammad ʿAli: 176
Hamadi, Rafiq: 207, 210
Hamza, Fuad: 155, 156, 157, 158, 160, 161, 162, 163, 164, 165, 166, 167, 168, 169
Hamza ibn ʿAli: 1, 3, 4, 15, 17, 18, 20, 22, 23, 24, 29, 30, 31, 32, 33, 34, 35, 36, 37, 38, 47, 49, 63, 67, 69, 70, 72, 98
Hamzeh, Nadim: 175
Hanafi doctrine: 99, 100,
Harem: 173
Harik, Judith: 75
Harran: 119, 120
Hasa, al: 165
Hasbayya: 61, 65, 125, 172, 208
Hashemites: 157, 159, 160, 168 .- Hussein bin ʿAli: 147,148,159
Hatum, Salim: 178
Haupoul, Charles de Beaufort d': 106, 110
Hawran: 106, 109, 115, 117, 118, 121, 122, 123, 124, 125, 126, 127, 131, 136, 138, 139, 140, 143, 144, 145, 146, 147, 148, 149
Hawrani, Akram al: 178
Haydar, Muhammad Rustum: 129, 130, 131, 132, 133, 134, 135, 136, 137, 138, 147

Hebraic: 16
Hebrew: 11
Hejaz: 157, 159, 161, 162, 164
Hesiod: 18
Heydar: 193
Heydaris (sect): 189, 193
Hibatallah, Ibn: 19
Hijaz: 1, 148
Ḥikma: 16, 43, 47, 56, 80
Hilton, James: 185
Hinduism: 186, 190, 202
Hitler: 166
Hitti, Philip: 10, 31, 61, 70, 174
Hizb Suriyya al-Jadida: 176, 177
Hizbullah: 213
HMS Lupin: 159, 161
Hodgson, Marshall: 37
Hogarth, D.G.: 159
Holomboe: 13
Hoss, Selim al: 208
Hourani, Albert: 111, 198
ḥudūd: 18, 37, 43, 49, 52, 65
Hungary: 146
Hunza: 192
Husayn, Muhammad Kamil: 30, 33
Hussein bin ʿAli (Sharif, King): 147, 148, 159

Ibadis: 191
Ibn ʿAmmar: 17
Ibn Abi al-Furn, Ahmad: 54
Ibn Abi Talib, ʿAli: 2, 35, 66, 71, 190
Ibn al-ʿIbri: 19
Ibn al-ʿAlqami, Muʾayyad al-Din Muhammad: 39
Ibn al-Athir: 19
Ibn al-Barbariyya: 17
Ibn al-Kurdi: 17
Ibn Gilda, Nasrallah: 9, 14, 36
Ibn Hisham: 12
Ibn Ilias, Abd al-Rahim: 3
Ibn Ismaʿil, Izadi Emir Muawiyyah: 189
Ibn Khaldun: 68
Ibn Khallikan: 19
Ibn Rushd: 65
Ibn Saud, ʿAbdul ʿAziz (King): 155, 156, 157, 158, 159, 160, 161, 162, 163, 164, 165, 166, 168, 169
Ibn Saud, Feisal bin ʿAbdul ʿAziz: 156, 158, 160, 162, 165
Ibn Sibat: 44, 46, 53, 54
Ibn Shuʿayb, Hisham: 3
Ibn Taghri-Birdi: 19
Ibn Wabra: 172
Ibn Wasifshah: 19
Ibn Yasir, Ammar: 65, 66, 70
Ibn Yunis, Mirshid: 120
Ibrahim Pasha: 141
Idlib: 173
Idrisi: 162
Ikhwan tribes: 159, 161
Ilam: 193
Imami Khojas (sect): 192
Imperial Library of Vienna: 14
Incarnation: 19, 20
Independence (Istiqlāl) Party: 156
India: 1, 192, 194
Indo-Pakistan: 188, 192
Indus: 192
Iqlim al-Ballan: 172
Iqlim al-Rihan: 172
Iqlim al-Tuffah: 172
Iqlim Jazzin: 172
Iran: 71, 82, 184, 185, 187, 188, 189, 192, 193
Iraq: 39, 82, 116, 158, 159, 160, 161, 164, 172, 193
Iraqi: 39, 158
Isfiya: 173

Islam: 1, 6, 20, 25, 35, 49, 66, 70, 79, 84, 87, 89, 90, 96, 97, 162, 172, 187, 191
Isma'ili(s): 1, 22, 29, 30, 31, 32, 33, 35, 164, 194; Isma'ilism: 192
Ismail Pasha: 118
Israel: 80, 81, 82, 86, 87, 88, 89, 90, 91, 171, 177, 200, 203
Israeli Knesset: 61
Istanbul: 39, 106, 107, 118, 119, 121, 122, 123, 129, 145, 149 .- Astaneh: 188 .- see *also* Constantinople
Italy: 146, 164
Izadi(s) (sect): 186, 189

Jabal al-A'la: 62, 172 .- see also Jabal al-Summaq
Jabal al-Anwar: 175
Jabal al-Arab: 62, 75, 173, 176 .- see also Jebel Druze
Jabal al-Summaq: 62, 172 .- see also Jabal al-'Ala
Jacobin: 21
Jamaat-khaneh: 188
Jamal Pasha, Ahmad: 143, 146, 147
Janbalat, Sa'id: 109
Janina (Yaniya): 120
Jansenism: 20
Jansenists: 16, 21
Jaramana: 148, 172
Jasim: 117
Jawad, Hafaa: 100
Jazīra: 188
Jebel Druze: 129, 173 .- see *also* Jabal al-Arab
Jeddah: 157, 158, 159, 160, 161, 162, 167, 168
Jerusalem: 129, 168
Jesuit(s): 16, 21, 175, 176
Jesus: 186
Jethro (Shu'ayb): 190
Jews: 22, 31, 44, 74, 88, 168 .- Jewish: 75, 194
Jiyyah: 211
Jordan: 62, 137, 168, 171, 173
Junaid: 193
Junayna: 120
Junblat(s): 199, 200, 202, 209, 212, 213
Junblat, Kamal: 62, 178, 199, 200, 201, 202, 203, 205, 208
Junblat, Walid: 197, 200, 207, 208, 210, 212

Ka'b Ibn Zuhayr: 19
Kaaba: 160
Kafar: 125
Kafarina: 125
Kaffiristan: 185, 192
Kalb: 172
Kant: 23
Karachi: 192
Karak: 124, 126
Karakaoum: 192
Kasan: 14
Kasaravi: 187
Kashgahr: 192
Kashmir: 192
Kastamonu: 120
Kazakhstan: 183, 188, 192
Keireddine, Salim: 183
Kermanshahan: 193
Kfar Matta: 173
Khaldeh: 211
Khalil, Anwar al-: 208
Khalkhala: 131
Khalwāt: 188
khalwa: 70, 71
Khalwatkadeh: 188
Khatib, Muhammad al-: 96
Khatiwar: 192
Khirbat 'Awad: 125

Khodaparastan: 189
Khomeini, Ayatollah: 71
Khondamir: 19
Khonsari: 39
Khorassan: 185, 192
Khosrow, Nasser: 191
Khurasan: 70
Kilaab: 172
Kindi, al-Miqdad ibn Aswad al-: 65, 66, 191
Kipling, Rudyard: 185
Kirmani, Hamid al-Din al-: 30
Kirmanshah: 21
Kizilbash Kurds: 82
Konya: 120
Kosovo: 120
Kulayb: 192
Kurdish: 174
Kurdistan: 193
Kutch: 192
Kuwait: 158, 159, 161; Kuwaitis: 159
Kyrgystan: 193

Labid: 19
Lahiq (al-Mukhtar): 17
Lahta: 120
Laja: 119, 124
Lakhm: 172, 175
Larkhanah: 192
Layish, Aharon: 70, 99
League of National Action (*ʿUṣbat al-ʿAmal al-Qawmī*): 176
Lebanese coast: 44
Lebanon: 36, 39, 43, 61, 63, 75, 76, 80, 81, 86, 87, 88, 91, 95, 100, 101, 102, 105, 107, 127, 109, 111, 139, 155, 156, 157, 164, 166, 168, 171, 172, 176, 177, 178, 200, 202, 213;
- Lebanese: 90, 148, 155, 203.- *see also:* Mount Lebanon
Lenin-Abad: 194
Levant: 156
Leyden: 14
Libya: 146
Libyan: 162
London: 14, 156, 157, 162, 165
Louis Philippe: 13
Louis XIV (King of France): 9, 36
Louis XVI (King of France): 20
Luristan: 193

Maʿarrat al-Nuʿman: 174
Maʿn: 172; Maʿni: 37
Maʿraba: 117
Mafʿala: 119, 125
Mahallat: 192
Majali, Tawfiq al-: 124
Majdal Shams: 120, 121
Majlis: 46, 47, 51, 65, 67, 70, 71
Makach-Qalah: 194
Makarem, Nassib: 174
Makarem, Sami: 10, 99, 100
Mamluk: 45, 53, 79, 141, 174
Mamoun: 190
Manicheanism: 186
Maqrizi: 18
Mardak al-Kafr: 119
Marja Square (Damascus): 146
Maronites: 106, 107, 110, 198, 200, 203
Maroun: 173
Maryam: 35, 69
Masamiyya: 120
Massʿoud, Muhammad Saʿid: 177
Massachusetts: 14
Massey, Fred: 174
Maundrell, Henry: 174
Mazandaran: 193
Mazdaic: 193
Mecca: 66, 130, 148, 157, 159, 160; Meccan: 70

Medina: 157, 159
Mediterranean: 107, 111, 148, 188
Mehmet V (Ottoman sultan): 120
Mesopotamia: 13, 156
Metn, al-: 172, 200
Michigan: 177
Middle East: 79, 89, 90, 107, 155, 173, 198, 200
Ministry of Public Works: 210
Miqdad: 117
Mirkhond: 19
Moltan: 192
Monastir: 120
Monotheists: 189
Moses: 87
Mount Carmel: 173
Mount Hermon: 36, 125
Mount Lebanon: 1, 36, 61, 62, 79, 105, 106, 108, 109, 111, 126, 144, 172, 173, 174, 175, 197, 198, 200, 209.
- see *also:* Lebanon
Muʾayyad, al-: 33
Muʾayyadi, Jilban al-: 53
Muʿaddi, Jamal: 87
Muʿizz, al-: 97
Mukhtar, al-: *see* Lahiq
Muʿtazila: 190
Mudri, Ahmad: 147
Mughayr: 125
Muhalla, al-: 17
Muhammad (the Prophet): 2, 19, 35, 65, 66, 69, 87, 186
Muhammad ʿAli Pasha: 110
Muhtar, Khalid: 207, 208
Mukalla: 163
Mukhtara: 109
Mulberry Trees: 144
mulūkhiyya: 72
Munich: 14, 36
Muqtabas al-: 126
Muqtana: 17, 20
Murabba: 164
Mushaashaiyah (sect): 185
Muslim: 23, 36, 52, 55, 62, 63, 73, 74, 79, 82, 83, 84, 85, 87, 88, 96, 99, 100, 109, 129, 138, 183, 185, 188, 189, 194, 199, 202
Mustali tayyebis (sect): 192
Mutaṣarrifiyya: 109, 111, 126
Mutair: 159
Muwaḥḥidūn (*Muwaḥḥid, Muwaḥḥida*): 1, 2, 3, 9, 97, 98, 99 189

Nabak al-: 124
Nablus: 16, 141, 142
Nahḍat al-ʿArab: 177
Najjar, ʿAbdallah al-: 79, 80, 82, 89, 91
Najran: 160, 163, 164, 189
Nakhchevan: 194
Namier: 165
Nammur, Nadim: 207, 209
Naples: 14
Napoleon: see Bonaparte
Nasafi, Muhammad al-: 191
Nasr, Murcel: 99, 100
Nasreddine, Hisham: 203, 208, 209
Nasser Eddin, Amin: 174
Nasser Eddin(s): 173
National Club (*Nādi al-Ahlī*): 176
National Movement: 202, 203
Natur, Salman: 61, 87, 88
Nawanagarm Jungarah: 192
Nawfal, Mahmoud: 177
Nazi Germany: 162
Near East: 15, 178
Neishpour: 191
Nejd: 157, 158
Netherlands: 11
New York: 39, 82, 177

Niffari, Muhammad ibn ʿAbd al-Jabbar al-: 39, 40
Nisan, Mordechai: 198
Nizaris (sect): 192
North America: 82, 176, 177, 194
Nuʿman, Qadi al-: 31, 35
Nuristan: 185
Nuristan: 192
Nusayris (sect): 30, 32, 193
Nuwayri, al-: 9, 18

Oman: 168, 191
Osh (Uzbekistan): 192
Ossetia: 194
Otaiba: 159
Ottoman(s): 79, 106, 107, 108, 110, 111, 115, 116, 117, 118, 119, 120, 121, 122, 124, 126, 129, 130, 136, 138, 139, 140, 141, 142, 143, 144, 145, 146, 147, 148, 149, 150, 155 .- empire: 79, 176
Oxford: 14, 36

Pakistan: 192
Palestine: 1, 36, 39, 61, 62, 73, 79, 156, 157, 163, 164, 165, 167, 168, 171, 172, 173, 175, 177 .- Palestinian(s): 74, 87, 88, 157, 166, 199, 202, 203
Parfitt, Canon Joseph T.: 174
Paris: 12, 13, 14, 18, 34, 36, 37, 129, 162, 166, 167
Patan: 192
Patriotism: 175
Penrice, John: 19
Pentateuch: 16
People's Army (*jaysh al-shaʿbi*): 202, 211, 212
Perceval, Caussin de: 14
Périllier, Louis: 61
Persian school: 191
Persian: 10, 11, 12, 39, 70
Pétis de la Croix, François: 9
Philby, Kim: 159
Philby, St. John: 159, 162
Pisa: 14
Place de Canons (Beirut): 155
Plato: 65, 186, 190
Plotinus: 186
Pococke, Richard: 174
Potlemy: 21
Prishtina: 121
Progressive Socialist Party: 63, 178, 179, 197, 200, 201, 202, 203, 205, 207, 208, 212
Protectorates: 162
Protestant: 175
Punjab: 192
Pythagoras: 65

qāʾim al-zamān: 38
Qaʾen (Iran): 192
Qabun, al-: 147
Qadri, Tahsin: 147
Qahtan: 176
Qahtaniyya: 176
Qanawat: 119
Qarabagh: 194
Qaramatis (*also* Qaramatian): 31, 185
Qasim, Amin: 96
Qasim, Samih al-: 87, 174
Qatar: 168
Qays, Ghaleb: 66
Qaysi: 175
Qazvin: 192
Qidhaʿa: 172, 175
Qom: 192
Qrayya: 120, 137, 138, 145, 146
Quhestan: 192
Qurʾan: 186
Qurashi, al-: 33

Qurnayel: 176
Quwatli, Shukri: 167

Rabāt: 188
Ramadan: 63
Rameh, al-: 174
Rashayya: 172, 173
Rawalpindi: 192
Reincarnation (*taqammus*): 62, 84, 190
Republican Independence Party (*Hizb al-Istiqlal al-Jumhuri*): 176
Rhodes: 119, 146
Rhomboid: 38
Riyadh: 162, 164, 165, 166, 168
Rogan, Eugene: 116
Roman: 131
Roosvelt, Franklin D.: 167, 168
Rosetta Stone: 22
Royal Navy: 158
Ruhi: 187
Rumelia: 119, 120, 121
Rushaydah: 173
Russia: 11, 12, 13, 146 .- Russian: 13 .- see *also:* Tsarist Empire
Ryan, Andrew: 160, 161, 165, 168

Sʿana, al-: 173
Sabees (Seveners): 191
Sacy, Antoine Silvestre de: 9, 10, 12, 13, 14, 15, 16, 17, 19, 20, 21, 22, 23, 24, 25, 26, 49
Safad: 51, 125, 173
Safadiyya: 173
Safwat, Najdat Fathi: 129
Sahawina: 125
Sahwat al-Balat: 125
Sakakini, Tahsin al-: 147
Salibi, Kamal: 108, 111, 198
Salih, Kanj: 121
Saljuk: 174
Salkhad: 120
Samaritans: 16
Saravan: 193
Sarbedaran: 185
Saudi Arabia: 156, 157, 159, 162, 163, 164, 165, 166, 167, 168, 189, 192, 193; Saudi Arabian(s): 159, 164, 169; Saudi National Guard: 168;
Saydah, Khalil: 147
Sayis: 51, 65
Sayyur, Adel: 208
Scaliger, Joseph: 16, 17
Schlicher, Linda: 148
Sehnaya: 172
Severus: 19
Shaʿir, Fahd al-: 178
Shadegan: 193
Shaghur: 53, 54
Shahbandar, ʿAbd al-Rahman al-: 147
Shahinshah: 71
Shamʿa, Rushdi al-: 124
Shangri-La: 185
Shaqa: 120
Sharifian: 159
Shawafneh: 173
Shaykhis: 193
Shayya, Jamil: 178
Shbekeh, al-: 173
Shiʿa: 22, 39, 71
Shiʿi: 1, 82, 129, 164, 184, 191, 213
Shihab, ʿAbdallah Ibn: 38
Shoueifat: 174
Shquf: 120
Shuʿayb (prophet): 87
Shuf, al-: 43, 75, 80, 125, 172, 173, 175, 200, 205
Shufi, Hammoud al-: 177
Shura, al-: 174
Sibawayh: 12
Siberia: 183, 187

Sijn: 119, 125
Sikkin: 17
Sind: 192
Sistani, al-: 191
Sitt Sarah: 67
Sitt Shaʿwani: 66
Sivas: 120
Skopji: 120
Sobhis: 193
Socrates: 65
Sorbonne: 129
South America: 83
Soviet Union: 156, 160, 161, 178, 183, 202
Spain: 11, 188 .- Spandiard: 13
Sprengling, Martin: 36
St. Maur: 14
St. Petersburg: 14
Stanhope, Lady Hester: 199
Strasbourg: 13
Stuedel: 12
Suez Crisis: 178
Sufism: 202 .- Sufi: 65, 66, 72, 194
Sulayman, al-: 175
Suleiman, ʿAbdullah: 160
Sumayya: 66
Sunnis: 22, 48, 49, 52, 53, 62, 87, 117, 184, 187, 194
Suwayda: 63, 118, 119, 145, 173, 174
Suwayhira: 120
Sweden: 11
Swiss: 13
Syria: 36, 61, 62, 79, 81, 82, 85, 88, 90, 91, 105, 106, 107, 108, 109, 110, 116, 117, 118, 119, 122, 130, 139, 146, 148, 149, 155, 156, 157, 164, 167, 171, 172, 173, 174, 176, 177, 193, 200, 212 .- Northern: 1 .- Southern: 1 .- Syrian: 36, 39, 80, 86, 115, 116, 126, 139, 140, 148, 155, 157, 172, 202
Syriac: 190
Syrian Nationalist Revolution: 139
Syrian Protestant College: 176
Syrian Scientific Society: 176
Syrian Social Nationalist Party: 208

Tajikstan: 185, 192, 193
Talesh: 193
Taliʿ, Amin: 176
Taliʿ, Rachid: 176
Tameem: 172
Tamimi, Ismaʿil Ibn Muhammad (Abu Ibrahim) al-: 19, 22, 29, 30, 31, 32, 33, 34, 67
Tamimi, Rafiq al-: 147
Tanukh: 43, 172, 175
Tanukhi, ʿIzz al-Din al-: 147
Tanukhi, Jamal al-Din ʿAbd Allah al- (al-Sayyid): 29, 34, 43, 44, 45, 46, 47, 48, 49, 50, 51, 52, 53, 54, 56, 68, 72, 74
Taqi al-Din, Halim: 99
Taqi Eddin, Amin: 174
Taqi Eddin, Saʿid: 174, 176
Taqi Eddins: 173
Taqiyya: 17, 53, 70, 71, 79, 80, 82, 87, 90, 185
Tarabay, Husayn: 121
Tarif, Amin: 86
Tarif, Muwaffaq: 86
Tarif, Salah: 61
Tarim: 192
Tassy, Garcin de: 13
Tatarstan: 192
tawḥīd (monotheism): 1, 2, 3, 49, 50, 53, 56, 62, 64, 67, 70, 72, 84, 95, 96, 97, 99, 100, 101, 102, 171, 190
Tayyʾ: 172
Tehran: 193
The independence (*Al-Istiqlāl*): 177

Tiberias: 142
Tilmisani: 19
Timoviev, Igor: 63
Torah: 16
Torino: 14
Transcaucasia: 188
Transjordan: 129, 159, 160, 164, 167, 168
Transmigration: 18, 24
Tresmegistus, Hermes: 24, 186
Truman, Harry: 168
Tsarit Empire: 187 .- see *also:* Russia
Tunisia: 171
Turab, al-: 175
Turk(s): 142, 144
Turkestan: 192
Turkey: 82, 156, 166, 167, 172, 188, 193
Turkish Alevites: 82
Turkish: 11, 116, 130, 141, 144, 167, 174, 175
Tuwaijiri, ʿAbdul ʿAziz al-: 168

ʿUbayd(s): 174
ʿUbayd, ʿAli: 174
ʿUbayd, Hamad: 178
ʿUbayd, Salameh: 174
Umm al-Rumman: 125
UNICEF: 210
Unionist Revolution: 145
United States of America: 36, 62, 90, 168, 174, 177, 178, 185, 208
University of Leiden: 14
Upper Galilee: 62, 75
Uppsala: 14
ʿUṣbat al-ʿAmal al-Qawmī: *see* League of National Action
Ush (Punjab): 192
Ushmuneyn: 19
Utrecht: 14
Uzbekistan: 192, 193

Vatican: 14, 36
Vichy: 167
Vienna: 14

Wadi al-ʿAjam: 124, 172
Wadi al-Taym: 43, 67, 172, 173, 175
Wahba, Hafez: 161
Wahhabis: 159
Wakkhan: 192
Walfa: 125
Weizmann, Chaim: 165
West Bank: 168
Worcester: 14
World War I: 108, 111, 140, 146, 155, 160, 162, 176, 177
World War II: 156, 166
Würzburg: 14
Wright, W.: 19

Xinjiang: 188

Yakne: 120
Yarkand: 192
Yassin, Yusuf: 157, 158, 162, 168
Yazd: 192
Yazidis (sect): 193
Yaziji, Nassif al-: 175
Yemen: 1, 160, 161, 162, 163, 164, 193
Yemeni: 175, 192

zāwiya: 188
Zaban, al-: 125
Zahra-Blok: 192
Zamakhashri, al-: 12
Zanjan: 193
Zawzan: 70
Zionism: 88, 163, 165
Zoroastrianism: 186, 190
Zuʿbi (family): 125